HTML5 Canvas

FOR

DUMMIES®

HTML5 Canvas

FOR

DUMMIES®

by Don Cowan

WILEY

John Wiley & Sons, Inc.

HTML5 Canvas For Dummies®

Published by
John Wiley & Sons, Inc.
111 River Street
Hoboken, NJ 07030-5774

www.wiley.com

Copyright © 2013 by John Wiley & Sons, Inc., Hoboken, New Jersey

Published by John Wiley & Sons, Inc., Hoboken, New Jersey

Published simultaneously in Canada

For general information on our other products and services, please contact our Customer Care Department within the U.S. at 877-762-2974, outside the U.S. at 317-572-3993, or fax 317-572-4002.

For technical support, please visit www.wiley.com/techsupport.

Wiley publishes in a variety of print and electronic formats and by print-on-demand. Some material included with standard print versions of this book may not be included in e-books or in print-on-demand. If this book refers to media such as a CD or DVD that is not included in the version you purchased, you may download this material at http://booksupport.wiley.com. For more information about Wiley products, visit www.wiley.com.

Library of Congress Control Number is available from the publisher.

ISBN 978-1-118-38535-7 (pbk); ISBN 978-1-118-41747-8 (ebk); ISBN 978-1-118-42082-9 (ebk); 978-1-118-45964-5 (ebk)

Manufactured in the United States of America

10 9 8 7 6 5 4 3 2 1

WILEY

About the Author

Don Cowan is a software designer, developer, and author with a history of pioneering work in a number of computing and mobile technologies, including programming languages, database systems, software architecture, graphics, and user interface. He's currently focused on developing software and writing books on the latest mobile and web platforms including Android, HTML5, and graphics capabilities such as HTML5 Canvas. As a developer and project manager at AT&T, Don worked on software and telecommunications systems all over the world including Brazil, the Netherlands, Germany, Japan, and South Africa.

Don also has a fine arts and graphics background. His paintings, etchings, and prints have sold around the world.

Don is a founding member of `marketimpacts.com` and is currently its Director of Software Engineering. He earned his Bachelor's degree in Mathematics from Northwestern University and Master's degree in Computer Science from the University of Illinois.

Follow Don on Twitter (@`donkcowan`) or read his blog at `www.donkcowan.com/blog`.

Dedication

To my daughter, Alana, and son, David, for their encouragement, support, and understanding. I love you both.

To my life partner, Christie Harrison, for her help and patience during the many months of my focus on this book. You're the best and I love you.

To our dog, Daisy. On top of her usual duties as our best friend, she performed beautifully as model and actress for two book chapters. And I love you, too.

To the Wiley team of editors for their patience and skill. Our collaboration was a high point in my life.

Author's Acknowledgments

Thanks to my agent, Carole Jelen, for discovering this opportunity and believing in me. You're a true professional.

Thanks to Wiley Acquisitions Editor Katie Feltman for giving me the chance to take on this exciting project. You were a huge help throughout the development and writing process.

Thanks to Wiley Senior Project Editor Kim Darosett, who is at the center of the action and makes sense of it all. Without you, I would have been lost in the woods.

Thanks to Wiley Copy Editor Debbye Butler who has managed to make a tech guy look like a polished author. Magic.

Thanks to Wiley Technical Editor Kelly Francis who has the eagle eyes to spot my errors and suggest just the right improvements. You're the best.

Thanks to Wiley Project Coordinator Patrick Redmond. All the pieces came together smoothly. You did a great job.

Thanks to Jack Fuller, a successful author and friend who took the time to lend his support and share his expertise. You're my author hero.

Thanks to Wayne Smith, a fellow techie and friend who gave just the right advice.

Thanks to David Highland, a friend and very smart guy who gave the right help at the right times.

And finally, thanks to all the relatives and friends who encouraged and supported me. You gave me hope during all those hours hunched over my keyboard.

Publisher's Acknowledgments

We're proud of this book; please send us your comments at http://dummies.custhelp.com. For other comments, please contact our Customer Care Department within the U.S. at 877-762-2974, outside the U.S. at 317-572-3993, or fax 317-572-4002.

Some of the people who helped bring this book to market include the following:

Acquisitions and Editorial

Senior Project Editor: Kim Darosett

Senior Acquisitions Editor: Katie Feltman

Copy Editor: Debbye Butler

Technical Editor: McClellan C. Francis

Editorial Manager: Leah Michael

Editorial Assistant: Leslie Saxman

Sr. Editorial Assistant: Cherie Case

Cover Photo: © merrymoonmary / iStockphoto

Cartoons: Rich Tennant (www.the5thwave.com)

Composition Services

Project Coordinator: Patrick Redmond

Layout and Graphics: Carl Byers, Jennifer Creasey, Joyce Haughey

Proofreader: Sossity R. Smith

Indexer: Infodex Indexing Services, Inc.

Special Help
Rebecca Whitney

Publishing and Editorial for Technology Dummies

    Richard Swadley, Vice President and Executive Group Publisher

    Andy Cummings, Vice President and Publisher

    Mary Bednarek, Executive Acquisitions Director

    Mary C. Corder, Editorial Director

Publishing for Consumer Dummies

    Kathleen Nebenhaus, Vice President and Executive Publisher

Composition Services

    Debbie Stailey, Director of Composition Services

Contents at a Glance

Table of Contents

Introduction

*T*o me, HTML5 Canvas is one of the most exciting Internet advancements since the development of the first web browsers in the 1990s. Canvas integrates motion graphics with browsers so that any web developers who are willing to develop JavaScript code can add compelling motion graphics and animation to their websites.

The browser-based graphics of Canvas differ from server-based graphics. The code to generate a Canvas display is executed on the client device by the browser, not on the server computer by the server host operating system. This means that you can add Canvas capabilities directly to your web pages without having to write server-side code.

In this book, you explore not only the technical aspects of Canvas, but the artistic aspects as well. You discover how to create compelling images that will capture your viewers' imaginations.

The HTML5 Canvas standard is gaining wide acceptance and implementation in the major browsers. This means that work you put into developing Canvas applications will produce results for many years or decades to come.

About This Book

HTML5 Canvas For Dummies is a beginner's guide to developing browser-based graphics applications. You don't need prior experience in computer graphics.

Canvas application code is written in HTML and JavaScript. Some experience in these languages is useful but not essential. I've designed the examples in the book to be as self-explanatory as possible. If you have programming experience but have not yet used JavaScript, you should still be able to understand and work with the code.

The HTML code needed to run the examples is minimal, and it's fairly easy to add Canvas code to the HTML of an existing website.

The examples are all self-contained. You can run an example without having to include it in a website. The examples (and source code) are available at www.dummies.com/go/html5canvas, and starting the Canvas application is as easy as clicking on an example file. You can easily access the code for reference or to use it for your own applications.

The examples are structured as mini-labs. It's easy to modify the code and observe the results on the Canvas display. This is a great way to learn, especially for graphics applications. The possibilities are infinite. You're encouraged to try experiments and see what happens.

Foolish Assumptions

Because you bought this book (for which I humbly thank you, by the way), I assume only two things about you: You are interested in finding out more about HTML5 Canvas, and you have a basic understanding of computer programming. Knowing JavaScript is helpful but not essential; you can learn what you need to know as you move through the book. Canvas applications are programmed mostly in JavaScript. There is a small amount of HTML to define Canvas areas on your web pages.

To begin developing Canvas applications, you need the following:

- A computer that runs a web browser that supports JavaScript code. Examples are
  - Windows XP (32 bit), Vista (32 or 64 bit), Windows 7 (32 or 64 bit), or Windows 8 (32 or 64 bit)
  - Mac OS X
  - Linux (i386)
- A text editor, such as Notepad for Windows or TextEdit for Mac. (Text editors are described in more detail in Chapter 2.)
- A code debugger such as Firefox Firebug. (See Chapter 2 for details on where you can download free code debuggers.)

Conventions Used in This Book

Code examples in this book use a monospace font to make them stand out from other text. An example is

```
context.strokeStyle = "black";
```

URL web references are in the same monospace font, for example:

```
www.mozilla.org/firefox
```

How This Book Is Organized

HTML5 Canvas For Dummies is divided into five parts, which I describe in the following sections.

Part 1: Looking at Canvas

Part I introduces Canvas, gives you a glimpse at how it works, and explains how to set up your Canvas development platform.

Part II: Drawing on Canvas

Part II introduces the basics of drawing on Canvas. You find out how to create and enhance basic objects as well as the fundamentals of adding movement and animation to your Canvas applications.

Part III: Breathing Life into Your Canvas

Part III steps up development and deals with artistic elements such as color, lifelike movement, and multimedia.

Part IV: Developing More Complex Applications

Part IV moves into more complex applications such as working in 3D.

Part V: The Part of Tens

Part V lists ten great HTML5 Canvas applications/websites and ten great Canvas development tools.

Bonus Chapter: Gaming with Canvas

If you're interested in finding out more about gaming, check out the "Gaming with Canvas" bonus chapter available as a PDF at www.dummies.com/go/html5canvas. This chapter shows you how to develop a Canvas arcade game.

eCheat Sheet

To give you a quick overview of the key points in this book, I've created an eCheat Sheet, which you can find online at www.dummies.com/cheatsheet/html5canvas. The eCheat Sheet lists Canvas functions and parameters in an easy to use format.

Icons Used in This Book

This icon indicates a helpful pointer you probably don't want to skip.

This icon represents something to keep in mind as you develop your Canvas applications.

This icon indicates information that's helpful but not essential to developing your applications. However, because this is a technical book, you like technical stuff, right?

This icon alerts you to potential problems you may encounter. It's a good idea to digest these pieces of information.

Where to Go From Here

I suggest starting with Chapter 1. There is progressive detail with each chapter building on the previous chapters. That said, I've tried to make each chapter as self-contained as possible — and you have the option of checking out the table of contents, skipping over chapters that don't interest you or that cover something you already know, and zeroing in on chapters that interest you the most. However you proceed, let your inner artist free and have some creative fun!

Occasionally, we have updates to our technology books. If this book does have technical updates, they will be posted at www.dummies.com/go/html5canvasupdates.

Part I
Looking at Canvas

The 5th Wave   By Rich Tennant

HORNER BROS.
MAKERS OF PREMIUM
BELLS & WHISTLES

"As a web site designer I never thought I'd say this, but I don't think your site has enough bells and whistles."

In this part . . .

*P*art I introduces you to HTML5 Canvas and the development platform to assemble as a base for creating your applications. I take a quick look behind Canvas to show you how the major pieces fit together and how it all works. I also show you what software and hardware you need and where to find these components.

1

A Quick Glimpse Behind the Canvas

Developers of the Canvas standard could have named their new creation anything they wanted. They could have called it an *area, pad, space,* or any number of other possibilities. They chose *Canvas,* with its obvious artistic implications. There is significant technical detail behind the implementation of Canvas, but at its core, the intent is to provide a new way to satisfy the urge for expression not so different from that behind prehistoric drawings on cave walls.

HTML5 Canvas is a digital version of the surfaces that have teased the imagination of mankind for thousands of years. Adding the power of computing to traditional media concepts creates an amazing combination. No need to imagine horses galloping or geese flying. Now they can move.

In this chapter, you get a first look at how HTML5 Canvas works and how to create your own compelling Canvas applications. You get a glimpse behind the Canvas to see what makes it tick.

Displaying Your Canvas on the Stage of the World Wide Web

Traditional artists working with traditional canvases face a tough task getting their work out into the world. They have to create their paintings, find galleries to show them, hope people notice them, and then maybe sell a few. This is a slow process indeed compared to the global exposure given to an HTML5 Canvas application.

Your Canvas application will sit within the framework of the Internet and World Wide Web. It will have instant and automatic distribution. Get a little buzz going and it could be seen by millions.

So what exactly *is* HTML5 Canvas? Well, stated briefly, HTML5 Canvas is a standard for applications written in JavaScript that run within a web page downloaded from a server and displayed by a browser on a client device. That's quite a mouthful and a bit difficult to absorb. As they say, a picture is worth a thousand words. Figure 1-1 shows how all the HTML5 Canvas pieces fit together.

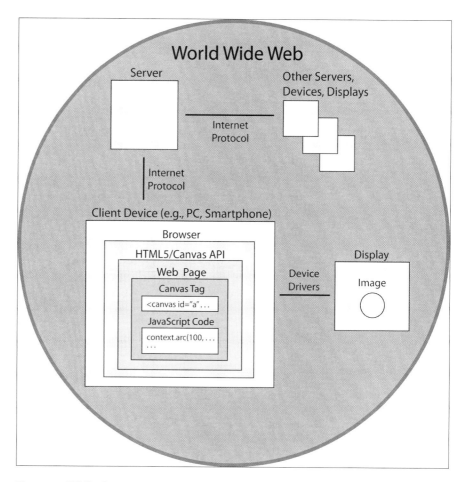

Figure 1-1: HTML5 Canvas on the World Wide Web.

Five great things about HTML5 Canvas

Canvas is a much anticipated feature of HTML5. Here are just a few of the great things about it:

- **It's interactive.** HTML5 Canvas can listen for and respond to user actions. Moving a mouse, pressing a button, tracing with a finger — these can all be sensed by your JavaScript code and used to drive application actions.

- **It's animated.** Objects can be made to move on an HTML5 Canvas . . . from simple bouncing balls to complex animations.

- **It's accessible.** All the major browsers now support HTML5 Canvas. Your Canvas application can be used on devices ranging from large computers to smartphones and tablets.

- **It's flexible.** An HTML5 Canvas can be used to display text, lines, shapes, images, videos . . . all with or without animation. It's a super-flexible medium.

- **It's growing rapidly.** HTML5 and the Canvas feature are steadily gaining popularity.

Client devices

Client devices include computers such as desktop PCs and mobile devices such as smartphones, tablets, and laptops. The client device is where your web browser resides and your Canvas is displayed. The website defining your Canvas is hosted on a server. Your web pages are downloaded from the server and displayed by your web browser.

Web browsers

Web browsers are software applications that construct and display web pages based on HyperText Markup Language (HTML) instructions. Major web browsers and their download sites are described next.

Desktop browsers

Desktop browsers can be downloaded from these developer sites:

- **Internet Explorer:** www.windows.microsoft.com/en-US/internet-explorer/downloads/ie

- **Firefox:** www.mozilla.org/firefox

- **Chrome:** www.google.com/chrome

- **Safari:** www.apple.com/support/safari

- **Opera:** www.opera.com

Mobile browsers

Mobile browsers are loaded on to mobile devices as apps that are downloaded from stores that are specific to the brand of device. To find browsers on app stores, search the store for *browser* or for a specific browser name, such as

- ✔ Internet Explorer
- ✔ Firefox
- ✔ Chrome
- ✔ Safari
- ✔ Opera

Websites and web pages

Websites are made up of web pages defined by HTML elements called *tags*. HTML tags define web page layout and content, including your Canvas. Listing 1-1 shows the code used to create the display in Figure 1-2. This is a simple example, but it demonstrates the basics needed to create a Canvas display.

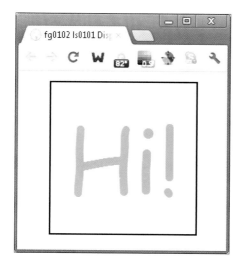

Figure 1-2: A simple Canvas display.

Listing 1-1:   Saying Hi on a Canvas

```html
<!DOCTYPE HTML>
<html>
<head>
<script>

// WINDOW LOAD function.
window.onload = function()
{
    // CANVAS definition standard variables.
    canvas  = document.getElementById("canvasArea");
    context = canvas.getContext("2d");

    // MESSAGE details centered on canvas.
    var mText = "Hi!"
    var xPos  = canvas.width/2;
    var yPos  = canvas.height/2;

    // TEXT format details.
    context.font        = "80pt Comic Sans MS";
    context.fillStyle   = "lime";
    context.textAlign   = "center";
    context.textBaseline = "middle";

    // FILL text.
    context.fillText(mText, xPos, yPos);
}
</script>
</head>
<body>

<div style = "width:200px; height:200px;
             margin:0 auto; padding:5px;">

<!-- CANVAS area definition -->
<canvas  id    = "canvasArea"
         width = "200"  height ="200"
         style = "border:2px solid black">
<!-- MESSAGE if browser doesn't support canvas -->
Your browser doesn't currently support HTML5 Canvas.
Please check www.caniuse.com/#feat=canvas for
information on browser support for canvas.
</canvas>

</div>
</body>
</html>
```

Here are some of the HTML tags used in Listing 1-1 and throughout the book:

- ✔ `<!DOCTYPE HTML>`: Declares the document for a web page
- ✔ `<html>`: Delineates HTML code
- ✔ `<head>`: Defines code containing information about your web page
- ✔ `<script>`: Delineates code areas such as your Canvas JavaScript
- ✔ `<body>`: Defines the main area of your webpage
- ✔ `<div>`: Provides web page formatting information
- ✔ `<canvas>`: Defines the Canvas area

HTML5

HTML5 is the latest version of the HyperText Markup Language. HTML defines how web pages function and how they're displayed. HTML5 contains many new and exciting features added to the previous version, HTML4. Major aspects of HTML5 include:

- ✔ **Improved interaction with the user:** Provides for fancier forms and more flexible user input.
- ✔ **Improved support of audio and video:** Provides native support for audio and video.
- ✔ **Geolocation:** Your application can determine where the client device is located if the device has location-sensing hardware.
- ✔ **Client-side data storage:** Your application can temporarily store data on the client device.
- ✔ **Canvas:** Powerful graphics display. Canvas is one of the most anticipated and important new HTML5 features.

For a complete list of new HTML5 features, visit

```
www.w3.org/TR/html5-diff/#new-elements
```

Canvas

The Canvas feature of HTML5 enables you to add dynamic displays within defined areas of your web pages. These displays can include sophisticated shapes, colors, text, video, audio, animation, and more. It's limited only, as they say, by your imagination.

The evolution of computer graphics

Computer graphics have been around since as far back as the 1960s. In the 1970s, video games began a push in the sophistication of graphics that continues today. However, until the introduction of Canvas, browser-based graphics relied mainly on vector manipulation. Vector graphics, such as Scalable Vector Graphics (SVG), draw images based on lines and curves defined by sets of data. Canvas, by contrast, is a "bit map" technology in which images are drawn based on the definition of the individual pixels (picture elements) of objects. This provides a greater degree of control over the display images. In practical terms, the Canvas bit map technology results in faster and more efficient rendering of displays that have large numbers of objects. This makes the development of browser applications such as games much more feasible.

The initial versions of Canvas were implemented by individual browser developers. The Apple WebKit browser was the first in 2004, followed by the Gecko (Firefox) browser in 2005 and the Opera browser in 2006. The HTML5 implementation of Canvas creates a common standard across all browsers. The most recent releases of all major web browsers support HTML5 Canvas.

To define Canvas areas (single or multiple) within your web page, use the new HTML5 <canvas> tag. Identify each Canvas with a unique id, as in this example from Listing 1-1:

```
<canvas  id    = "canvasArea"
         width = "200"  height ="200"
         style = "border:2px solid black">
</canvas>
```

JavaScript code

It's your JavaScript code that will draw images on your Canvas. Without JavaScript, a Canvas is just a blank space.

JavaScript, developed by Netscape in the mid-1990s, is a different language than Java, although its developers were influenced by Java, which was developed by Sun Microsystems in the early 1990s.

Here is the JavaScript from Listing 1-1 that created the display in Figure 1-2:

```
// WINDOW LOAD function.
window.onload = function()
{
   // CANVAS definition variables.
   canvas  = document.getElementById("canvasArea");
   context = canvas.getContext("2d");

   // MESSAGE details centered on canvas.
   var mText = "Hi!"
   var xPos  = canvas.width/2;
   var yPos  = canvas.height/2;

   // TEXT format details.
   context.font        = "80pt Comic Sans MS";
   context.fillStyle   = "lime";
   context.textAlign   = "center";
   context.textBaseline = "middle";

   // FILL text.
   context.fillText(mText, xPos, yPos);
}
```

The JavaScript code in the sample listings is structured to be as easy as possible to understand. The focus of this book is on Canvas features and capabilities, not on programming languages. I've commented the code heavily and avoided complex coding structures. For a concise JavaScript language reference, see

```
http://docs.webplatform.org/wiki/javascript/tutorials
```

Device drivers

A *device driver,* which is usually built into client computers, smartphones, and tablets, is a software/firmware layer between an application and a device, such as a display. The display driver does the work of displaying the individual pixels that form the images on your Canvas.

Displays

Displays can be built into the client device or function as separate devices attached to the client. There's a huge variety of displays ranging from those that are measured in feet to those measured in inches. Displays are made up of individual picture elements (pixels), each of which is controlled by the device driver to show a color specified by software on the client device, such as your Canvas application code.

The Interplanetary Internet

The World Wide Web may need a new name. It's about to reach out beyond our planet. NASA is developing a technology that extends the Internet and web to extraterrestrial locations. Known as the "Interplanetary Internet," it uses Disruption-Tolerant Networking (DTN) to sustain super long-distance connections without data loss. Get ready to draw images of "ET" on your Canvas. (Search for *DTN* on www.nasa.gov to get the latest updates.)

Images

Canvas images are constructed pixel by pixel *(bit mapped),* as opposed to *vector graphics,* which are drawn based on points along specified lines. The dimensions of a Canvas are specified in pixels, and the images you create with your application code are based on pixel dimensions.

Remote devices

A *remote* device is located away from the client device containing your HTML and JavaScript code.

Internet Protocol

Client devices communicate with servers and other devices around the world via the *Internet Protocol* suite. Internet Protocol is the communications glue that holds the Internet and World Wide Web together. It's a layered structure of messaging and rules for exchanging information across telecommunications systems.

Servers

Servers are the computing devices that host the website that contains your Canvas application. Even though the task of constructing and displaying a web page and Canvas is delegated to the client device, the server plays an important role. The server stores your HTML and JavaScript code and downloads it to the client when a user selects one of your web pages for display. The server can also host images and data that can be retrieved and used by your Canvas application.

HTML5 Canvas applications

The applications for HTML5 Canvas are limitless. Here are a few important ones:

- **Advertising:** The interactivity and animation of HTML5 Canvas are ideal for attracting the attention needed for successful advertising.

- **Art & decoration:** HTML5 Canvas provides intricate control of color and images for creating artistic and decorative surfaces.

- **Education & training:** Text, images, videos, diagrams, and other HTML5 Canvas features can be combined to produce effective education and training applications.

- **Entertainment:** The web is growing as a platform for delivering entertainment. HTML5 Canvas video, images, and graphics are a great base for developing entertaining applications.

- **Gaming:** The HTML5 Canvas fine grain, pixel level control of displays, and the many methods for creating animation offer lots of possibilities for gaming applications.

- **Data representation:** HTML5 Canvas provides features to combine the power of access to global data sources with the imagery of graphs and charts.

Seeing a Canvas Application in Action

One of the great things about developing Canvas applications is how quickly you can see your work produce results. Here's an overview of the Canvas development sequence, which is covered in detail in Chapter 2:

1. **Create your HTML5 and JavaScript code using a text editor.**

   For example, you can use a text editor such as Notepad on a PC or TextEdit on a Mac.

2. **Save your Notepad or TextEdit file in a directory on your computer with the .HTML or .HTM extension.**

3. **Double-click the .HTML or .HTM file in your directory to display your Canvas.**

   Your Canvas appears in your default browser.

To get you jump-started with this process, access the examples for this book, as described in the following sections. The examples are self-contained, and each one includes all the code necessary to display a Canvas.

Using your browser to display a sample Canvas

You can download the sample applications in this book two ways:

⟋ **Download the files from** http://www.dummies.com/go/html5canvas. After the download has completed, double-click the downloaded folder to open it and access the individual .HTM files. You can then move these files to any other folder you choose. To start an individual example, double-click the .HTM file.

⟋ **Access individual example web pages:** Go to http://donkcowan.com/ html5-canvas-for-dummies#examples/ and click individual example page links.

As an example, to display the Canvas in Figure 1-2, access the code from Listing 1-1, as follows:

1. **Point your browser to** http://donkcowan.com/html5-canvas-for-dummies#examples/ **to access the sample code for individual listings in the book.**

   You should see a list of samples, including Listing 1-1 Saying Hi on Canvas.

2. **Click the listing (for example, Listing 1-1 Saying Hi on Canvas).**

   You should see the Canvas display appear (refer to Figure 1-2). That's it — a simple two-step process to reach the sample code.

Using the sample code

The example listings have a number of uses:

⟋ **Experimenting with the code:** The sample code is a great way to understand how Canvas JavaScript code functions. Modify the code and watch the effect on the display.

⟋ **Using the code to seed your applications:** The samples provide a base for developing your own applications.

⟋ **Referencing the code:** It's easy to forget how to code a particular Canvas task. A quick check of the sample code can be a big aid during application development.

To use the sample code directly on http://donkcowan.com/html5-canvas-for-dummies#examples/, do the following:

1. **Use your browser to access the sample listings from the book.**

   Follow the two preceding steps to access the sample you're interested in.

2. **Right-click (Ctrl+click on the Mac) on the page displaying the Canvas.**

   The menu of options for the web page appears (see Figure 1-3.)

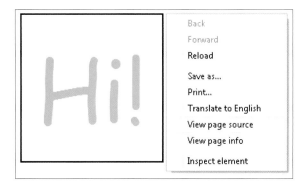

Figure 1-3: Canvas displays a menu of options.

3. **Click View Page Source to display the HTML and JavaScript code generating the Canvas display.**

4. **Highlight the code that you want to copy.**

5. **Right-click (Ctrl+click on the Mac) on the page displaying the code and select Copy from the options, as shown in Figure 1-4.**

6. **Open your text editor and paste the code into your application.**

   Right-click (Ctrl+click on the Mac) the page displaying the code and select Paste from the options.

```
 1  <!DOCTYPE HTML>  <!-- HTML to define a web page -->
 2  <html>
 3  <head>
 4  <script>  <!-- JavaScript to display canvas -->
 5
 6  // SUMMARY: Displays text in the center of a canvas.
 7
 8  // A. WINDOW LOAD function.
 9  window.onload = function()
10  {
11
12       Copy                                                        Ctrl+C
13       Search Google for '<!DOCTYPE HTML>  <!-- HTML to define a web page...'
14
15       Inspect element
16       var mText  = "Hi!"
17       var xPos   = canvas.width/2;
18       var yPos   = canvas.height/2;
19
20       // A3. TEXT format details.
21       context.font         = "90pt Comic Sans MS";
22       context.fillStyle    = "lime";
23       context.textAlign    = "center";
24       context.textBaseline = "middle";
25
26       // A4. FILL text.
27       context.fillText(mText, xPos, yPos);
```

Figure 1-4: The Canvas code menu of options.

To download, save, and then use the sample code on your computer, do the following:

1. **Download the Zip file from** www.dummies.com/go/html5canvas **and store the files where you want them on your computer.**

   Move the entire folder or individual file to a new location if you choose to.

2. **Right-click (Ctrl+click on the Mac) the desired file and select Open With** *your text editor* **(Notepad, for example) from the options, as shown in Figure 1-5.**

   The file containing the code from the sample application opens in the text editor.

For your convenience, the image, audio, and video files referenced by the sample JavaScript code are stored on a server at www.marketimpacts.com. This means that the sample applications will execute without your having to adjust the code for file location.

The image, audio, and video files are also available in the Zip file you downloaded from www.dummies.com/go/html5canvas. To reference image, audio, or video files that you reuse from the download or create yourself, you'll need to change the JavaScript file references to point to the server where you store the files. I explain this process in more detail in Chapter 4.

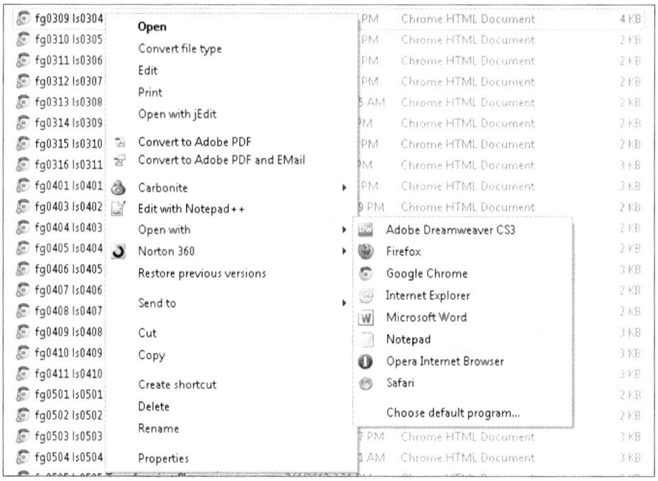

Figure 1-5: Opening the code file on your computer.

Why develop for HTML5 Canvas

HTML5 Canvas is an attractive platform for software development. Here are five reasons why.

✓ **Develop once, run anywhere:** HTML5 Canvas is supported by recent releases of the major web browsers, which run on a wide variety of devices from large computers to mobile devices. Code written using HTML5 tags and JavaScript code will work on all these devices.

✓ **Toolkit availability:** The tools needed to develop a Canvas application are not extensive or expensive — a computer, browser, text editor, and code debugger. For advanced development, such as sophisticated games, a number of third-party libraries are available to facilitate coding.

✓ **It's a well-accepted standard:** Although it will take time for all the features of HTML5 to be implemented in all browsers, HTML5 Canvas is a solid and accepted standard that will be around for many, many years.

✓ **Demand for interaction and animation:** Web users today want to interact with websites and see entertaining movement and animation. HTML5 Canvas gives developers a solid platform for serving these needs.

✓ **The mobile market:** HTML5 Canvas is increasingly supported on mobile devices. It offers a way to develop applications for smartphones and tablets without having to program for individual operating systems such as iOS and Android.

2

Setting Up Your Canvas Platform

In This Chapter

Understanding the tools you need to develop a Canvas application

Testing and tuning your system for Canvas applications

Checking browser support for HTML5 and Canvas

Choosing a text editor

Exploring tools for editing and debugging your HTML5 and JavaScript code

*G*ood news! The tools you need to start developing HTML5 Canvas applications aren't extensive or expensive. The basic tools you need are a web browser, a text editor, and a code debugger, all of which are likely already installed on your computer or available through free downloads.

In this chapter, you find out about the hardware and software needed to run Canvas applications and how to set up your Canvas development platform.

Testing Canvas Performance on Your System

The hardware and software you use will affect the performance of your Canvas applications. Components of your system that can significantly impact performance include the

- **Central Processing Unit (CPU):** Performs calculations for the operating system and applications
- **Random Access Memory (RAM):** Integrated circuit memory that allows direct, rapid access to any data
- **Graphics Processing Unit (GPU):** Integrated circuit dedicated to displaying images on a screen
- **Web browser brand and version:** Constructs web pages for display based on HTML and JavaScript code
- **Web browser support for GPU hardware acceleration:** Off-loads computing related to screen displays from the CPU to the GPU

Most of today's desktop and laptop computers run HTML and JavaScript code fast enough to produce smooth, good-looking results. However, the performance of Canvas applications varies across hardware systems and browser software. To test your system for Canvas performance, do the following:

1. **Point your browser to** `http://donkcowan.com/html5-canvas-for-dummies#examples/`**, and click the link for Listing 9-2.**

   You see a Canvas application with rotating concentric circles, as shown in Figure 2-1. (The details of this application are covered in Chapter 9.)

2. **Check the frame rate (in frames per second) at the lower left of the Canvas area.**

   The *frame rate* tells you how many times per second your system is able to draw the moving circles. This performance is influenced by your computer hardware and browser software.

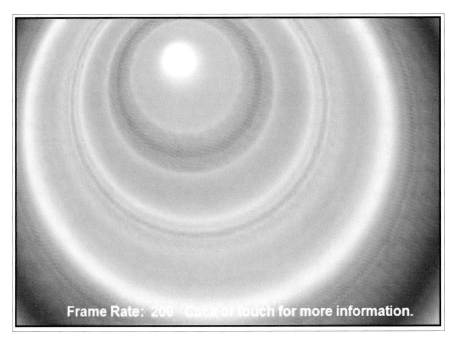

Frame Rate: 200 Click or touch for more information.

Figure 2-1: Canvas performance test application.

Table 2-1 shows the results running on my computer, which has the following profile:

- Windows 7 Operating System
- Intel Quad i7 M620 CPU (Central Processing Unit)
- 2.67 GHz (Gigahertz cycle time)
- 8GB RAM (Gigabytes of Random Access Memory)
- NVIDIA Quadro FX 2800M GPU (Graphics Processing Unit)
- GPU hardware acceleration enabled on supported browsers

Table 2-1		Canvas Performance on a PC	
Browser	*Version*	*GPU Acceleration*	*Frames per Second*
Internet Explorer	9	Yes	250
Chrome	20	Yes	200
Safari	5	Yes	110
Opera	11	No	70
Firefox	13	No	80

After testing a number of Canvas applications on my computer, I found that some using animation heavily don't perform well on browsers scoring fewer than 200 frames per second. How well your browser displays a Canvas depends on the specifics of the Canvas application and on your computer.

In Table 2-1, you can see there's quite a bit of variation between browsers . . . an order of magnitude between the faster and slower browsers. Browser performance changes with new browser releases. Because of the gaining popularity of HTML5 Canvas, browser developers are motivated to continually improve the performance of Canvas on their products.

Tuning Your Display

Canvas applications create images by manipulating individual pixels on a portion of the display screen — the Canvas area. Pixel manipulation is at the heart of HTML5 Canvas. Pixels are the raw material onto which your Canvas images are projected. Get to know them and love them.

Understanding pixels

Without using a magnifying glass, you can't differentiate individual pixels. Even though they're thousands of small "bit players," you should have a basic understanding of their characteristics and how they function:

✔ **Pixel structure:** The term *pixel* comes from a combination of the terms *picture* and *element.* A pixel is the smallest application-controllable element on a display screen. Displays create a pixel color by combining three or four basic *subpixel* colors such as red, green, and blue … or cyan, magenta, yellow, and black. In your JavaScript code, you can define thousands of colors that are generated by the display hardware using varying proportions of these basic subpixel colors.

The arrangement of the red, green, and blue subpixels on a computer monitor screen is shown in Figure 2-2. Typically, the hardware combines a horizontal group of three subpixels to create a single color pixel that becomes part of the display image.

To define the dimensions of a Canvas for your applications, choose a height and width in pixels. A Canvas that is 400 pixels wide and 200 pixels high contains 80,000 pixels, for example.

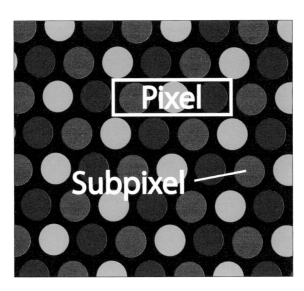

Figure 2-2: Display pixels.

✔ **Display resolution:** The display resolution is the number of pixels on the screen. Resolution is usually expressed in width and height such as "1440 x 900," meaning 1,440 pixels wide by 900 pixels high. Most computers have display resolutions that are at least 1024 x 600 pixels. That's a total of 614,400 pixels. Higher-end tablet devices can also reach this resolution.

✔ **Pixel density:** The width and height in inches of a display can vary independently of the resolution in pixels. In other words, some displays have more pixels per square inch than others. This measurement is called PPI (pixels per inch), or *pixel density*. The greater the pixel density for a given screen size, the greater the perceived quality of the display. It's counterintuitive, but for displays, bigger isn't necessarily better. A larger display with a lower pixel density might appear less "sharp." Even small displays with a high pixel density can produce amazing images.

Adjusting your display

Your Graphics Processing Unit (GPU), also referred to as a *video card,* is the hardware and firmware that control display pixels. The *video driver* is software that allows programs such as your JavaScript code to interface with the GPU. The GPU, the driver, and their settings can have a significant impact on the quality of your Canvas displays.

On many systems, you can check and adjust the performance of your GPU by using a control panel. Figure 2-3 shows the control panel for an NVDIA video card.

Consider taking the following actions to improve the performance of your graphics system:

✔ **Adjust your GPU settings.** Adjust the settings for your Graphics Processing Unit by using a control panel such as the one shown in Figure 2-3. Which settings are available depends on the brand and model of your GPU.

✔ **Enable GPU acceleration.** For Nvidia Control Panel in Figure 2-3, this is controlled on the Set PhysX configuration tab under 3D Settings. Click the Enabled radio button to turn it on.

✔ **Adjust image settings for performance versus quality.** These settings are shown in Figure 2-3. For the Nvidia Control Panel, a rotating object shows the effect of your choice. Choose a setting that looks best to you on your computer.

To locate your CPU control panel:

- *On a PC:* Choose Start⌐Control Panel⌐*Your GPU Control Panel.*

- *On a Mac:* Choose ⌘⌐System Preferences⌐Displays⌐*Your GPU Control Panel.*

✓ **Turn off other applications.** If other applications are running, they'll use CPU cycles and reduce the performance of your Canvas application.

✓ **Install the latest video drivers.** Not having the latest release can negatively affect your Canvas performance. Check the manufacturer's website for information on the latest driver releases.

If you want to upgrade your GPU, many options are available. An Internet search for GPU or video cards will list a wide variety of manufacturers and retailers. You don't necessarily want to design a Canvas application tuned to the most powerful user devices. If you're developing an application that will be available on the Internet, it will be viewed by users with a wide variety of devices.

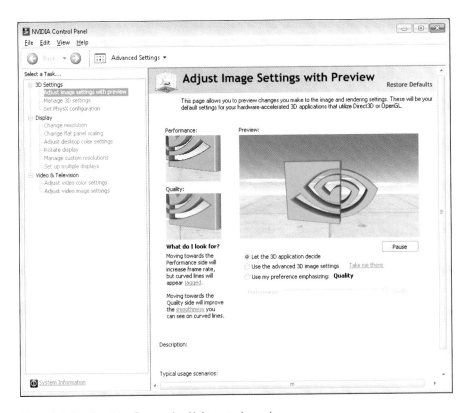

Figure 2-3: The Graphics Processing Unit control panel.

Turning on browser GPU hardware acceleration

Most web browsers have implemented GPU hardware acceleration in recent releases. Using acceleration, functions that would normally be performed by your application software code in the CPU are delegated to hardware in the GPU. This can result in dramatic increases in the performance of graphics displays.

You can't be certain whether viewers of your Canvas application will have hardware acceleration turned on for their browsers. However, because motion graphics are becoming much more common on web pages, browser support for hardware acceleration is improving, and more users are enabling it.

Follow these steps (as of this writing) to turn on browser GPU hardware acceleration (GPU hardware acceleration is automatically turned on by the Safari browser):

Internet Explorer

1. **Click the Tools icon at the upper right of the browser screen.**

2. **Select Internet Options from the drop-down menu.**

3. **In the Internet Options dialog box, click the Advanced tab.**

4. **To turn on acceleration, uncheck the Use Software Rendering box.**

5. **Restart your browser.**

Chrome

1. **Enter** about:flags **in the browser search bar address box and search on that page.**

2. **Click the Enable link under Override Software Rendering List.**

3. **Click the Enable link under GPU Compositing on All Pages.**

4. **Restart your browser.**

Opera

1. **Enter** about:config **in the browser search bar address box and search on that page.**

2. **Enter** acceleration **in the search bar of the config page and press enter.**

3. **Change the Enable Hardware Acceleration box to 1.**

4. **Restart your browser.**

Firefox

1. **Enter** about:config **in the browser search bar address box and search on that page.**
2. **Enter** render **in the filter box and look for** `gfx.font_rendering.directwrite.enabled`**.**
3. **Double-click this entry to toggle the value to True.**
4. **Restart your browser.**

Testing Your Application on Mobile Devices

Since the introduction of the iPhone in 2007, followed by Android, Windows, and others, websites can now be easily viewed on a wide variety of mobile devices. Although you don't need a mobile device to develop an HTML5 Canvas application, you might want to test your application on a smartphone or tablet to see how it performs.

Mobile screen resolutions range from about 160 x 100 pixels for smaller smartphones to around 1024 x 600 pixels for larger tablets. At the low end of the range, viewing a website can be difficult. On the higher-end smartphones and tablets, accessing websites is becoming easy and common.

Mobile devices generally lag computers in their support for HTML5 and Canvas. You can test the level of HTML5 support for your mobile devices by going to www.html5test.com, as shown in Figures 2-5 through 2-7.

Even if your device shows as supporting Canvas, not all websites using Canvas will necessarily work on your phone or tablet. If a Canvas application uses WebGL, or other additional features that are not supported on your device, the application won't function.

Keep in mind that average mobile device processors and video hardware aren't as powerful as those in desktop or laptop computers. This means that a Canvas application may not work as well on your mobile device as it does on your desktop or laptop.

To test your mobile device for Canvas performance, follow the same steps in the earlier section "Testing Canvas Performance on Your System" and note the frame rate for your phone.

Table 2-2 shows the results running on my smartphone, which has the following profile:

- ✔ Samsung Galaxy Nexus SCH 1515
- ✔ 1.2 GHz Dual-Core Processor
- ✔ Android 4.0 Operating System

Table 2-2	Canvas Performance on a Smartphone	
Browser	*Version*	*Frames per Second*
Chrome Mobile	Beta	20
Opera Mobile	12	8
Android	4	9
Dolphin HD	8	14

Measuring Web Browser Support for HTML5 Canvas

Web browser support for HTML5 Canvas is a work in progress. Browser developers are continuing to add HTML5 feature support and performance improvements.

Examining HTML5 Canvas support

HTML5 is the fifth and latest version of the markup language for displaying content on the World Wide Web. HTML standards are defined by the World Wide Web Consortium (W3C), which is targeting 2014 for the completion of the HTML5 recommendation. It will likely take some years after that for all web browsers to support the complete set of HTML5 features.

The world, however, isn't waiting for completion of the standard to begin using HTML5. Many HTML5 features, including Canvas, are already implemented in recent releases of the major browsers.

The table in Figure 2-4 from `www.caniuse.com/#feat=canvas` shows the level of implementation for HTML5 Canvas for the major browsers as of this writing.

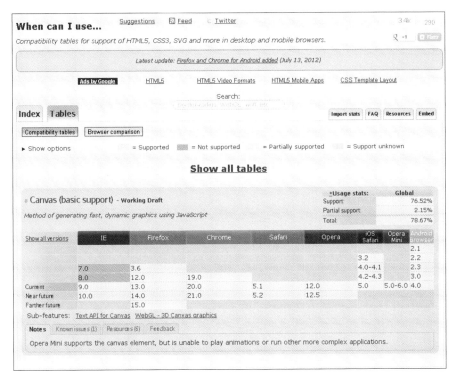

Courtesy Alexis Deveria.

Figure 2-4: Browser support for HTML5 Canvas.

Testing the browsers you use

Test the browsers on your computers and mobile devices for HTML5 support by using the HTML5 Test at `www.html5test.com`. It produces an overall rating for a browser version on a scale of 0-500 and checks ratings for individual features. An overall rating of over 400 is a decent score. These ratings will rise as browser developers add HTML5 functionality.

To test your Canvas applications on the major browsers, load recent versions of Internet Explorer, Firefox, Chrome, Safari, and Opera onto your computer. Open your completed application with each browser to check its performance. (See Chapter 1 for details on where to download these browsers.)

Using Text Editors

HTML5 Canvas application code is represented by sequences of text characters. Use a text editor to create and edit your code. You can't use a word processor, such as Microsoft Word, because it inserts special control characters
to give the document the desired formatting, such as you see in this book. A
text editor doesn't insert formatting characters.

Standard text editors

Computers usually come with a standard text editor already installed, such as
Notepad (shown Figure 2-5) with Windows, and TextEdit (shown in Figure 2-6)
with Mac OS X. They provide basic, no-frills text editing.

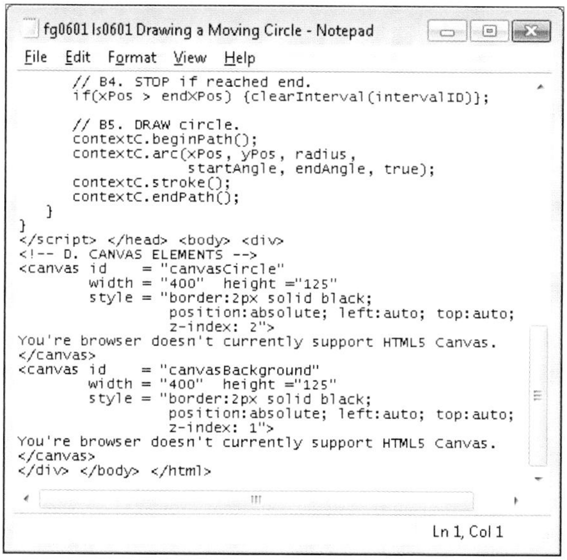

Figure 2-5: Windows Notepad text editor.

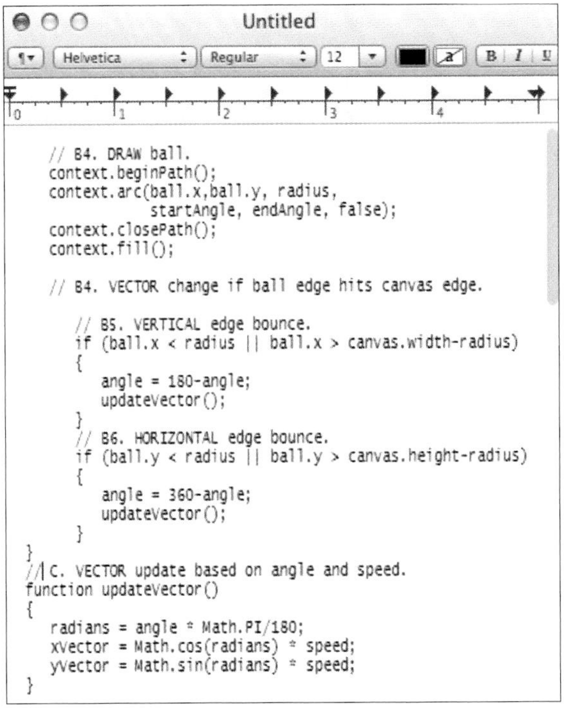

```
// B4. DRAW ball.
context.beginPath();
context.arc(ball.x,ball.y, radius,
            startAngle, endAngle, false);
context.closePath();
context.fill();

// B4. VECTOR change if ball edge hits canvas edge.

    // B5. VERTICAL edge bounce.
    if (ball.x < radius || ball.x > canvas.width-radius)
    {
        angle = 180-angle;
        updateVector();
    }
    // B6. HORIZONTAL edge bounce.
    if (ball.y < radius || ball.y > canvas.height-radius)
    {
        angle = 360-angle;
        updateVector();
    }
}
// C. VECTOR update based on angle and speed.
function updateVector()
{
    radians = angle * Math.PI/180;
    xVector = Math.cos(radians) * speed;
    yVector = Math.sin(radians) * speed;
}
```

Figure 2-6: Mac OS X TextEdit text editor.

Alternatives to standard text editors

There are many alternatives to standard text editors. These enhanced editors provide features such as:

- ✓ **Colored element and indentation highlighting:** For easier differentiation of code elements

- ✓ **Find and replace:** For easier multiple changes to the same piece of code

- ✓ **Drag-and-drop:** To more easily rearrange your code

- ✓ **Split screen editing:** To be able to edit multiple files side-by-side

- ✓ **Zoom controls:** To make your code larger or smaller

Here are a few popular ones you may want to check out:

- **Notepad++:** Shown in Figure 2-7, Notepad++ is one of the most popular alternatives to standard Windows Notepad. It's free and can be downloaded from `www.notepad-plus-plus.org`.

- **jEdit:** Shown in Figure 2-8, jEdit is a popular text editor that can be used with Windows, Mac OS, Unix, and Linux. jEdit is free and can be downloaded from `www.jedit.org`.

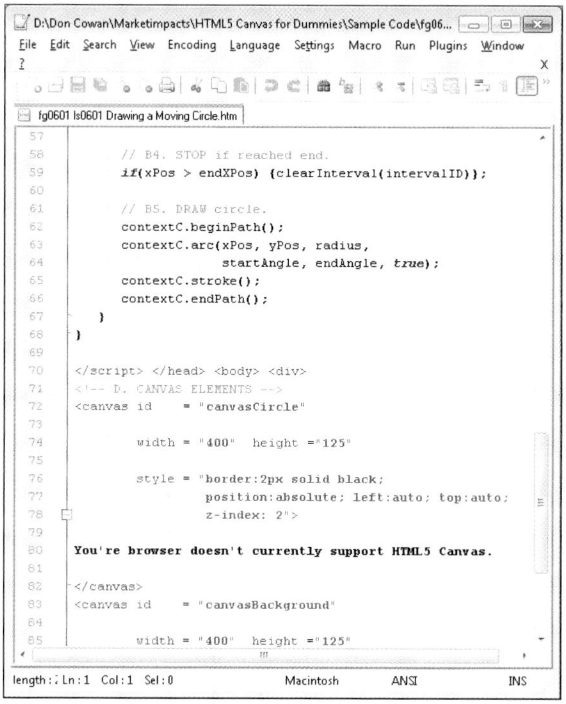

Figure 2-7: Notepad++ text editor.

```
jEdit - fg0601 ls0601 Drawing a Moving Circle.htm                    ☐ ☐ ✕
File  Edit  Search  Markers  Folding  View  Utilities  Macros  Plugins  Help

☐ ☐ ☐ ☒ ☐ ☐ ☐ ☐ ✂ ☐ ☐ ☐ ☐ ☐ ☐ ─

☐ fg0601 ls0601 Drawing a Moving Circle.htm (D:\Don Cowan\Marketimpacts\HTM... ▼

            // B4. STOP if reached end.
            if(xPos > endXPos) {clearInterval(intervalID)};

            // B5. DRAW circle.
            contextC.beginPath();
            contextC.arc(xPos, yPos, radius,
                         startAngle, endAngle, true);
            contextC.stroke();
            contextC.endPath();
        }
    }

    </script> </head> <body> <div>
    <!-- D. CANVAS ELEMENTS -->
    <canvas id    = "canvasCircle"

            width = "400"  height ="125"

            style = "border:2px solid       ;
                     position:absolute; left:auto; top:auto;
                     z-index: 2">

    You're browser doesn't currently support HTML5 Canvas.

    </canvas>
    <canvas id    = "canvasBackground"

            width = "400"  height ="125"

1,1 (0/2332)                    (html,none,Cp1252)         MG 26/121Mb 11:47 AM
```

Figure 2-8: The jEdit text editor.

Saving HTML5 Canvas application files

After you've entered the HTML5 Canvas application code in your favorite text editor, save the file with the `.htm` or `.html` extension. To do this, click Save and then, in the Save As dialog box, select All Files from the Save As Type drop-down list, and append `.htm` or `.html` to the filename (see Figure 2-9). Then click Save.

With the `.htm` or `.html` file extension, when you click the filename, your default browser opens the file as a web page, and your Canvas is displayed. To edit your code, open the file with a text editor, such as Notepad or jEdit.

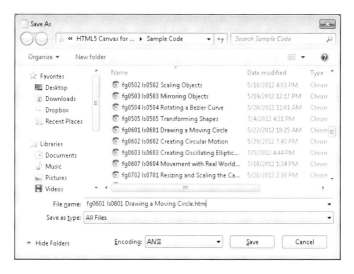

Figure 2-9: Saving HTML5 Canvas application files.

Using Code Debuggers

It's virtually impossible to develop Canvas applications without a code debugger. HTML and JavaScript are interpreted languages, so there's no compiler used to check for syntax errors. Program code is executed by the browser. Your code can also contain logic errors and other problems that are difficult to diagnose.

As a result, when your code contains errors, you'll often see nothing happen. Your Canvas simply remains blank. You'll have no indication where to look for the cause of failure. This is, in fact, usually what happens the first time you run your application code. You see nothing. Yikes, what do you do now?

Code debuggers to the rescue. A *debugger* lets you set code breakpoints (places where execution stops) and examine application variables during execution. You can step through your code and follow exactly what's happening to determine where failures occur and what's causing them.

Firefox Firebug

Shown in Figure 2-10, the Firefox Firebug browser extension is a popular and powerful debugging tool. It's free, and you can download and add it to your Firefox browser by following these steps:

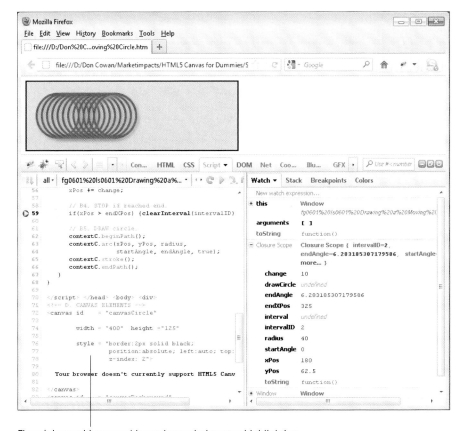

Firerainbow add-on provides color-coded syntax highlighting.

Figure 2-10: Firefox Firebug debugger extension with the Firerainbow add-on.

1. **If you don't have the latest version of Firefox installed on your computer, go to** `www.firefox.com`. **Click Firefox Free Download and install the browser.**

2. **Using the Firefox browser, go to** `www.getfirebug.com`, **and then click the Install Firebug button.**

   It's important to use Firefox in this step so that Firebug will be automatically installed as a Firefox extension.

3. **Start Firebug in the Firefox browser by choosing Tools⇨Web Developer⇨Firebug⇨Open Firebug.**

There's currently no way to save changes to your code by using Firebug. It's necessary when using Firebug for debugging to make any code changes using your text editor. When debugging, I open side-by-side windows with Firefox/Firebug in one window and my text editor in the other. It's easy to make changes in the text editor window, save them, and then run the test in the Firefox window using Firebug.

Every so often, your operating system might think that the text editor file you're trying to save is being used by another program. In this instance, it's necessary to delete the file before resaving it. Just make sure you have your code safely in the open text editor window before you delete the file. Otherwise, you'll lose all your valuable work!

Firerainbow

Firerainbow is an add-on to Firebug that provides color-coded syntax highlighting for easier differentiation of programming elements. You can download it for free at `http://firerainbow.binaryage.com`. You can see the effect of Firerainbow in the lower left window of Figure 2-10.

Other browsers' debugging tools

The other major browsers also provide JavaScript debugging tools. To access these tools, follow these steps for individual browsers:

Chrome

1. **Open the browser.**
2. **Choose Tools⬎Developer Tools.**
3. **Click the Scripts tab.**

Internet Explorer

1. **Open the browser.**
2. **Choose Tools⬎Developer Tools.**
3. **Click the Script tab.**

Opera

1. **Open the browser.**
2. **Open the webpage at** `http://dev.opera.com/articles/view/opera-developer-tools.`

3. Drag the Developer Console button to your toolbar.

4. Click the Developer Console button you just created.

5. Click the JS tab.

Safari

1. Open the browser.

2. Open the web page `http://extensions.apple.com`.

3. Click Install Now for the Firebug Lite extension.

4. Click the Firebug Lite button you just created.

5. Click the Script tab.

Part II
Drawing on Canvas

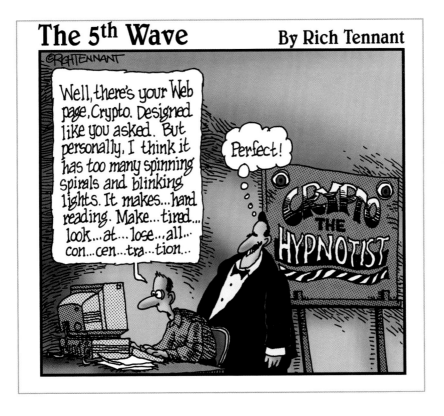

In this part . . .

In Part II, I explain the basics of drawing on your Canvas. You discover how to create, enhance, and transform fundamental objects such as text, lines, rectangles, circles, and images. I also cover the basics of creating moving and animated objects.

3

Creating Objects

*I*t's time to start creating on your Canvas, beginning with basic objects that you'll be turning into *objets d'art*. In this chapter, you discover how to draw basic objects and enhance them with colors, patterns, shadows, and more. In later chapters, you find out how to build on these basic objects to create more complex structures, make them move, and interact with viewers.

Positioning Objects on a Canvas

Every artist faces the challenge of making that first mark on a blank canvas. First though, you need to figure out where your virtual Canvas is and how you get at it.

Defining a web page to hold your Canvas

You need to do a couple things before you start working on your Canvas. Like a painter needs to mount his canvas on a frame, your Canvas has to be "mounted" on a web page. Listing 3-1 shows the basic HTML code to hold one or more Canvases and the JavaScript code you'll write to draw on those Canvases. Listing 3-1 displays the simple web page shown in Figure 3-1.

Listing 3-1: Web Page HTML Code

```
<!DOCTYPE HTML>   <!-- HTML document            -->
<html>            <!-- Beginning of HTML code    -->
<head>            <!-- Header                     -->
<script>          <!-- JavaScript code            -->

<!-- Place your JavaScript code here.             -->
</script>         <!-- End of JavaScript code     -->
</head>           <!-- End of header              -->

<body>            <!-- Body of web page           -->

<!-- Formatting for contents                      -->
<div Style = "width:200px; height:200px;
            margin:0 auto; padding:5px;">

<!-- Place your Canvas definitions here.          -->

<!-- Place other web page contents here.          -->
Web page contents.
</div>            <!-- End of formatting          -->
</body>           <!-- End of body                -->
</html>           <!-- End of html document       -->
```

Figure 3-1: Web page display.

A full discussion of HTML tags and website design is well beyond the scope of this book. So in this section, I give you a basic description of the HTML code needed to display your Canvas.

The layout of a web page is delineated by using a notation called *tags*. Tags are enclosed in angle brackets < > that tell the browser you're defining an aspect of your web page.

Each web page element is defined using a start tag, such as `<head>` and, in most cases, an end tag such as `</head>`. Some elements don't need an end tag because they contain all their defining information in the start tag.

Between the start and end tags, there can be:

- Other elements, such as a Canvas
- Attributes, such as dimensions
- Content, such as text and images

Tag information is used by the browser to format web page segments. The tags themselves are not displayed.

To define a web page and position a Canvas within it, take these steps:

1. **Define a document type tag.**

   All HTML documents must start with the `<!DOCTYPE HTML>` tag. There's no end tag used for document type, so it looks like this:

   ```
   <!DOCTYPE HTML>
        .
        Place all your other HTML tags and content here.
        .
   ```

2. **Define HTML tags.**

   The `<HTML>` and `</HTML>` tags delineate the beginning and end of the web page and are positioned as follows:

   ```
   <HTML>
        .
        Define your web page here.
        .
   </HTML>
   ```

3. **Define header tags.**

   The `<head>` and `</head>` tags enclose the code that contains information about the web page. I recommended that you place your JavaScript code in the header as is done in Listing 3-1 and all the code samples in this book:

   ```
   <head>
        .
        Place your <script> tags and JavaScript code here.
        .
   </head>
   ```

4. Define script tags.

The `<script>` and `</script>` tags enclose the code that will be used to control actions on the screen. Place the JavaScript that draws on your Canvas inside the script tags:

```
<script>
  .
  Place your JavaScript code here.
  .
</script>
```

5. Define body tags.

The `<body>` and `</body>` tags delineate the main area of the web page to be displayed:

```
<body>
  .
  Define the display area of your web page,
including your Canvas, here.
  .
</body>
```

6. Define formatting tags.

Formatting tags, such as the `<div>` and `</div>` tags in Listing 3-1, provide the browser with instructions on how to format content, such as:

```
<div   style = "width:500px; height:200px; margin:0 auto; padding:5px;">
</div>
```

Defining your Canvas

The two-dimensional space on which your application draws objects is referred to as the *2D Canvas context*. That's quite a mouthful. The word *context* indicates that your Canvas contains more information than just object positioning. Your JavaScript code will add contextual information such as color and shadows. Using the 2D Canvas context, you'll be able to create interesting and powerful images.

The code in Listing 3-2 displays the Canvas shown in Figure 3-2. Listing 3-2 includes a compressed version of the element tags shown in Listing 3-1. This compression is done to conserve space in code listings in this book.

Figure 3-2: Displaying a Canvas.

Listing 3-2:   Code to Display a Canvas

```
<!DOCTYPE HTML> <html> <head> <script>

// A. WINDOW LOAD function.
window.onload = function()
{
   // A1. CANVAS definition standard variables.
   canvas  = document.getElementById("canvasArea");
   context = canvas.getContext("2d");

   // A2. MESSAGE details. Center on canvas.
   var mText = "Hi!"
   var xPos  = canvas.width/2;
   var yPos  = canvas.height/2;

   // A3. TEXT format details.
   context.font         = "80pt Comic Sans MS";
   context.fillStyle    = "lime";
   context.textAlign    = "center";
   context.textBaseline = "middle";

   // A4. FILL text.
   context.fillText(mText, xPos, yPos);
}
</script> </head> <body>
<div   style = "width:500px; height:200px; margin:0 auto; padding:5px;">

<!-- A5. CANVAS area definition.  -->
<canvas id   = "canvasArea"  width = "500"  height = "200"
        style = "border:2px solid black">
Your browser doesn't currently support HTML5 Canvas.
</canvas> </div> </body> </html>
```

To display a Canvas within a web page, use the following steps in developing your code:

1. **Define your Canvas by using `<canvas>` and `</canvas>` tags.**

   Add HTML5 `<canvas>` and `</canvas>` tags to Listing 3-1. Don't worry about whether you're referring to the correct Canvas feature. There's only one HTML5 Canvas!

   You can, however, have more than one Canvas defined for your application. Identify each Canvas with a unique `id`, as shown in this example from A5 of Listing 3-2:

   ```
   <canvas   id = "canvasArea">
   .
   .
   .
   </canvas>
   ```

   You could have another with a different `id`:

   ```
   <canvas   id = "canvasArea2">
   .
   .
   .
   </canvas>
   ```

   In Listing 3-1 and other examples in this book, the Canvas is the only content. In most real applications, a Canvas will be positioned within other web page content.

2. **Add specifications inside the `<canvas>` tag detailing the dimensions of the Canvas and style of the Canvas border.**

   Here's an example:

   ```
   width = "500"  height = "200"
   style = "border:2px solid black"
   ```

   For more information on style options, see `www.w3.org/TR/CSS2`.

3. **Between the `<canvas>` and `</canvas>` tags, add the text that will be displayed if HTML5 Canvas isn't supported by the browser displaying your web page.**

   For example:

   ```
   Your browser doesn't currently support HTML5 Canvas.
   ```

4. **Create a window `onload` function that will be initiated when the web page is loaded. The `onload` function is the starting point for executing JavaScript code in your application.**

Here's an example in A of Listing 3-2:

```
window.onload = function(){ . . . }
```

5. **Use a JavaScript statement to create a variable identifying a specific Canvas. Within that statement, use the `getElementById()` function to retrieve the Canvas element.**

Here's an example in A1 of Listing 3-2:

```
var canvas = document.getElementById("canvasArea");
```

6. **Use a JavaScript statement to create a variable referring to the 2D context for that Canvas. Use the `getContext()` function to retrieve the context.**

Here's an example in A1 of Listing 3-2:

```
var context = canvas.getContext("2d");
```

7. **Refer to the context variable in subsequent JavaScript statements to draw on the Canvas.**

Here's an example in A3 of Listing 3-2:

```
context.fillStyle = "black";
```

The string of references to get from your JavaScript code to your Canvas is a bit confusing. The following shorthand should help you remember the sequence:

JavaScript code➪Context variable➪Canvas variable➪Canvas tag.

Absolute positioning

In a 2D space, positions are referenced using *x* and *y* coordinates. The *x* axis extends horizontally, and the *y* axis extends vertically. As shown in Figure 3-3, the center has a position *x* = 0 and *y* = 0. This can also be expressed as (0, 0).

This method of positioning objects, known as the Cartesian coordinate system, goes all the way back to the 17th century. The word *Cartesian* comes from the work of the French mathematician and philosopher Rene Descartes (1596–1650). The Cartesian

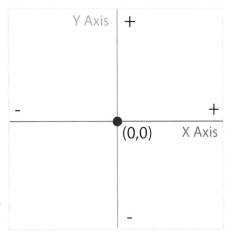

Figure 3-3: Cartesian coordinate space.

coordinate system, shown in Figure 3-3, specifies a point in a plane using a pair of numbers indicating distances from the intersection of the x and y axes.

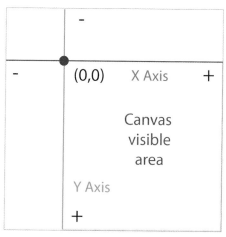

Figure 3-4: Canvas coordinate space.

Unlike a standard Cartesian coordinate space, the Canvas space doesn't have visible negative points. Using negative coordinates won't cause your application to fail, but objects positioned using negative coordinate points won't appear in the display.

Also, as shown in Figure 3-4, the x and y coordinate positions on a Canvas progress from (0, 0) to the right and *downward* to the maximum dimensions of the Canvas space. Therefore, a Canvas that is 400 pixels wide by 200 pixels high has a maximum pixel position of (399, 199).

If you've used Cartesian coordinates in the past, you may forget that on a Canvas space, y coordinates increase downward instead of upward. (I have a mathematics background, so this happens to me all the time.) If you make this mistake, you may be mystified about why you're seeing incorrect Canvas images. Add the *y coordinate direction* to your checklist of common coding errors.

Relative positioning

In addition to specifying numbered pixel positions, such as (240, 145), variables, such as (xPos, yPos), can be used for positioning. Furthermore, these location variables can be defined relative to other variables. This allows positioning relative to locations on the Canvas other than the (0, 0) point used for absolute positioning. Relative positioning by using variable names has a number of advantages over absolute positioning:

- Better documentation of the meaning of object positions
- Improved code understandability
- Enhances the ability to reuse code, such as drawing multiple objects with the same function
- Improved flexibility in changing the position of objects on the Canvas, such as when creating object motion or animation

To use relative positioning, as shown in Figure 3-5, follow these steps:

1. **Define variables to hold anchor position coordinates and values.**

   These variables will be used to calculate object positions. For example, you might want to position objects relative to a starting position with a delta offset:

   ```
   var xStart = 240;    var yStart = 145;
   var delta1 = 35;     var delta2 = 40;
   ```

2. **Define variables to hold your object *x* and *y* coordinate positions.**

   Use the variables from Step 1 to calculate the *x* and *y* coordinates for an object, such as:

   ```
   var xPos = xStart + delta1;
   var yPos = yStart + delta2;
   ```

3. **Use position variables to reference object locations.**

   Use your calculated *x* and *y* coordinates from Step 2 in JavaScript statements, such as those used to display text on your Canvas:

   ```
   var mText = "Text to be displayed."
   context.fillText(mText, xPos, yPos);
   ```

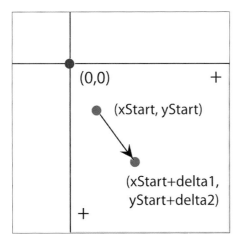

Figure 3-5: Relative positioning on a Canvas.

Drawing Rectangles

Rectangles are one of the most common and easiest to draw Canvas objects. The code in Listing 3-3 created the rectangles shown in Figure 3-6.

Listing 3-3: Drawing Rectangles

```
<!DOCTYPE HTML> <html> <head> <script>

// A. WINDOW LOAD function.
window.onload = function()
{
    // A1. CANVAS definition standard variables.
    canvas  = document.getElementById("canvasArea");
    context = canvas.getContext("2d");

    // A2. LAYOUT of first rectangle.
    var xPos  = 20;     var yPos   = 20;
    var width = 100;    var height = 50;

    // A3. DISPLAY rectangles.
    context.fillStyle   = "hotpink";
    context.fillRect      (xPos,      yPos,     width,     height);
    context.lineWidth   = 4;
    context.strokeStyle = "royalblue";
    context.strokeRect    (xPos+130, yPos,     width,     height);
    context.fillStyle   = "darkorange";
    context.fillRect      (xPos+260, yPos,     width,     height);
    context.clearRect     (xPos+285, yPos+10, width-50, height-20);
}
</script> </head> <body>
<div    style = "width:400px; height:90px; margin:0 auto; padding:5px;">
<canvas id    = "canvasArea"
        width = "400"  height = "90"  style = "border:2px solid black">
Your browser doesn't currently support HTML5 Canvas.
</canvas> </div> </body> </html>
```

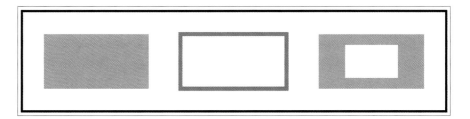

Figure 3-6: Rectangles.

In this section and those that follow, I won't be discussing the standard code to display a web page and Canvas (as demonstrated in Listings 3-1 and 3-2). Other than changes to the dimensions of the Canvas in the `<div>` and `<canvas>` tags, the code is the same for each listing.

To create a rectangle, follow these steps:

1. **Define variables to control positioning.**

   As shown in A2 of Listing 3-3, define variables used to draw the rectangles, such as positioning coordinates:

   ```
   var xPos = 20;    var yPos = 20;
   ```

2. **Using references to the Canvas context, define attributes of the rectangles.**

   For example, here's a fill color shown in A2:

   ```
   context.fillStyle = "hotpink";
   ```

   You can find a more complete discussion of object attributes in the next section.

3. **Create your rectangles using the function for the type of rectangle desired:**

   - `fillRect()`: A rectangle that's filled as specified in attributes such as `fillStyle`. An example is the first rectangle in Figure 3-6:

     ```
     context.fillRect(xPos, yPos, width, height);
     ```

   - `strokeRect()`: A rectangle that's outlined as specified in attributes such as `strokeStyle` and `lineWidth`. An example is the second rectangle in Figure 3-6:

     ```
     context.strokeRect(xPos+130, yPos,  width, height);
     ```

   - `clearRect()`: A rectangle that creates a cleared space. This is demonstrated in the third rectangle of Figure 3-6:

     ```
     context.clearRect(xPos+285, yPos+10, width-50, height-20);
     ```

Defining Object Attributes

The choices you make for object attributes can help your Canvas application stand out and attract users. The attributes discussed in this section include

- **Colors:** Fill your object with any of thousands of color variations.

- **Gradients:** Vary the colors within an object.

✓ **Patterns:** Fill your object with a repeated pattern.

✓ **Transparency:** Let another image or background show through your object.

✓ **Shadows:** Generate shadows below, above, or to the side of your objects.

✓ **Clipping:** Set a mask that will remove designated portions of your object.

You can apply these attributes to a variety of object types, such as lines, circles, rectangles, and multi-sided shapes. To assign an attribute to an object, follow these steps:

1. **Define the attribute in the Canvas context.**

   For example, set the `fillStyle` for objects to be drawn in black:

   ```
   context.fillStyle = "black";
   ```

2. **Create objects that you want to have the attribute.**

   When an object is drawn, the existing context attributes are applied. So, say that after the statement in Step 1, you use the following function:

   ```
   context.fillText("Hi", xPos, yPos);
   ```

   The result is that the word *Hi* is drawn in black on the Canvas at position x = xPos, y = yPos.

   After the `fillStyle` is set to black, you can draw a single object or multiple objects by using this style. As long as the context `fillStyle` attribute is set to black, objects drawn will have a black `fillStyle`.

3. **Change the attribute for other objects.**

   To change the `fillStyle` of the next objects drawn, add code to change the `fillStyle` attribute. For example, changing the `fillStyle` to orange:

   ```
   context.fillStyle = "orange";
   ```

The terms `fillStyle` and `fillText` are similar, which creates a bit of confusion. The term `fillStyle` is an *attribute* that is assigned a value using an = operation. The term `fillText` is a *function* that is executed using the parameters inside parentheses ( ). Another way to understand this distinction is to remember that the attributes will not appear on the Canvas until an object is drawn using a function.

Colors

Apply color to object fills and *strokes* (lines) by using the `fillStyle` and `strokeStyle` context attributes. For example:

```
context.fillStyle   = "orange";
context.strokeStyle = "red";
```

You can specify the color of an object in a number of ways, including

Color Specification	Example
Color keywords	`cornflowerblue`
Hexadecimal values	`#6495ED`
RGB (red, green, blue)	`rgb(100, 149, 237)`
HSL (hue, saturation, lightness)	`hsl(219, 58%, 93%)`

Color keywords

There are basic and extended keywords for a wide variety of colors, as shown in Figure 3-7. See `www.w3.org/TR/css3-color/#svg-color` for additional details.

Hexadecimal values

Using a hexadecimal representation for red, green, and blue values allows the creation of more than 16 million different colors. This is useful when designing color variations or matching a very specific color. As an example, the extended color `"cornflowerblue"` has a hexadecimal value of `"#6495ED"`.

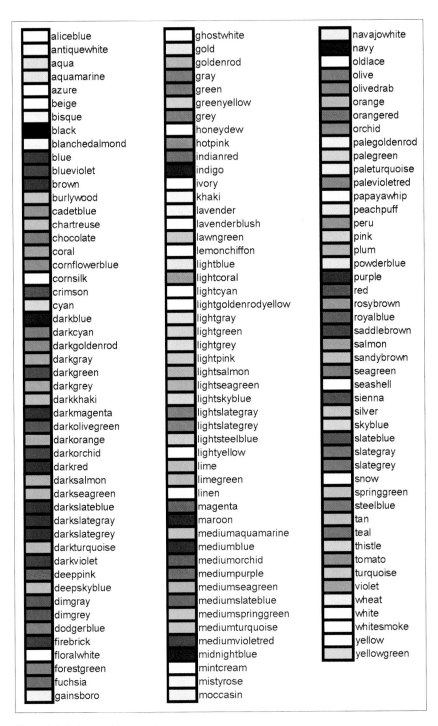

aliceblue	ghostwhite	navajowhite
antiquewhite	gold	navy
aqua	goldenrod	oldlace
aquamarine	gray	olive
azure	green	olivedrab
beige	greenyellow	orange
bisque	grey	orangered
black	honeydew	orchid
blanchedalmond	hotpink	palegoldenrod
blue	indianred	palegreen
blueviolet	indigo	paleturquoise
brown	ivory	palevioletred
burlywood	khaki	papayawhip
cadetblue	lavender	peachpuff
chartreuse	lavenderblush	peru
chocolate	lawngreen	pink
coral	lemonchiffon	plum
cornflowerblue	lightblue	powderblue
cornsilk	lightcoral	purple
crimson	lightcyan	red
cyan	lightgoldenrodyellow	rosybrown
darkblue	lightgray	royalblue
darkcyan	lightgreen	saddlebrown
darkgoldenrod	lightgrey	salmon
darkgray	lightpink	sandybrown
darkgreen	lightsalmon	seagreen
darkgrey	lightseagreen	seashell
darkkhaki	lightskyblue	sienna
darkmagenta	lightslategray	silver
darkolivegreen	lightslategrey	skyblue
darkorange	lightsteelblue	slateblue
darkorchid	lightyellow	slategray
darkred	lime	slategrey
darksalmon	limegreen	snow
darkseagreen	linen	springgreen
darkslateblue	magenta	steelblue
darkslategray	maroon	tan
darkslategrey	mediumaquamarine	teal
darkturquoise	mediumblue	thistle
darkviolet	mediumorchid	tomato
deeppink	mediumpurple	turquoise
deepskyblue	mediumseagreen	violet
dimgray	mediumslateblue	wheat
dimgrey	mediumspringgreen	white
dodgerblue	mediumturquoise	whitesmoke
firebrick	mediumvioletred	yellow
floralwhite	midnightblue	yellowgreen
forestgreen	mintcream	
fuchsia	mistyrose	
gainsboro	moccasin	

Figure 3-7: Colors and keywords.

Hexadecimal numbers use a base of 16 symbols to represent values, to allow specifying larger numbers with the same number of symbols as a number system with a smaller base, such as the familiar base 10 system of digits 0 through 9. To convert a number between base systems, you can use a conversion website such as

```
www.statman.info/conversions/hexadecimal.html
```

RGB and HSL values

Colors can also be defined by using numeric values for combinations of RGB (red, green, blue) or HSL (hue, saturation, lightness). HSL is also referred to as HSV (hue, saturation, value).

RGB specifies numbers for the level of red, green, and blue in numbers from 0 to 255:

```
rgb(24,50,150)
```

For example, to create a fillStyle using this color:

```
context.fillStyle = "rgb(24,50,150)"
```

HSL specifies a number for hue and percentages for saturation and lightness:

```
hsl(30,50%,75%)
```

- **Hue** indicates the position on a circular color wheel starting with red at the zero degree point and wrapping back to red at 360 degrees.
- **Saturation** indicates the amount of color from 0% to 100%.
- **Lightness** indicates the purity of color from 0% to 100%.

To create a fillStyle with the hsl format, use the following line:

```
context.fillStyle = "hsl(30, 50%, 75%)"
```

The best way to understand the real meaning of these numbers is to experiment with a color design tool such as http://kuler.adobe.com (shown in Figure 3-8).

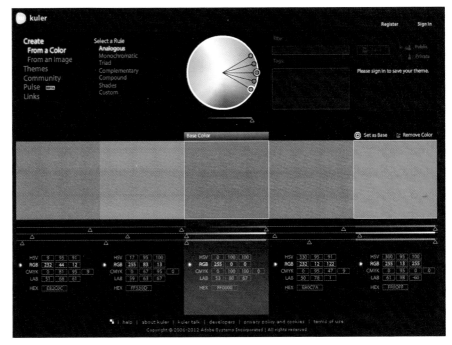

Figure 3-8: Color picker.

Gradients

Gradients create transitions between colors, and they can be linear or radial:

- ✓ **Linear gradients** transition their colors, as shown in the first three squares and line at the bottom of Figure 3-9.

- ✓ **Radial gradients** transition their colors as shown in the last two squares in Figure 3-9.

The objects in Figure 3-9 were created by using the code in Listing 3-4.

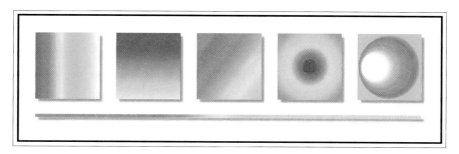

Figure 3-9: Linear and radial gradients.

Listing 3-4:   Creating Gradients

```
<!DOCTYPE HTML> <html> <head> <script>

// A. WINDOW LOAD function.
window.onload = function()
{
    // A1. CANVAS definition standard variables.
    canvas  = document.getElementById("canvasArea");
    context = canvas.getContext("2d");

    // A2. LAYOUT of first object.
    var xPos  = 20;   var yPos   = 20;   var gap = 20;
    var width = 80;   var height = 80;

    // A3. ATTRIBUTES.
    context.shadowOffsetX = 4;
    context.shadowOffsetY = 4;
    context.shadowBlur    = 3;
    context.shadowColor   = "gray";
    context.lineWidth     = 4;

    // A4. LINEAR HORIZONTAL gradient.
    var gradLH = context.createLinearGradient(
              20,                              // Start x
              0,                               // Start y
              100,                             // End x
              0);                              // End y

    // A5. LINEAR VERTICAL gradient.
    var gradLV = context.createLinearGradient(
              0,                               // Start x
              0,                               // Start y
              0,                               // End x
              100);                            // End y
```

(continued)

Listing 3-4 *(continued)*

```
// A6. LINEAR DIAGONAL gradient.
var gradLD = context.createLinearGradient(
            xPos+(2*width)+(2*gap),              // Start x
            yPos,                                 // Start y
            xPos+220+width,                       // End x
            yPos+height);                         // End y


// A7. CENTERED RADIAL gradient.
var gradRC = context.createRadialGradient(
            xPos+(3*width)+(3*gap)+(width/2),    // Inner circle x
            yPos+(height/2),                      // Inner circle y
            5,                                    // Inner circle radius
            xPos+(3*width)+(3*gap)+(width/2),    // Outer circle x
            yPos+(height/2),                      // Outer circle y
            50);                                  // Outer circle radius


// A8. OFFSET RADIAL gradient.
var gradRO = context.createRadialGradient(
            xPos+(4*width)+(4*gap)+(width/4),    // Inner circle x
            yPos+(height/2),                      // Inner circle y
            15,                                   // Inner circle radius
            xPos+(4*width)+(4*gap)+(width/2),    // Outer circle x
            yPos+(height/2),                      // Outer circle y
            40);                                  // Outer circle radius


// A9. COLORS.
gradLH.addColorStop( 0, "deeppink"    );
gradLH.addColorStop(.3, "orange"      );
gradLH.addColorStop(.6, "lime"        );
gradLH.addColorStop( 1, "yellow"      );
gradLV.addColorStop( 0, "red"         );
gradLV.addColorStop(.4, "blueviolet"  );
gradLV.addColorStop( 1, "gold"        );
gradLD.addColorStop( 0, "fuchsia"     );
gradLD.addColorStop(.5, "orange"      );
gradLD.addColorStop( 1, "springgreen" );
gradRC.addColorStop( 0, "red"         );
gradRC.addColorStop(.5, "turquoise"   );
gradRC.addColorStop( 1, "olive"       );
gradRO.addColorStop( 0, "yellow"      );
gradRO.addColorStop(.7, "magenta"     );
gradRO.addColorStop( 1, "limegreen"   );


// A10. LINEAR gradient objects.
context.fillStyle    = gradLH;
context.fillRect     (xPos+(0*width)+(0*gap), yPos, width, height);
context.fillStyle    = gradLV;
context.fillRect     (xPos+(1*width)+(1*gap), yPos, width, height);
```

```
       context.fillStyle    = gradLD;
   context.fillRect       (xPos+(2*width)+(2*gap), yPos, width, height);
   context.strokeStyle = gradLD;
   context.beginPath();
   context.moveTo         (xPos,                   yPos+height+gap);
   context.lineTo         (xPos+(5*width)+(4*gap), yPos+height+gap);
   context.stroke();

   // A11. RADIAL gradient objects.
   context.fillStyle    = gradRC;
   context.fillRect       (xPos+(3*width)+(3*gap), yPos, width, height);
   context.fillStyle    = gradRO;
   context.fillRect       (xPos+(4*width)+(4*gap), yPos, width, height);
}
</script> </head> <body>
<div    style = "width:525px; height:150px; margin:0 auto; padding:5px;">
<canvas id     = "canvasArea"  width = "525"  height ="150"

               style = "border:2px solid black">
Your browser doesn't currently support HTML5 Canvas.
</canvas> </div> </body> </html>
```

To create gradients, follow these steps:

1. **Create gradient variables by using either `createLinearGradient()` or `createRadialGradient()`, depending on whether you want a linear or radial shape to your color transitions.**

   The `createLinearGradient()` function has four parameters, which specify x and y starting and ending positions:

   ```
   var gradLH = context.createLinearGradient(StartX, StartY, EndX, EndY);
   ```

   Set the value of the x and y coordinates to determine the angle of the gradient and influence the size of color bands generated. The x and y coordinates are relative to the top-left corner of the Canvas.

   - To create a horizontal gradient, set the y parameters to zero.
   - To create a vertical gradient, set the x parameters to zero.

   See A4–5 in Listing 3-4 for linear horizontal (`gradLH`) and linear vertical (`gradLV`) gradient code examples:

   ```
   var gradLH = context.createLinearGradient(20, 0, 100,   0);
   var gradLV = context.createLinearGradient(0,  0,   0, 100);
   ```

These two statements generated the first two objects in Figure 3-9. Use the code in Listing 3-4 to experiment with different values for these parameters and observe the results.

The `createRadialGradient()` function has six parameters, defining the *x* position, *y* position, and radius for two circles:

```
var gradRC = context.createRadialGradient(
            innerCircleX, innerCircleY, innerCircleRadius,
            outerCircleX, outerCircleY, outerCircleRadius,);
```

To create a radial gradient centered in an object, the *x* and *y* values must be set to the desired position within the object. A7–8 in Listing 3-4 demonstrate centering a radial in a square (`gradRC`) and placing one offset to the side (`gradRO`). Here's the centered radial gradient:

```
var gradRC = context.createRadialGradient(
            xPos+(3*width)+(3*gap)+(width/2),    // Inner circle x
            yPos+(height/2),                     // Inner circle y
            5,                                   // Inner circle radius

            xPos+(3*width)+(3*gap)+(width/2),    // Outer circle x
            yPos+(height/2),                     // Outer circle y
            50);                                 // Outer circle radius
```

The gradient *x* and *y* parameters are positions relative to the top-left corner of the Canvas, *not the object using the gradient.* To make the gradient positioning relative to an object, the *x* and *y* values must be adjusted to lie within the object. (See A6–8 in Listing 3-4.)

2. **Use the `addColorStop()` function to add colors to the gradient.**

The first parameter determines where a color begins. The second parameter determines the color.

Here's an example in code section A9 of Listing 3-4:

```
gradLH.addColorStop( 0, "deeppink" );
gradLH.addColorStop(.3, "orange"   );
gradLH.addColorStop(.6, "lime"     );
gradLH.addColorStop( 1, "yellow"   );
```

3. **Set the `fillStyle` to the gradient that has been defined.**

Here's an example in code sections A10–11 of Listing 3-4:

```
context.fillStyle = gradLH;
```

In addition to using gradients with simple shapes like squares and lines, gradients can be applied to more complex, multi-sided shapes. The process is the same. After the `fillStyle` has been set to a gradient, objects drawn will use that gradient.

4. **Create the object using the appropriate function.**

   The object will be filled with the gradient because the context has been set with the gradient `fillStyle` in Step 3. Sections A10–11 in Listing 3-4 demonstrate creating a number of objects with a gradient applied. One example is

```
context.fillRect(xPos+(2*width)+(2*gap), yPos, width, height);
```

Patterns

Patterns create repeated images. The patterns in Figure 3-10 were created with the code in Listing 3-5.

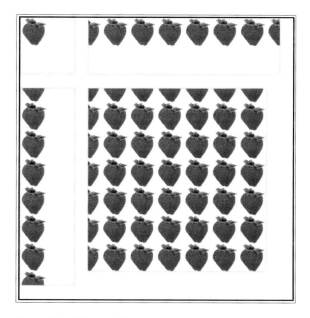

Figure 3-10: Objects with patterns.

Listing 3-5: Using Patterns

```
<!DOCTYPE HTML> <html> <head> <script>

// A. WINDOW LOAD function.
window.onload = function()
{
    // A1. CANVAS definition standard variables.
    canvas  = document.getElementById("canvasArea");
    context = canvas.getContext("2d");

    // A2. IMAGE variables and sources.
    var smallImage = new Image();
    smallImage.src = "http://marketimpacts.com/storage/Strawberry50px.png";

    // B. PATTERN creation.
    smallImage.onload = function()
    {
        // B1. ATTRIBUTES.
        context.shadowOffsetX = 4;      context.shadowOffsetY = 4;
        context.shadowBlur    = 10;     context.shadowColor   = "lavender";

        // B2. REPEAT pattern variables.
        var repeatPattern   = context.createPattern(smallImage, "repeat"   );
        var noRepeatPattern = context.createPattern(smallImage, "no-repeat");
        var repeatXPattern  = context.createPattern(smallImage, "repeat-x" );
        var repeatYPattern  = context.createPattern(smallImage, "repeat-y" );

        // B3. PATTERN objects.
        context.fillStyle = repeatPattern;
        context.fillRect    (125, 125, 325, 325);
        context.strokeRect (125, 125, 325, 325);
        context.fillStyle = noRepeatPattern;
        context.fillRect    (0, 0, 100, 100);
        context.strokeRect (0, 0, 100, 100);
        context.fillStyle = repeatXPattern;
        context.fillRect    (125, 0, 350, 100);
        context.strokeRect (125, 0, 350, 100);
        context.fillStyle = repeatYPattern;
        context.fillRect    (0, 125, 100, 350);
        context.strokeRect (0, 125, 100, 350);
    }
}
</script> </head> <body>
<div    style = "width:500px;  height:500px; margin:0 auto; padding:5px;">
<canvas  id   = "canvasArea"  width = "500"  height = "500"
         style = "border:2px solid black">
Your browser doesn't currently support HTML5 Canvas.
</canvas> </div> </body> </html>
```

As shown in Figure 3-10, four types of patterns can be generated:

- **Repeat:** The object is filled with the repeated image, as shown in the lower right of Figure 3-10.

- **No Repeat:** The image is drawn only once in the object, as shown in the upper left of Figure 3-10.

- **Repeat X:** The image is repeated across the horizontal length of the object, as shown in the upper right of Figure 3-10.

- **Repeat Y:** The image is repeated down the vertical height of the object, as shown in the lower left of Figure 3-10.

As of this writing, the major browsers have different implementations of pattern generation. The Repeat pattern is consistent across browsers.

The browser creates patterns by starting at the upper left of the Canvas at position (0, 0). Notice in Figure 3-10 that even when patterns are drawn inside a space that does not start at (0, 0), the pattern is drawn using the (0, 0) starting point. You can change this starting point by *translating* the (0, 0) point to another position, as explained in Chapter 5.

To use patterns, do the following:

1. **Create a variable to hold the image and reference the source on a website.**

   In the Listing 3-5, a 50 pixel square image of a ball is used. This is shown in code section A2:

   ```
   var smallImage = new Image();
   smallImage.src = "http://marketimpacts.com/storage/Strawberry50px.png";
   ```

2. **Create the function to be executed when the image is loaded.**

   Here's an example in code section B of Listing 3-5:

   ```
   smallImage.onload = function()
   { . . . }
   ```

3. **Define any attributes you want applied to the image.**

   For example, in B1 of Listing 3-5, shadow attributes are established:

   ```
   context.shadowOffsetX = 4;    context.shadowOffsetY = 4;
   context.shadowBlur    = 10;    context.shadowColor   = "gray";
   ```

4. **Create pattern variables by using the `createPattern()` function.**

An example is shown in B2 of Listing 3-5:

```
var repeatPattern = context.createPattern(smallImage,"repeat");
```

5. **Finally, create the objects using the pattern.**

In B3 of Listing 3-5, the `fillStyle` attribute is used to establish the type of repetition, and the `fillRect()` function is used to fill the objects with the pattern. The `strokeRect()` function is used in the example to show the outline of the rectangle being filled. One example is

```
context.fillStyle = repeatPattern;
context.strokeRect (125, 125, 325, 325);
context.fillRect   (125, 125, 325, 325);
```

Objects including rectangles, circles, lines, and those that are complex and multi-sided can be filled with patterns. Once the `fillStyle` has been set to a pattern, that pattern will be used when an object is drawn.

Transparency

Object transparency is created by using the `globalAlpha` attribute. This attribute indicates the degree of transparency from 0 to 1, where 0 is fully transparent and 1 is fully opaque. Figure 3-11 shows objects created by the code in Listing 3-6 using varying degrees of `globalAlpha`.

To create color blends using transparency, overlap images as demonstrated in Figure 3-11.

The term *alpha* comes from the concept of "alpha channels" developed in the late 1970s to carry information about how to modify an original image, or channel. It's called `globalAlpha` because it applies globally to the entire Canvas context to which it's assigned.

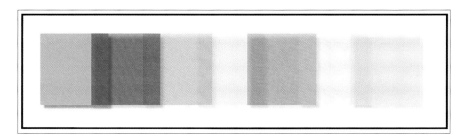

Figure 3-11: Object transparency.

Listing 3-6: Using Transparency

```
<!DOCTYPE HTML> <html> <head> <script>

// A. WINDOW LOAD function.
window.onload = function()
{
   // A1. CANVAS definition standard variables.
   canvas  = document.getElementById("canvasArea");
   context = canvas.getContext("2d");

   // A2. LAYOUT of first object.
   var xPos   = 20;   var yPos   = 20;   var gap = -20;
   var width  = 80;   var height = 80;

   // A3. SHADOW attributes.
   context.shadowOffsetX = 4;      context.shadowOffsetY = 4;
   context.shadowBlur    = 3;      context.shadowColor   = "gray";

   // A4. OBJECTS with global alpha.
   context.globalAlpha = 1;
   context.fillStyle   = "orange";
   context.fillRect    (xPos+(0*width)+(0*gap), yPos, width, height);
   context.globalAlpha = .5;
   context.fillStyle   = "blue";
   context.fillRect    (xPos+(1*width)+(1*gap), yPos, width, height);
   context.globalAlpha = .25;
   context.fillStyle   = "red";
   context.fillRect    (xPos+(2*width)+(2*gap), yPos, width, height);
   context.globalAlpha = .25;
   context.fillStyle   = "limegreen";
   context.fillRect    (xPos+(3*width)+(3*gap), yPos, width, height);
   context.globalAlpha = .4;
   context.fillStyle   = "magenta";
   context.fillRect    (xPos+(4*width)+(4*gap), yPos, width, height);
   context.globalAlpha = .25;
   context.fillStyle   = "gold";
   context.fillRect    (xPos+(5*width)+(5*gap), yPos, width, height);
   context.globalAlpha = .4;
   context.fillStyle   = "turquoise";
   context.fillRect    (xPos+(6*width)+(6*gap), yPos, width, height);
}
</script> </head> <body>
<div    style = "width:490px;   height:125px; margin:0 auto; padding:5px;">
<canvas id     = "canvasArea"
        width = "490"  height = "125" style  = "border:2px solid black">
Your browser doesn't currently support HTML5 Canvas.
</canvas> </div> </body> </html>
```

To create transparency in an object, do the following:

1. **Set the context `globalAlpha` attribute to the desired level of transparency.**

   After you set this attribute, whatever colors are used to fill an object or stroke will be altered when the object is created. This is demonstrated in A4 of Listing 3-6, which includes this example:

   ```
   context.globalAlpha = .5;
   ```

2. **Set the `fillStyle` for the objects that you will draw.**

   In the following sample code from A4, the `fillStyle` is set to blue, and the `globalAlpha` setting from Step 1 example will make the blue 50% transparent.

   ```
   context.fillStyle = "blue";
   ```

   An alternative way to set the transparency is to use a fourth parameter in an `rgb` specification for a color. For example, use the following code to set the color blue to a 50% transparency level:

   ```
   context.fillStyle = "rgb(0,0,255,.5)"
   ```

3. **Create the object.**

   Use the appropriate function to create your object. In code section A4 in Listing 3-6, the transparency will be applied to a rectangle:

   ```
   context.fillRect(xPos+(1*width)+(1*gap), yPos, width, height);
   ```

Shadows

To create shadows, as demonstrated in Figure 3-12 and Listing 3-7, follow these steps:

1. **Set shadow attributes in the Canvas context.**

   Set context shadow attributes as in A3–5 of Listing 3-7:

   - *Shadow x and y offsets:* The distance of the shadow from the original object.
   - *Shadow blur:* The amount of blurring applied.
   - *Shadow color:* The color of the shadow, which can be different than the color of the original object.

   An example is

   ```
   context.shadowOffsetX = 4;  context.shadowOffsetY = 4;
   context.shadowBlur    = 3;  context.shadowColor   = "gray";
   ```

2. Draw the objects that you want to have a shadow.

Draw objects with shadow attributes defined to generate the accompanying shadows as is shown in this example from A3–5 of Listing 3-7:

```
context.fillRect(x1Pos, yPos, length, height);
```

Figure 3-12: Object shadows.

Listing 3-7:   Creating Shadows

```
<!DOCTYPE HTML> <html> <head> <script>

// A. WINDOW LOAD function.
window.onload = function()
{
   // A1. CANVAS definition standard variables.
   canvas  = document.getElementById("canvasArea");
   context = canvas.getContext("2d");

   // A2. LAYOUT parameters.
   var x1Pos  = 25;    var x2Pos  = 175;   var x3Pos  = 325;
   var yPos   = 10;
   var length = 100;   var height = 25;

   // A3. RECTANGLE with shadow.
   context.shadowOffsetX = 4;
   context.shadowOffsetY = 4;
   context.shadowBlur    = 3;
   context.fillStyle     = "deeppink";
   context.shadowColor   = "gray";
   context.fillRect     (x1Pos, yPos, length, height);

   // A4. RECTANGLE with shadow.
   context.shadowOffsetX = 8;
   context.shadowOffsetY = 8;
   context.shadowBlur    = 3;
   context.strokeStyle   = "aqua";
   context.shadowColor   = "lightgreen";
   context.lineWidth     = 9;
   context.strokeRect   (x2Pos, yPos, length, height);
```

(continued)

Listing 3-7 *(continued)*

```
   // A5. RECTANGLE with shadow.
   context.shadowOffsetX = 30;
   context.shadowOffsetY = 30;
   context.shadowBlur    = 9;
   context.fillStyle     = "darkorange";
   context.shadowColor   = "greenyellow";
   context.fillRect      (x3Pos, yPos, length, height);
}
</script> </head> <body>
<div    style = "width:500px;  height:80px;  margin:0 auto; padding:5px;">
<canvas id    = "canvasArea"
        width = "500"  height = "80"  style  = "border:2px solid black">
Your browser doesn't currently support HTML5 Canvas.
</canvas> </div> </body> </html>
```

Clipping

Clipping is a function that restricts the area of a Canvas that can be drawn on to the size and shape of an object. For example, Figure 3-13 shows how a rectangular clipping region was used to eliminate portions of text. Notice that the sides, top, and bottom of the words "Hi there!" have been shaved off by the clipping region. The code in Listing 3-8 created this display.

Figure 3-13: Clipping objects.

Listing 3-8:   Clipping Objects

```
<!DOCTYPE HTML> <html> <head> <script>

// A. WINDOW LOAD function.
window.onload = function()
{
   // A1. CANVAS definition standard variables.
   canvas  = document.getElementById("canvasArea");
   context = canvas.getContext("2d");
```

```
    // A2. MESSAGE details. Center on canvas.
    var mText = "Hi there!"
    var xPos  = canvas.width/2;    var yPos  = canvas.height/2;

    // A3. TEXT format details.
    context.font         = "60pt Comic Sans MS";
    context.fillStyle    = "hotpink";
    context.textAlign    = "center";
    context.textBaseline = "middle";

    // A4. CLIPPING region.
    context.rect(40, 40, 320, 50);
    context.clip();

    // A5. FILL text.
    context.fillText(mText, xPos, yPos);
}
</script> </head> <body>
<div    style = "width:500px;  height:90px; margin:0 auto; padding:5px;">
<canvas id     = "canvasArea"
        width = "400"  height = "150"  style  = "border:2px solid black">
Your browser doesn't currently support HTML5 Canvas.
</canvas> </div> </body> </html>
```

To establish a clipping region, follow these steps:

1. **Create a clipping shape by using the appropriate function.**

   Use a function such as the `rect()` function to create the clipping shape:

   ```
   rect(xPos, yPos, width, height)
   ```

   Here's an example from A4 of Listing 3-8:

   ```
   context.rect(40, 40, 320, 50);
   ```

   Other shapes, such as a circle, can also be used to establish the clipping region.

2. **Use the `clip()` function to create a clipping region.**

   Code section A4 of Listing 3-8 demonstrates this:

   ```
   context.clip();
   ```

   The clipping region will have the shape of the area created in Step 1.

3. **Draw the shape to be clipped by using the appropriate function.**

   Here's an example from code section A5 in Listing 3-8:

   ```
   context.fillText(mText, xPos, yPos);
   ```

   Thus, the shape created in Step 1 is used to clip the shape created in Step 3.

Displaying Text

You've already seen an example of displaying text in a Canvas application in Chapter 1. It's a common and important function. Text even has its own Application Programming Interface (API).

To display text, first set the characteristics of the text by assigning values to the appropriate context attributes, such as:

```
context.font      = "italic bold 12px Arial";
context.fillStyle = "black";
context.textAlign = "center";
```

Then apply the `fillText()` method to the context passing as parameters the text to be displayed and its coordinates on the Canvas:

```
context.fillText(mText, xPos, yPos);
```

An example is shown earlier in Figure 3-2, which was generated using the code in Listing 3-2.

Font attributes

You can set a number of font properties by using `context.font`: style, weight, size, and face. These are based on Cascading Style Sheet (CSS) specifications. Not all values are required. If values aren't specified, the defaults are applied. The format of the statement to assign font attributes is

```
context.font = "style weight size face";
```

For example:

```
context.font = "italic bold 20px arial";
```

Font style

Styles available include:

- `normal` (the default)
- `italic`
- `oblique` (similar to italic, usually associated with sans-serif faces)
- `inherit` (style comes from the parent element)

Font weight

Weights available include

- ✔ normal (the default)
- ✔ bold | bolder
- ✔ lighter
- ✔ 100 | 200 | 300 | 400 | 500 | 600 | 700 | 800 | 900
- ✔ inherit (weight comes from the parent element)

Font size

Font sizes can be specified in:

- ✔ px (pixels) for exact size
- ✔ pt (points) for exact size
- ✔ em (ems) 1 em is equal to the font size set for the web page

Canvas font sizes are normally specified in pixels or points. The range of font sizes available depends on the browser displaying the web page. Most browsers support sizes in the hundreds of pixels. If you're using large sizes, test your application on the major browsers to verify they can handle your text.

Font face

Font faces, also referred to as type faces, give text their individual appearance. The font faces supported depend on the browser displaying the web page. Browsers don't support the wide variety of font faces found on word processors. One way to deal with this restricted selection is to specify a font family name for the font face: sans-serif, serif, or monospace. If you want to specify an individual font name, some choices that are generally supported by browsers are

- ✔ **Sans-serif:** Arial, Verdana
- ✔ **Serif:** Georgia, Times New Roman, Times
- ✔ **Monospace:** Courier New, Courier

Text baseline

The textBaseline attribute controls the vertical positioning of text relative to a virtual baseline upon which most letters in a line of text sit. The attribute instructs the browser what position *on the text* to place along the baseline. The baseline in Figure 3-14 is shown as a red line across the Canvas.

		|middle	|alphabetic	|ideographic	|bottom
|top	|hanging				

Figure 3-14: Text baselines.

Some of the `textBaseline` attributes produce counterintuitive results. For example, using the `top` value places text lower on the Canvas than using the `bottom` value.

The code in Listing 3-9 produced Figure 3-13, which shows the positioning options for `textBaseline`:

- `top`: The baseline is above the text.
- `hanging`: The baseline is above the text.
- `middle`: The baseline is through the middle of the text.
- `alphabetic`: The baseline is at the base of letters without a lower loop, such as the letter e.
- `ideographic`: The baseline is below the text, touching the bottom of characters with a descending loop, such as g.
- `bottom`: The baseline is below the text.

Listing 3-9:   Using Text Baselines

```
<!DOCTYPE HTML> <html> <head> <script>

// A. WINDOW LOAD function.
window.onload = function()
{
    // A1. CANVAS definition standard variables.
    canvas  = document.getElementById("canvasArea");
    context = canvas.getContext("2d");

    // A2. TEXT variables.
    var xPos = 75;     var yPos = canvas.height/2;

    // A3. ATTRIBUTES.
    context.font      = "10pt Arial";   context.fillStyle   = "black";
    context.textAlign = "right";        context.strokeStyle = "hotpink";
    context.lineWidth = 1;

    // A4. BASELINE.
    context.beginPath();
```

```
context.moveTo(0, yPos);
context.lineTo(canvas.width, yPos);
context.stroke();

// A5. TEXT BASELINE examples.
context.textBaseline = "top";
context.fillText("|top",         xPos*1, yPos);
context.textBaseline = "hanging";
context.fillText("|hanging",     xPos*2, yPos);
context.textBaseline = "middle";
context.fillText("|middle",      xPos*3, yPos);
context.textBaseline = "alphabetic";
context.fillText("|alphabetic",  xPos*4, yPos);
context.textBaseline = "ideographic";
context.fillText("|ideographic", xPos*5, yPos);
context.textBaseline = "bottom";
context.fillText("|bottom",      xPos*6, yPos);
}
</script> </head> <body>
<div    style = "width:500px; height:50px; margin:0 auto; padding:5px;">
<canvas id    = "canvasArea"  width = "500"  height = "50"
        style = "border:2px solid black">
Your browser doesn't currently support HTML5 Canvas.
</canvas> </div> </body> </html>
```

There are some `textBaseline` implementation differences between browsers. Watch for these variations, especially when using the `hanging` or `ideographic` attributes. If your application requires very precise positioning, test your font face with your characters by using Listing 3-9.

To test the text baseline using Listing 3-9, follow these steps:

1. **Change the font attribute in A3:**

   ```
   context.font = "10pt Verdana";
   ```

2. **Change the text in A5:**

   ```
   context.fillText("New text to test.", xPos*1, yPos);
   ```

To set the `textBaseline` in your application, use the following steps:

1. **Set the `textBaseline` attribute in the Canvas context.**

   An example from A5 of Listing 3-9 is

   ```
   context.textBaseline = "middle";
   ```

2. **Use the `fillText()` function to display text.**

   An example from A5 of Listing 3-9 is

   ```
   context.fillText("middle", xPos*3, yPos);
   ```

Text alignment

The textAlign attribute controls the horizontal positioning of text relative to a virtual vertical line running through the center of a word. The attribute instructs the browser what position *on the text* to place along the vertical center point. The vertical center point in Figure 3-15 is shown as a red line down the Canvas.

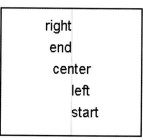

Figure 3-15: Text alignment.

This produces some counterintuitive results. For example, using the left value places text farther to the right on the Canvas than when using the right value.

The code in Listing 3-10 produced Figure 3-15, which shows the positioning options for textAlign:

✔ right: The alignment line is to the right of the text.

✔ end: The alignment line is to the right of the text.

✔ center: The alignment line is through the center of the text.

✔ left: The alignment line is to the left of the text.

✔ start: The alignment line is to the left of the text.

Listing 3-10:   Using Text Alignments

```
<!DOCTYPE HTML> <html> <head> <script>

// A. WINDOW LOAD function.
window.onload = function()
{
    // A1. CANVAS definition standard variables.
    canvas  = document.getElementById("canvasArea");
    context = canvas.getContext("2d");

    // A2. TEXT variables.
    var xPos  = canvas.width/2;
    var yPos  = 30;

    // A3. ATTRIBUTES.
    context.font        = "15pt Arial";
    context.fillStyle   = "black";
    context.strokeStyle = "hotpink";
    context.lineWidth   = 1;

    // A4. CENTERLINE.
    context.beginPath();
```

```
        context.moveTo(xPos, 0);
        context.lineTo(xPos, canvas.height);
        context.stroke();

        // A5. TEXT BASELINE examples.
        context.textAlign = "right";
        context.fillText(   "right",  xPos, yPos*1);
        context.textAlign = "end";
        context.fillText(   "end",    xPos, yPos*2);
        context.textAlign = "center";
        context.fillText(   "center", xPos, yPos*3);
        context.textAlign = "left";
        context.fillText(   "left",   xPos, yPos*4);
        context.textAlign = "start";
        context.fillText(   "start",  xPos, yPos*5);
    }
</script> </head> <body>
<div    style = "width:200px; height:175px; margin:0 auto; padding:5px;">
<canvas id    = "canvasArea"  width = "200"  height = "175"
        style = "border:2px solid black">
Your browser doesn't currently support HTML5 Canvas.
</canvas> </div> </body> </html>
```

There are some `textAlign` implementation differences between browsers. If your application requires very precise positioning, test your font face with your characters using Listing 3-10.

To test text alignment using Listing 3-10, follow these steps:

1. **Change the font attribute in A3:**

   ```
   context.font = "10pt Verdana";
   ```

2. **Change the text in A5:**

   ```
   context.fillText("New text to test.", xPos*1, yPos);
   ```

To set the `textAlign` attribute in your application, use the following steps:

1. **Set the `textAlign` attribute in the Canvas context.**

   An example from A5 of Listing 3-10 is

   ```
   context.textAlign = "center";
   ```

2. **Use the `fillText()` function to display text.**

   An example from A5 of Listing 3-10 is

   ```
   context.fillText("center", xPos, yPos*3);
   ```

Drawing Lines

Drawing a line is a basic Canvas function that you'll use to create objects from simple, single line segments to complex, multiple segment shapes. Figure 3-16 shows examples of lines created by the code in Listing 3-11. The lines to the left demonstrating end caps are single segment, simple lines. The three objects to the right demonstrating join options are a bit more complex and use multiple line segments.

Figure 3-16: Drawing lines.

Listing 3-11: Drawing Lines

```
<!DOCTYPE HTML> <html> <head> <script>

// A. WINDOW LOAD function.
window.onload = function()
{
    // A1. CANVAS definition standard variables.
    canvas  = document.getElementById("canvasArea");
    context = canvas.getContext("2d");

    // A2. VARIABLES.
    var width  = 60;   var height = 75;   var gap    = 50;

    // A3. ATTRIBUTES of lines.
    context.strokeStyle  = "red";   context.lineWidth    = 20;
    context.shadowOffsetX = 4;      context.shadowOffsetY = 4;
    context.shadowBlur   = 7;       context.shadowColor   = "gray";

    // A4. DRAW lines.
    //      xStart yStart cap
    //      ------ ------ -------
    drawLine(25,    25,    "butt"  );
    drawLine(25,    75,    "square");
    drawLine(25,    125,   "round" );

    // A5. DRAW joins.
    //      xStart                 yStart join
```

```
//           ---------------------  ------  -------
drawJoin(175+(0*gap)+(0*width), 120,    "miter");
drawJoin(175+(1*gap)+(1*width), 120,    "bevel");
drawJoin(175+(2*gap)+(2*width), 120,    "round");

// B. LINE DRAWING function.
function drawLine(xStart, yStart, cap)
{
   // B1. ATTRIBUTES of lines.
   context.lineCap = cap;

   // B2. DRAW lines.
   context.beginPath();
   context.moveTo(xStart,             yStart);
   context.lineTo(xStart+1.5*width, yStart);
   context.stroke();
}
// C. LINE JOINING function.
function drawJoin(xStart, yStart, join)
{
   // C1. ATTRIBUTES of lines.
   context.lineCap = "round";

   // C2. DRAW lines.
   context.beginPath();
   context.moveTo(xStart,             yStart);
   context.lineTo(xStart+(width/2), yStart-height);
   context.lineTo(xStart+width,     yStart);
   context.lineJoin = join;
   context.stroke();
}
}
</script> </head> <body>
<div     style = "width:500px; height:160px; margin:0 auto; padding:5px;">
<canvas id    = "canvasArea"  width = "500"  height = "160"
        style = "border:2px solid black">
Your browser doesn't currently support HTML5 Canvas.
</canvas> </div> </body> </html>
```

Line attributes

A number of attributes can be used in drawing a line. Two examples as shown in code segment A3 of Listing 3-11 (in the preceding section) are

```
context.strokeStyle = "red";
context.lineWidth   = 20;
```

Attributes that can be used for lines include

- **Colors:** Fill your line with any of thousands of color variations.
- **Gradients:** Vary the colors within a line.
- **Patterns:** Fill your line with a repeated pattern.
- **Transparency:** Let another image or background show through your line.
- **Shadows:** Generate shadows below, above, or to the side of your line.
- **Clipping:** Set a mask that will remove designated portions of your line.
- **Width:** Set the width of your line.
- **Caps:** Control the shape of the caps on the ends of your line.
- **Joins:** Set a mask that will remove designated portions of your object.

Line caps

As shown earlier in Figure 3-16, there are three types of line caps:

- `butt`: The line is square ended *without* adding any length.
- `square`: The line is square ended *with* added length.
- `round`: The line is round ended *with* added length.

Line joins

As shown earlier in Figure 3-16, there are three types of line joins:

- `miter`: The lines are joined with a pointed tip.
- `bevel`: The lines are joined with a squared tip.
- `round`: The lines are joined with a rounded tip.

Line construction

To construct a line, use these steps:

1. Define functions to draw lines.

In most of your applications, you'll be drawing lots of different kinds of lines. It's a good practice to define functions for appropriate groups of line types. In Listing 3-11, two functions are defined, drawLine() in code section B to draw simple, single segment lines, and drawJoin() in code section C to draw examples of joining two lines:

```
function drawLine(xStart, yStart, cap)
{ . . . }
function drawJoin(xStart, yStart, join)
{ . . . }
```

2. **Use the beginPath() method to start a new line path.**

This method doesn't actually draw the line; it just says "clear the decks; we're starting a new line." And remember, you have to include a reference to the Canvas context, as in B2 of Listing 3-11:

```
context.beginPath();
```

3. **Use the moveTo() function to move to the beginning position of the line.**

Specify as parameters the *x* and *y* coordinates for the start of the line as in B2 and C2:

```
context.moveTo(xStart, yStart);
```

4. **Use the lineTo() function to define a line.**

Specify as parameters the *x* and *y* coordinates of the endpoint of the line. Use multiple lineTo() functions used to create multiple line segments as in C2:

```
context.lineTo(xStart+(width/2), yStart-height);
context.lineTo(xStart+width, yStart);
```

5. **Use the stroke() function to draw the line segment(s).**

The stroke will be made using the attributes currently defined in the Canvas context as in B2 and C2:

```
context.stroke();
```

4

Enhancing Objects

In This Chapter

Drawing multi-sided shapes

Drawing curves

Overlapping shapes

Creating randomized shapes

Displaying images

*1*t's time to start getting a bit fancier with your Canvas objects. The preceding chapters show you how to draw basic objects. In this chapter, you discover how to make more complex objects and how to place them on the Canvas in more sophisticated ways.

Drawing Multi-Sided Shapes

To create multi-sided shapes, you extend the number of lines drawn in a path. (See Chapter 3 for details on creating lines.) As an example, Listing 4-1 shows the code used to create the objects in Figure 4-1.

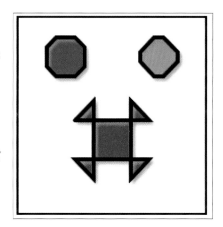

Figure 4-1: Multi-sided shapes.

Listing 4-1: Drawing Multi-Sided Shapes

```
<!DOCTYPE HTML> <html> <head> <script>

// A. WINDOW LOAD function.
window.onload = function()
{
    // A1. CANVAS definition variables.
    canvas  = document.getElementById("canvasArea");
    context = canvas.getContext("2d");

    // A2. ATTRIBUTES of shapes.
    context.strokeStyle   = "black";
    context.lineCap       = "round";   context.lineWidth    = 4;
    context.shadowOffsetX = 3;         context.shadowOffsetY = 3;
    context.shadowBlur    = 5;         context.shadowColor   = "gray";

    // A3. SHAPE 1.
    var xPos    = 50;    var yPos    = 40;
    var fLength = 20;    var cLength = 2;
    var color   = "blue"
    drawShape(xPos, yPos, fLength, cLength, color);

    // A4. SHAPE 2.

    var xPos    = 150;   var yPos    = 40;
    var fLength = 20;    var cLength = 4;
    var color   = "green"
    drawShape(xPos, yPos, fLength, cLength, color);

    // A5. SHAPE 3.
    var xPos    = 100;   var yPos    = 125;
    var fLength = 20;    var cLength = .5;
    var color   = "purple"
    drawShape(xPos, yPos, fLength, cLength, color);

    // B. DRAW shape function.
    function drawShape(xPos, yPos, fLength, cLength, color)
    {
```

```
// B1. CALCULATE short length.
var sLength = fLength/cLength;

// B2. PATH segments.
context.beginPath();
context.moveTo(xPos-(sLength), yPos-(fLength));
context.lineTo(xPos+(sLength), yPos-(fLength));
context.lineTo(xPos+(fLength), yPos-(sLength));
context.lineTo(xPos+(fLength), yPos+(sLength));
context.lineTo(xPos+(sLength), yPos+(fLength));
context.lineTo(xPos-(sLength), yPos+(fLength));
context.lineTo(xPos-(fLength), yPos+(sLength));
context.lineTo(xPos-(fLength), yPos-(sLength));
context.lineTo(xPos-(sLength), yPos-(fLength));

// B3. DRAW shape.
context.fillStyle = color;
context.fill();
context.stroke();
    }
}
</script> </head> <body>
<div   style = "width:200px;  height:200px;  margin:0 auto; padding:5px;">
<canvas id   = "canvasArea" width = "200"  height = "200"
      style = "border:2px solid black">
Your browser doesn't currently support HTML5 Canvas.
</canvas> </div> </body> </html>
```

To create a multi-sided shape, follow these steps:

1. **Set object attributes that you want to apply to all the shapes you'll draw.**

    Here's sample code from A2 of Listing 4-1:

    ```
    context.strokeStyle = "black";
    context.lineWidth   = 4;
    ```

2. **Define key shape characteristics and call the function used to create the shapes.**

   See the example shown in A3–5 of Listing 4-1. The characteristics from this coding example include the *x* and *y* coordinate positions of the shape, the lengths used to calculate line segments, and the fill color:

   ```
   var xPos    = 50;    var yPos    = 40;
   var fLength = 20;    var cLength = 2;
   var color   = "blue"
   ```

3. **Define a function to create shapes.**

   Create a function to draw your shapes as is done in code segment B of Listing 4-1. It's a good programming practice to isolate repetitive code in a separate function. Exactly what code is included depends on the needs of your application and how you choose to partition functionality.

   ```
   function drawShape(xPos, yPos, fLength, cLength, color)
   { . . . }
   ```

   Call this function to create individual shapes as in A3–5:

   ```
   drawShape(xPos, yPos, fLength, cLength, color);
   ```

4. **Within the shape-creating function, calculate any variables needed for shape adjustments.**

   For example, here's the variable sLength in B1 of Listing 4-1:

   ```
   var sLength = fLength/cLength;
   ```

5. **Within the shape-creating function, define the individual line segments that will form the shape.**

   Here is a sample from B2 of Listing 4-1:

   ```
   context.beginPath();
   context.moveTo(xPos-(sLength), yPos-(fLength));
   context.lineTo(xPos+(sLength), yPos-(fLength));
   context.lineTo(xPos+(fLength), yPos-(sLength));
   ```

6. **Create the shape.**

   Finally, create the shape, as in B3 of Listing 4-1:

   ```
   context.fillStyle = color;
   context.fill();
   context.stroke();
   ```

Notice that the shapes created in Figure 4-1 demonstrate quite a bit of variation based on the variables used to calculate line segments.

Drawing Curves

Learning the techniques to draw curves is important because without them, creating complex non-linear paths would be virtually impossible. By specifying just a few parameters, you can draw complex and interesting shapes.

Curves can take a number of forms, as described in the following sections:

- Arcs
- Circles
- Rounded corners
- Bezier curves
- Quadratic curves
- Multi-segment curves

Arcs

An *arc* is a section of a virtual circle. When drawing an arc, you don't draw the circle; rather, you draw as though the circle were there. Figure 4-2 shows the aspects of arcs and circles used to draw an arc.

Arcs are formed by the `arc()` function, which takes six parameters:

```
arc(x, y, radius, startAngle, endAngle, anticlockwise)
```

There are some very counterintuitive aspects to the way these parameters are defined and used, so read the following parameter definitions carefully:

- **X:** The *x* coordinate of the center of the virtual circle used to form the arc. Note that this is *not* the point at which drawing of the arc begins. In Figure 4-2, if you were drawing an arc from point S to point E, the starting point for drawing would be S, not the coordinates `(x,y)`. The arc is, however, positioned on the Canvas using the `(x,y)` coordinates. Another way to say this is that the arc will never touch the `(x,y)` point on the Canvas.

- **Y:** The *y* coordinate of the center of the arc virtual circle.

- **Radius:** The radius of the virtual circle containing the arc. The radius is used to determine the distance from `(x,y)` for every point on the arc as it is drawn.

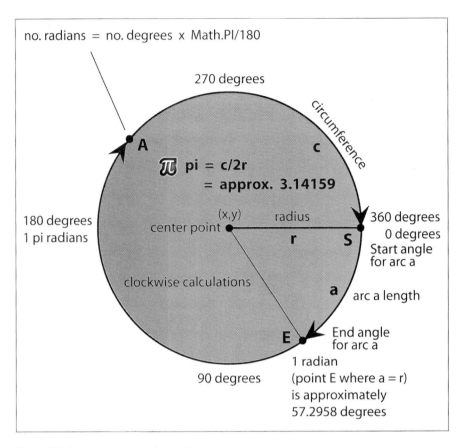

Figure 4-2: Arc parameters and calculations.

✔ **startAngle:** The position on the virtual circle in radians of the start point for drawing the arc. The zero point for measurement is at the 3 o'clock position on the circle (not 12 o'clock as you might assume). If you're using degree as a reference for the angle, convert degrees to radians with the `Math.PI()` function:

```
startAngle = angleInDegrees * Math.PI/180
```

For reasons I won't fully explore here, using radians instead of degrees for the angle parameters is considered more efficient. Radians are a more mathematical concept than degrees.

✔ **endAngle:** The position on a circle in radians of the endpoint for drawing the arc.

✏ **anticlockwise:** Indicates whether the arc should be drawn in a clockwise or anticlockwise direction. A value of `true` draws the arc in an anti-clockwise direction, and a value of `false` draws the arc in a clockwise direction. This is a bit confusing, but this is how the parameter is configured. Figure 4-2 shows calculations for a clockwise direction.

Figure 4-3 shows arcs drawn by the code in Listing 4-2. The code to draw the arcs is contained in the `drawArc()` function in code section B of the listing. In addition to the six parameters needed by the `arc()` function, two additional parameters are added to the `drawArc()` function: `lineColor` and `fillColor`.

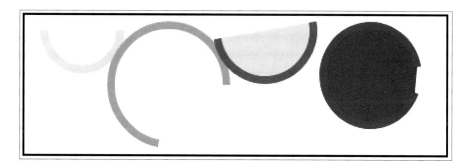

Figure 4-3: Arcs.

Listing 4-2: Drawing Arcs

```
<!DOCTYPE HTML> <html> <head> <script>

// A. WINDOW LOAD function.
window.onload = function()
{
    // A1. CANVAS definition variables.
    canvas  = document.getElementById("canvasArea");
    context = canvas.getContext("2d");

    // A2. ARCS.
    //       x    y  radius startAngle endAngle antiC   line       fill
    //       ---- --- ------ ---------- -------- -----  ------    --------
    drawArc ( 60, 15, 40,      0,       180, false, "aqua",  "yellow");
    drawArc (150, 70, 60,      0,       100,  true, "green", "white" );
    drawArc (250, 15, 50,    350,       170, false, "red",   "pink"  );
    drawArc (360, 60, 50,    350,        20,  true, "blue",  "purple");

    // B. DRAW arc function.
    function drawArc(xPos, yPos, radius, startAngle, endAngle,
                 anticlockwise, lineColor, fillColor)
    {
```

(continued)

Listing 4-2 *(continued)*

```
        // B1. ANGLES in radians.
        var startAngle = startAngle * (Math.PI/180);
        var endAngle   = endAngle   * (Math.PI/180);


        // B2. RADIUS.
        var radius = radius;


        // B3. ATTRIBUTES.
        context.strokeStyle = lineColor;
        context.fillStyle   = fillColor;
        context.lineWidth   = 8;


        // B4. SHAPE.
        context.beginPath();
        context.arc(xPos, yPos, radius, startAngle, endAngle, anticlockwise);
        context.fill();
        context.stroke();

    }
}
</script> </head> <body>
<div    style = "width:440px; height:140px; margin:0 auto; padding:5px;">
<canvas id    = "canvasArea" width = "440" height = "140"
        style = "border:2px solid black">
Your browser doesn't currently support HTML5 Canvas.
</canvas> </div> </body> </html>
```

Follow these steps to draw an arc:

1. **Create a function to draw your arcs.**

   Create a function that will do the repetitive tasks of generating your arcs, as in code section B of Listing 4-2:

   ```
   function drawArc(xPos, yPos, radius, startAngle, endAngle,
                    anticlockwise, lineColor, fillColor)
   { . . . }
   ```

   Then call the function using various parameter values, such as this statement from code section A2:

   ```
   drawArc(60, 15, 40, 0, 180, false, "aqua", "yellow");
   ```

2. **Calculate angles in radians.**

   If you're starting with angles in degrees, as is the case in Listing 4-2, convert the angles to radians as is done in B1:

   ```
   var startAngle = startAngle * (Math.PI/180);
   var endAngle   = endAngle   * (Math.PI/180);
   ```

3. Set the values and attributes of the arc to be drawn.

Here's an example from code sections B2–3:

```
var radius        = radius;
context.strokeStyle = lineColor;
context.fillStyle   = fillColor;
context.lineWidth   = 8;
```

4. Draw the arcs.

Set the arc path using the `beginPath()` and `arc()` functions. Then use the `fill()` and `stroke()` functions to create the arc fill and line. It's not necessary to use both the `fill()` and `stroke()` functions as is done in B4 of Listing 4-2. If you want to create only a fill or only a stroke, use only that function.

```
context.beginPath();
context.arc(xPos, yPos, radius, startAngle, endAngle, anticlockwise);
context.fill();
context.stroke();
```

Circles

A *circle* is simply an arc that ends where it started. As in the old saying, it goes "full circle." Figure 4-2 shows the aspects of arcs and circles used to draw a circle. Circles are formed using the `arc()` function, which takes six parameters:

```
arc(x, y, radius, startAngle, endAngle, anticlockwise)
```

Here's the lowdown on these parameters:

- ✔ **X:** The *x* coordinate of the center of the circle.
- ✔ **Y:** The *y* coordinate of the center of the circle.
- ✔ **Radius:** The radius of the circle.
- ✔ **startAngle:** The position on the circle in *radians* of the start point for drawing the arc. Because a full circle is being drawn, it doesn't matter what starting and ending angles are used as long as they designate the same point.
- ✔ **endAngle:** The position on the circle in radians of the endpoint for drawing the arc.
- ✔ **Anticlockwise:** Indicates whether the arc should be drawn in a clockwise or anticlockwise direction. Because a full circle is being drawn, it doesn't matter whether the `true` or `false` value is used.

Figure 4-4 shows circles drawn by the code in Listing 4-3. The code to draw the circles is contained in the `drawCircle()` function in code section B. In addition to the parameters needed by the `arc()` function, two additional parameters are added to the `drawCircle()` function: `lineColor` and `fillColor`.

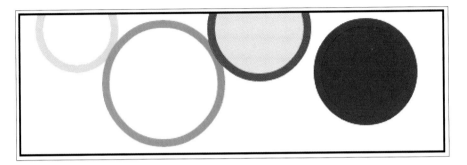

Figure 4-4: Circles.

Listing 4-3: Drawing Circles

```
<!DOCTYPE HTML> <html> <head> <script>

// A. WINDOW LOAD function.
window.onload = function()
{
    // A1. CANVAS definition variables.
    canvas  = document.getElementById("canvasArea");
    context = canvas.getContext("2d");

    // A2. CIRCLES.
    //           x    y   radius  line     fill
    //          ---- ---- ------ ------   --------
    drawCircle( 60,  15,  40,    "aqua",  "yellow");
    drawCircle(150,  70,  60,    "green", "white" );
    drawCircle(250,  15,  50,    "red",   "pink"  );
    drawCircle(360,  60,  50,    "blue",  "purple");

    // B. DRAW circle function.
    function drawCircle(xPos, yPos, radius, lineColor, fillColor)
    {
        // B1. ANGLES in radians.
        var startAngle =   0 * (Math.PI/180);
        var endAngle   = 360 * (Math.PI/180);

        // B2. RADIUS.
```

```
        var radius = radius;

        // B3. ATTRIBUTES.
        context.strokeStyle = lineColor;
        context.fillStyle   = fillColor;
        context.lineWidth   = 8;

        // B4. SHAPE.
        context.beginPath();
        context.arc(xPos, yPos, radius, startAngle, endAngle, false);
        context.fill();
        context.stroke();
    }
}
</script> </head> <body>
<div    style = "width:440px;  height:140px; margin:0 auto; padding:5px;">
<canvas    id = "canvasArea" width = "440"  height = "140"
        style = "border:2px solid black">
Your browser doesn't currently support HTML5 Canvas.
</canvas> </div> </body> </html>
```

To draw circles, do the following:

1. **Create a function to draw your circles.**

   Create a function that will do the repetitive tasks of generating your circles, as in code section B of Listing 4-3:

   ```
   function drawCircle(xPos, yPos, radius, lineColor, fillColor)
   { . . . }
   ```

   Then, as in A2 of Listing 4-3, call the drawCircle() function various parameter values, such as:

   ```
   drawCircle(60, 15, 40, "aqua", "yellow");
   ```

2. **Calculate angles in radians.**

   Because the circle is starting and ending in the same position, the start and end angles can be the same for every circle and set in the function drawCircle(), as is done in B1 of Listing 4-3:

   ```
   var startAngle =   0 * (Math.PI/180);
   var endAngle   = 360 * (Math.PI/180);
   ```

3. **Set the values and attributes of the arc to be drawn.**

   Here's an example from code sections B2–3:

   ```
   var radius          = radius;
   context.strokeStyle = lineColor;
   context.fillStyle   = fillColor;
   context.lineWidth   = 8;
   ```

4. **Draw the circles.**

   Set the arc path using the `beginPath()` and `arc()` functions. Then use the `fill()` and `stroke()` functions to create the arc fill and line. It's not necessary to use both the `fill()` and `stroke()` functions as is done in B4 of Listing 4-3. If you want to create only a fill or only a stroke, use only that function.

   Notice that the last parameter in the `arc()` function, which is the anticlockwise parameter, is set to false. This will cause all circles to be drawn in a clockwise direction. Also notice that portions of the circles lie outside the Canvas area. This doesn't cause the code to fail; the points outside the Canvas area will simply not be displayed.

   ```
   context.beginPath();
   context.arc(xPos, yPos, radius, startAngle, endAngle, false);
   context.fill();
   context.stroke();
   ```

Rounded corners

Figure 4-5 shows a rounded corner drawn by the code in Listing 4-4. To draw a rounded corner, use the `arcto()` function, which has five parameters:

```
arcto(xBeginning, yBeginning, xEnd, yEnd, radius)
```

Here's more on these parameters:

- **xBeginning:** *X* coordinate of the beginning of the corner arc
- **yBeginning:** *Y* coordinate of the beginning of the corner arc
- **xEnd:** *X* coordinate of the end of the corner arc
- **yEnd:** *Y* coordinate of the end of the corner arc
- **Radius:** Radius of the corner arc

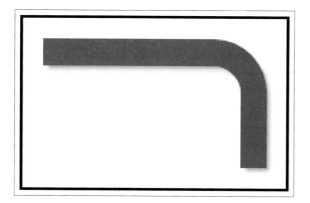

Figure 4-5: Rounded corners.

Listing 4-4: Drawing Rounded Corners

```
<!DOCTYPE HTML> <html> <head> <script>

// A. WINDOW LOAD function.
window.onload = function()
{
    // A1. CANVAS definition variables.
    canvas  = document.getElementById("canvasArea");
    context = canvas.getContext("2d");

    // A2. LAYOUT parameters.
    var xPos   = 25;  var yPos   = 25;  var width = 150;
    var height = 75;  var radius = 30;

    // A3. ATTRIBUTES of lines and arc.
    context.strokeStyle   = "red";      context.lineWidth    = 20;
    context.lineCap       = "square";   context.shadowOffsetX = 3;
    context.shadowOffsetY = 3;          context.shadowBlur   = 5;
    context.shadowColor   = "gray";

    // A4. STARTING point.
    context.beginPath();
    context.moveTo(xPos, yPos);

    // A5. TOP line path.
    context.lineTo(xPos+width-radius, yPos);

    // A6. CORNER arc path.
    context.arcTo(xPos+width, yPos, xPos+width, yPos+radius, radius);

    // A7. SIDE line path.
```

(continued)

Listing 4-4 *(continued)*

```
    context.lineTo(xPos+width, yPos+height);

    // A8. DRAW image.
    context.stroke();
}
</script> </head> <body>
<div    style = "width:200px; height:125px; margin:0 auto; padding:5px;">
<canvas id    = "canvasArea" width = "200" height = "125"
        style = "border:2px solid black">
Your browser doesn't currently support HTML5 Canvas.
</canvas> </div> </body> </html>
```

Follow these steps to create a rounded corner:

1. **Define variables you'll use to calculate the positions of the lines and arc that will be used to construct the corner.**

   Examples from A2 of Listing 4-4 include

   ```
   var xPos   = 25;  var yPos   = 25;  var width  = 150;
   var height = 75;  var radius = 30;
   ```

2. **Set the attributes of the lines and arc.**

   Here are examples from A3 of Listing 4-4:

   ```
   context.strokeStyle = "red";
   context.lineWidth   = 20;
   ```

3. **Set the starting point for the shape.**

   Here's an example from A4 of Listing 4-4:

   ```
   context.beginPath();
   context.moveTo(xPos, yPos);
   ```

4. **Form the lines that intersect with the rounded corner.**

   See code sections A5 and A7 in Listing 4-4:

   ```
   context.lineTo(xPos+width-radius, yPos);
   context.lineTo(xPos+width, yPos+height);
   ```

5. **Using the `arcto()` function, form the arc that creates the rounded corner.**

   Here's an example in code section A6 of Listing 4-4:

   ```
   context.arcTo(xPos+width, yPos, xPos+width, yPos+radius, radius);
   ```

6. Draw the shape.

Finally, draw the entire shape as in A8 of Listing 4-4:

```
context.stroke();
```

Bezier curves

A *Bezier curve* (named after the French engineer Pierre Bezier) is a path between two points that's shaped by control points lying outside what would be the straight line between the two points. Figure 4-6 shows a Bezier curve drawn by the code in Listing 4-5. The start point (S) and endpoint (E) are also shown along with the control points (1 and 2) used to form the curve.

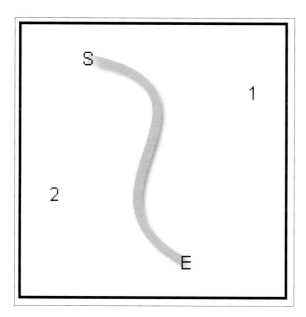

Figure 4-6: A Bezier curve.

Essentially, the control points "pull" the line toward them. The code in Listing 4-5 is constructed so that you can easily experiment with the control points in section A2 to see how moving them changes the shape of the line. The mathematics of how the curve is drawn is beyond the scope of this book. However, watching how the curve responds to control point changes is the best way to understand the dynamics of the curve (something like a baseball player learning to throw a ball by watching how it moves through the air rather than digesting the mathematics of every type of throw).

Listing 4-5:   Drawing Bezier Curves

```
<!DOCTYPE HTML> <html> <head> <script>

// A. WINDOW LOAD function.
window.onload = function()
{
    // A1. CANVAS definition variables.
    canvas  = document.getElementById("canvasArea");
    context = canvas.getContext("2d");

    // A2. LAYOUT parameters.
    var xStart    = 50;    var yStart    = 25;
    var xControl1 = 175;   var yControl1 = 50;
    var xControl2 = 25;    var yControl2 = 125;
    var xEnd      = 125;   var yEnd      = 175;

    // A3. ATTRIBUTES of curve.
    context.strokeStyle   = "orange";    context.lineWidth     = 7;
    context.shadowOffsetX = 3;           context.shadowOffsetY = 3;
    context.shadowBlur    = 5;           context.shadowColor   = "gray";

    // A4. STARTING point.
    context.beginPath();
    context.moveTo(xStart, yStart);

    // A5. BEZIER curve.
    context.bezierCurveTo(xControl1, yControl1,
                          xControl2, yControl2, xEnd, yEnd);
    // A6. DRAW curve.
    context.stroke();

    // A7. DISPLAY control points.
    displayPoint(xStart,    yStart,    "S");
    displayPoint(xControl1, yControl1, "1");
    displayPoint(xControl2, yControl2, "2");
    displayPoint(xEnd,      yEnd,      "E");

    // B. DISPLAY POINT function.
    function displayPoint(xPos, yPos, text)
    {
        // B1. ATTRIBUTES.
        context.font        = "10pt Arial";
        context.fillStyle   = "black";
        context.textAlign   = "center";
        context.textBaseline = "middle";
        context.shadowColor = "white";

        // B2. DISPLAY text.
        context.fillText(text, xPos, yPos);
```

```
    }
}
</script> </head> <body>
<div  style = "width:200px;  height:200px;  margin:0 auto; padding:5px;">
<canvas id  = "canvasArea"  width = "200"  height = "200"
       style = "border:2px solid black">
Your browser doesn't currently support HTML5 Canvas.
</canvas> </div> </body> </html>
```

To draw a Bezier curve, do the following:

1. **Define the variables required to form the curve.**

   Code section A2 of Listing 4-5 is an example:

   ```
   var xStart     = 50;    var yStart    = 25;
   var xControl1 = 175;    var yControl1 = 50;
   var xControl2 = 25;     var yControl2 = 125;
   var xEnd      = 125;    var yEnd      = 175;
   ```

2. **Define the attributes for the curve.**

   Here is an example from A3 of Listing 4-5:

   ```
   context.strokeStyle = "orange";
   context.lineWidth   = 7;
   ```

3. **Set the starting point for the curve.**

   Here's an example in code section A4:

   ```
   context.beginPath();
   context.moveTo(xStart, yStart);
   ```

4. **Define the Bezier curve itself.**

   See the code in section A5. This requires two control points and an endpoint:

   ```
   context.bezierCurveTo(xControl1, yControl1,
                    xControl2, yControl2, xEnd, yEnd);
   ```

5. **Draw the curve using the `stroke()` function.**

   Here's an example in code section A6:

   ```
   context.stroke();
   ```

Quadratic curves

A *quadratic curve* is a form of Bezier curve. Instead of using two control points, as shown earlier, in Figure 4-6, a quadratic curve uses only one, as shown in Figure 4-7. (The code that generated this curve is shown in Listing 4-6.)

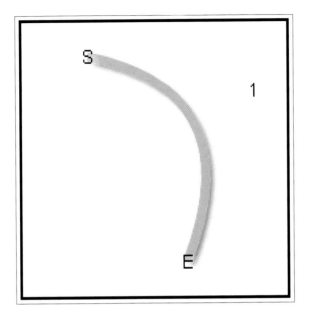

Figure 4-7: A Quadratic curve.

Listing 4-6: Drawing Quadratic Curves

```
<!DOCTYPE HTML> <html> <head> <script>

// A. WINDOW LOAD function.
window.onload = function()
{
    // A1. CANVAS definition variables.
    canvas  = document.getElementById("canvasArea");
    context = canvas.getContext("2d");

    // A2. LAYOUT parameters.
    var xStart    = 50;   var yStart  = 25;    var xControl1 = 175;
    var yControl1 = 50;   var xEnd    = 125;   var yEnd      = 175;

    // A3. ATTRIBUTES of curve.
    context.strokeStyle   = "orange";   context.lineWidth    = 7;
    context.shadowOffsetX = 3;          context.shadowOffsetY = 3;
    context.shadowBlur    = 5;          context.shadowColor   = "gray";

    // A4. STARTING point.
    context.beginPath();
    context.moveTo(xStart, yStart);

    // A5. QUADRATIC curve.
```

```
context.quadraticCurveTo(xControl1, yControl1, xEnd, yEnd);

// A6. DRAW curve.
context.stroke();

// A7. DISPLAY control points.
displayPoint(xStart,    yStart,    "S");
displayPoint(xControl1, yControl1, "1");
displayPoint(xEnd,      yEnd,      "E");

// B. DISPLAY POINT function.
function displayPoint(xPos, yPos, text)
{
   // B1. ATTRIBUTES.
   context.font         = "10pt Arial";   context.fillStyle    = "black";
   context.textAlign    = "center";       context.textBaseline = "middle";
   context.shadowColor  = "white";

   // B2. DISPLAY text.
   context.fillText(text, xPos, yPos);
}
}
</script> </head> <body>
<div  style   = "width:200px;  height:200px;  margin:0 auto; padding:5px;">
<canvas id    = "canvasArea"   width = "200"   height = "200"
        style = "border:2px solid black">
Your browser doesn't currently support HTML5 Canvas.
</canvas> </div> </body> </html>
```

To draw a quadratic curve, do the following:

1. Define the variables required to form the curve.

Code section A2 of Listing 4-6 is an example:

```
var xStart     = 50;   var yStart   = 25;   var xControl1 = 175;
var yControl1 = 50;   var xEnd     = 125;  var yEnd      = 175;
```

2. Define the attributes for the curve.

Here are some examples from A3 of Listing 4-6:

```
context.strokeStyle = "orange";
context.lineWidth   = 7;
```

3. Define the starting point for the curve.

Here's an example in code section A4:

```
context.beginPath();
context.moveTo(xStart, yStart);
```

4. Define the Quadratic curve itself.

See the example in code section A5. This requires two control points and an endpoint:

```
context.quadraticCurveTo(xControl1, yControl1, xEnd,  yEnd);
```

5. Finally, draw the curve using the `stroke()` function.

See code section A5:

```
context.stroke();
```

Multi-segment curves

Drawing curves using a function with more than two control points is too mathematically complex and processor-cycle consuming to be practical. So, to create curves with additional control points, string together Bezier curves (or other types of curves), as shown in Figure 4-8 and earlier, in Listing 4-7.

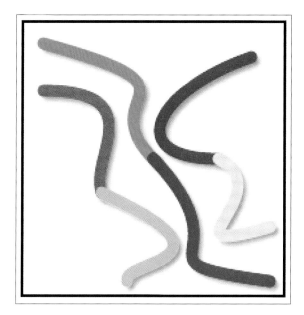

Figure 4-8: Multi-segment curves.

Listing 4-7:   Drawing Multi-Segment Curves

```
<!DOCTYPE HTML> <html> <head> <script>


// A. WINDOW LOAD function.
window.onload = function()
{
    // A1. CANVAS definition variables.
    canvas  = document.getElementById("canvasArea");
    context = canvas.getContext("2d");


    // A2. CURVES.
    //        xS   yS   xC1  yC1  xC2  yC2  xE   yE   color
    //        ---- ---- ---- ---- ---- ---- ---- ---- -------
    drawCurve( 15,  15, 150,  50,  50,  50, 100, 100, "green" );
    drawCurve(100, 100, 175, 175,  75, 175, 190, 190, "blue"  );
    drawCurve( 15,  50, 100,  50,  50, 100,  60, 125, "red"   );
    drawCurve( 60, 125, 175, 175,  75, 175,  80, 190, "orange");
    drawCurve(175,  25, 100,  50,  75, 100, 150, 100, "purple");
    drawCurve(150, 100, 200, 125, 100, 175, 190, 150, "pink"  );
}
// B. DRAW CURVE function.
function drawCurve(xStart, yStart, xControl1, yControl1,
                   xControl2, yControl2, xEnd, yEnd, color)
{
    // B1. ATTRIBUTES.
    context.strokeStyle  = color;        context.lineWidth    = 9;
    context.lineCap      = "round"       context.shadowOffsetX = 3;
    context.shadowOffsetY = 3;           context.shadowBlur   = 5;
    context.shadowColor  = "gray";


    // B2. STARTING point.
    context.beginPath();
    context.moveTo(xStart, yStart);


    // B3. BEZIER curve.
    context.bezierCurveTo(xControl1, yControl1,
                          xControl2, yControl2,
                          xEnd,       yEnd);
    // B4. DRAW curve.
    context.stroke();
}
</script> </head> <body>
<div    style = "width:200px;   height:200px; margin:0 auto; padding:5px;">
<canvas id    = "canvasArea"    width = "200"  height = "200"
        style = "border:2px solid black">
Your browser doesn't currently support HTML5 Canvas.
</canvas> </div> </body> </html>
```

To draw multi-segment curves, do the following:

1. **Create a function to draw your curves.**

   Create a function that will do the repetitive tasks of generating your curves, as in code section B of Listing 4-7:

   ```
   function drawCurve(xStart, yStart, xControl1, yControl1,
                      xControl2, yControl2, xEnd, yEnd, color)
   { . . . }
   ```

   Call the function to draw a curve, as in section A2:

   ```
   //          xS   yS   xC1  yC1  xC2  yC2  xE   yE   color
   //          ---- ---- ---- ---- ---- ---- ---- ---- -------
   drawCurve( 15,  15, 150,  50,  50,  50, 100, 100, "green" );
   drawCurve(100, 100, 175, 175,  75, 175, 190, 190, "blue"  );
   ```

2. **Define the attributes for the curve.**

   Here are some examples from B1 of Listing 4-7:

   ```
   context.strokeStyle = "color";
   context.lineWidth   = 9;
   ```

3. **Define the starting point for the curve.**

   See the code section B2:

   ```
   context.beginPath();
   context.moveTo(xStart, yStart);
   ```

4. **Define the curve itself.**

   See the example in B3. In this example, it is a Bezier curve that requires two control points and an endpoint:

   ```
   context.bezierCurveTo(xControl1, yControl1,
                         xControl2, yControl2,
                         xEnd,      yEnd);
   ```

5. **Draw the curve using the `stroke()` function.**

   See code section B4:

   ```
   context.stroke();
   ```

Compositing Objects

Compositing is a word you don't hear often. It's the verb associated with the noun composite. Figure 4-9 shows examples of the composite options generated by the code in Listing 4-8.

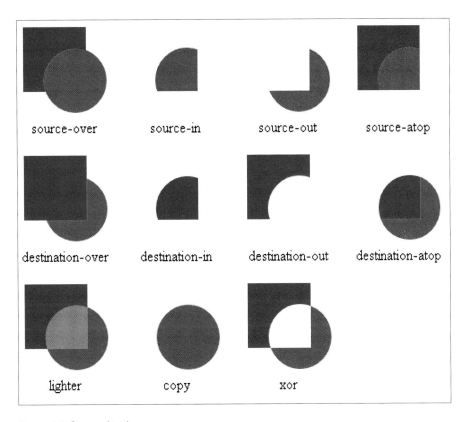

Figure 4-9: Composite shapes.

Listing 4-8:   Compositing Shapes

```
<!DOCTYPE HTML> <html> <head> <script>

// A. WINDOW LOAD function.
window.onload = function()
{
   // A1. DRAW individual shapes examples.
   drawShapes("source-over");
   drawShapes("source-in");
   drawShapes("source-out");
   drawShapes("source-atop");
   drawShapes("destination-over");
   drawShapes("destination-in");
   drawShapes("destination-out");
   drawShapes("destination-atop");
   drawShapes("lighter");
```

(continued)

Listing 4-8 *(continued)*

```
    drawShapes("copy");
    drawShapes("xor");
}
// B. DRAW function.
function drawShapes(type)
{
    // B1. CANVAS ID.
    canvas  = document.getElementById(type);
    context = canvas.getContext("2d");

    // B2. VARIABLES.
    var squareOffset = 15;  var squareSide   = 70;
    var circleOffset = 73;  var circleRadius = 35;

    // B3. SQUARE.
    context.fillStyle = "blue";
    context.fillRect(squareOffset, squareOffset, squareSide, squareSide);

    // B4. COMPOSITE attribute.
    context.globalCompositeOperation = type;

    // B5. CIRCLE.
    context.fillStyle = "red";
    context.beginPath();
    context.arc(circleOffset, circleOffset, circleRadius, 0, Math.PI*2, true);
    context.fill();
}
</script>
<style type="text/css"> td {text-align:center;}
</style> </head> <body>

<!-- C. TABLE of composite shapes. -->
<table border="0" align="center">
<tr> <td>
<canvas id="source-over"      width="120" height="110">
</canvas><br/><l>source-over</l>
</td> <td>
<canvas id="source-in"        width="120" height="110">
</canvas><br/><l>source-in</l>
</td> <td>
<canvas id="source-out"       width="120" height="110">
</canvas><br/><l>source-out</l>
</td> <td>
<canvas id="source-atop"      width="120" height="110">
</canvas><br/><l>source-atop</l>
</td> </tr> <tr> <td>
<canvas id="destination-over" width="120" height="110">
</canvas><br/><l>destination-over</l>
```

```
</td> <td>
<canvas id="destination-in"   width="120" height="110">
</canvas><br/><l>destination-in</l>
</td> <td>
<canvas id="destination-out"  width="120" height="110">
</canvas><br/><l>destination-out</l>
</td> <td>
<canvas id="destination-atop" width="120" height="110">
</canvas><br/><l>destination-atop</l>
</td> </tr> <tr> <td>
<canvas id="lighter"          width="120" height="110">
</canvas><br/><l>lighter</l>
</td> <td>
<canvas id="copy"             width="120" height="110">
</canvas><br/><l>copy</l>
</td> <td>
<canvas id="xor"              width="120" height="110">
</canvas><br/><l>xor</l>
</td> </tr> </table> </body> </html>
```

In the following sections, I discuss the various compositing options and show you how to draw composite shapes.

Compositing options

Compositing is performed based on the setting for the attribute `global CompositeOperation`. You have 11 compositing options to control how objects appear when placed relative to one another (refer to Figure 4-9):

- `source-over`
- `source-in`
- `source-out`
- `source-atop`
- `destination-over`
- `destination-in`
- `destination-out`
- `destination-atop`
- `lighter`
- `copy`
- `xor`

The *source object* is the object drawn first and is a blue square in the examples in Figure 4-9. The *destination shape,* a red circle in the examples, is drawn second after the `globalCompositeOperation` attribute is set.

Not all browsers implement all of the compositing options in the same way. If compositing is an important part of your application, make sure you test your code on the major browsers.

Creating a table to hold the examples

To display examples of multiple compositing options, I created a table using HTML code, as shown in section C of Listing 4-8:

```
<table border="0" align="center">
<tr>
<td>
<canvas id="source-over"  width="120" height="110">
</canvas><br/><l>source-over</l>
</td>
<td>
<canvas id="source-in"    width="120" height="110">
</canvas><br/><l>source-in</l>
</td>
.
.
.
</table>
```

I used a table to prevent the composite option chosen for one set of objects from interfering with the options chosen for other sets. This example also demonstrates the use of multiple Canvas areas on a single web page.

Drawing the composite shapes

To use compositing drawing shapes, do the following:

1. **Create a function to draw your objects.**

   Create a function that will do the repetitive tasks of drawing your objects, as in code section B of Listing 4-8:

   ```
   function drawShapes(type)
   { . . . }
   ```

The function, which takes the compositing type as a parameter, is called from section A1, as follows:

```
drawShapes("source-over");
drawShapes("source-in");
```

2. Based on the compositing type, retrieve the Canvas ID and 2D context.

See code section B1 of Listing 4-8:

```
canvas  = document.getElementById(type);
context = canvas.getContext("2d");
```

3. Define any variables needed to create the shapes.

See the example in code section B2:

```
var squareOffset = 15;   var squareSide = 70;
```

4. Draw the destination shape (the first, or bottom, shape).

In Listing 4-8, this is the blue square:

```
context.fillRect(squareOffset, squareOffset,squareSide, squareSide);
```

5. Set the composite type as an attribute for the context.

See the example in B4:

```
context.globalCompositeOperation = type;
```

6. Draw the source shape (the second, or top, shape).

In Listing 4-8 code, in section B5, the source shape is the red circle:

```
context.beginPath();
context.arc(circleOffset,circleOffset,circleRadius,0,Math.PI*2,true);
context.fill();
```

The two shapes are displayed according to the composite attribute set in Step 5.

Randomizing Shapes

Randomizing shapes is useful for creating interesting and varied Canvas images. It's also a powerful tool for imitating the variations found in nature. Figure 4-10 is an example of randomly sized, colored, and positioned circles. The code used to create the circles is in Listing 4-9.

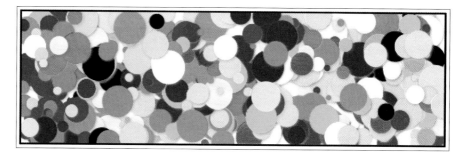

Figure 4-10: Random circles.

Listing 4-9: Randomizing Circles

```
<!DOCTYPE HTML> <html> <head> <script>

// A. WINDOW LOAD function.
window.onload = function()
{
    // A1. CANVAS definition variables.
    canvas  = document.getElementById("canvasArea");
    context = canvas.getContext("2d");

    // A2. PARAMETERS for circles.
    var numCircles = 500;
    var maxRadius  = 20;
    var minRadius  = 3;
    var colors     =
    ["aqua", "black", "blue", "fuchsia", "green", "cyan",  "lime",  "maroon",
     "navy", "olive", "purple", "red", "silver", "teal", "yellow", "azure",
     "gold", "bisque", "pink", "orange"];
    var numColors  = colors.length;

    // A3. CREATE circles.
    for(var n=0; n<numCircles; n++)
    {
        // A4. RANDOM values for circle characteristics.
        var xPos       =  Math.random() * canvas.width;
        var yPos       =  Math.random() * canvas.height;
        var radius     =  minRadius + (Math.random() * (maxRadius-minRadius));
        var colorIndex =  Math.random() * (numColors-1);
        colorIndex     =  Math.round(colorIndex);
        var color      =  colors[colorIndex];

        // A5. DRAW circle.
        drawCircle(context, xPos, yPos, radius, color);
    }
```

```
};
// B. CIRCLE drawing function.
function drawCircle(context, xPos, yPos, radius, color)
{
    //B1. PARAMETERS for shadow and angles.
    var startAngle       = (Math.PI/180)*0;
    var endAngle         = (Math.PI/180)*360;
    context.shadowColor  = "gray";
    context.shadowOffsetX = 1;
    context.shadowOffsetY = 1;
    context.shadowBlur    = 5;

    //B2. DRAW CIRCLE
    context.beginPath();
    context.arc(xPos, yPos, radius, startAngle, endAngle, false);
    context.fillStyle = color;
    context.fill();
}
</script> </head> <body>
<div    style = "width:500px;    height:150px; margin:0 auto; padding:5px;">
<canvas id    = "canvasArea" width = "500"  height = "150"
        style = "border:2px solid black">
Your browser doesn't currently support HTML5 Canvas.
</canvas> </div> </body> </html>
```

To create a randomized object, use the `Math.random()` function to generate a random number between 0 and 1. Then apply that number to a variable
used to produce a random shape. In Listing 4-9, a random number is generated based on the width of the Canvas:

```
var xPos = Math.random() * canvas.width;
```

To include randomized objects in your application, do the following:

1. Create a function to draw your objects.

Create a function that will do the repetitive tasks of generating your
objects, which are circles in code section B of Listing 4-9:

```
function drawCircle(context, xPos, yPos, radius, color)
{ . . . }
```

The function is called, as in A5:

```
drawCircle(context, xPos, yPos, radius, color);
```

2. **Create code to repeatedly call the draw function.**

   See A3 of Listing 4-9:

   ```
   for(var n=0; n<numCircles; n++)
   { . . . }
   ```

3. **Set variables that you will use to generate random shape characteristics.**

   For example, as shown in A2 of Listing 4-9, maximum and minimum radius can be used to generate randomly sized circles:

   ```
   var maxRadius = 20;
   var minRadius = 3;
   ```

4. **Use the `Math.random()` function to generate values that you use as parameters for drawing your objects.**

   See the example in A4:

   ```
   var yPos   = Math.random() * canvas.height;
   var radius = minRadius + (Math.random() * maxRadius - minRadius);
   ```

5. **Draw randomized shapes.**

   Draw your objects as in code section B of Listing 4-9, which draws a circle based on parameters for random position, radius, and color:

   ```
   context.beginPath();
   context.arc(xPos, yPos, radius, startAngle, endAngle, false);
   context.fillStyle = color;
   context.fill();
   ```

Displaying Images

Images are a great way to add dimensionality to your Canvas application. They can be anything from photographs to illustrations and graphics. Figure 4-11 shows a series of images created by the code in Listing 4-10.

Figure 4-11: Images.

The second image is drawn by enlarging the first one, which produces fuzziness. The third image is drawn using a larger source image, which eliminates this distortion. The fourth image also contains distortion, because it's a "blow-up" of a section of the third image. Use source image sizes that, as a rule, closely match the size of the displayed image.

Listing 4-10: Displaying Images

```
<!DOCTYPE HTML> <html> <head> <script>

// A. WINDOW LOAD function.
window.onload = function()
{
   // A1. CANVAS definition variables.
   canvas  = document.getElementById("canvasArea");
   context = canvas.getContext("2d");

   // A2. IMAGE sources.
   var smallImage = new Image();
   var largeImage = new Image();
   smallImage.src = "http://marketimpacts.com/storage/Strawberry50px.png";
   largeImage.src = "http://marketimpacts.com/storage/Strawberry100px.png";

   // A3. VARIABLES.
   var smallImageXPos   = 40;       var smallImageYPos   = 55;
   var smallImageWidth  = 75;       var smallImageHeight = 75;
   var largeImageXPos   = 225;      var largeImageYPos   = 10;
   var sourceCropX      = 25;       var sourceCropY      = 25;
   var sourceCropWidthX = 50;       var sourceCropWidthY = 50;
   var imageWidth       = 80;       var imageHeight      = 80;

   // A4. ATTRIBUTES.
   context.shadowOffsetX = -3;      context.shadowOffsetY = 3;
   context.shadowBlur    = 8;       context.shadowColor   = "gray";

   // B. LOAD image of small ball.
   smallImage.onload = function()
   {
      // B1. DRAW image.
      context.drawImage(smallImage, smallImageXPos, smallImageYPos);

      // B2. DRAW image with resizing.
      context.drawImage(smallImage, smallImageXPos+80, smallImageYPos-25,
                   smallImageWidth, smallImageHeight);
   }
   // C. LOAD image of large ball.
   largeImage.onload = function()
   {
      // C1. DRAW image.
```

(continued)

Listing 4-10 *(continued)*

```
        context.drawImage(largeImage, largeImageXPos, largeImageYPos);

        // C2. DRAW image with cropping.
        context.drawImage (largeImage, sourceCropX, sourceCropY,
                           sourceCropWidthX, sourceCropWidthY,
                           largeImageXPos+140, largeImageYPos+10,
                           imageWidth, imageHeight);
    }
}
</script> </head> <body>
<div    style = "width:500px;  height:125px;  margin:0 auto; padding:5px;">
<canvas id    = "canvasArea"  width = "500"  height = "125"
        style = "border:2px solid black">
Your browser doesn't currently support HTML5 Canvas.
</canvas> </div> </body> </html>
```

To display images, do the following:

1. **Store the images that your application will access on a server.**

   Most often, you'll use the same server hosting your website, but it can be any server accessible via the Internet.

2. **Load the image files from the server.**

   Code section A2 in Listing 4-10 contains the code to load images into your application.

   First, create variables to hold your images, such as:

   ```
   var smallImage = new Image();
   ```

   Next, access the source for your images, such as

   ```
   "http://marketimpacts.com/storage/Strawberry50px.png";
   ```

   Finally, create functions that will be invoked when your images load, such as shown in code sections B and C:

   ```
   largeImage.onload = function()
   { . . . }
   ```

3. **Set the variables and attributes you'll use for drawing your images on the Canvas.**

   See these examples from A3 and A4 in Listing 4-10:

   ```
   var smallImageXPos  = 40;        var smallImageYPos = 55;
   context.shadowColor = "gray";
   ```

4. **Draw your images on the Canvas using the `drawImage()` function.**

   This function has different parameters for drawing:

   - Images the same size and composition as the original
   - Images that are resized from the original
   - Images that are cropped from the original

   To draw an image the same size and composition as the original, use `drawImage()`, as shown in B1 and C1 of Listing 4-10. The parameters are

   ```
   drawImage(image, xPosition, yPosition);
   ```

   This code draws the `image` with its upper left corner at (`xPosition`, `yPosition`) using the original image dimensions.

5. **Resize images.**

   To draw an image using different dimensions than the original, use `drawImage()` as shown in B2 of Listing 4-10:

   ```
   drawImage(image, xPosition, yPosition, width, height);
   ```

   This line draws image at (`xPosition`, `yPosition`) using `width` and `height`.

6. **Crop images.**

   To draw an image with cropping, use `drawImage()`, as shown in B2 of Listing 4-10:

   ```
   drawImage(image, sourceCropX, sourceCropY, xPosition, yPosition,
           width, height);
   ```

   This code draws an image at (`xPosition`, `yPosition`) using `width` and `height` with cropping of the original image starting at (`sourceCropX`, `sourceCropY`).

5

Transforming Objects

. . . .

In This Chapter

Applying a transform matrix

Using Canvas states

Using the transform matrix for rotation, scaling, mirroring, and skewing objects

Applying multiple transforms

. . . .

*W*e've all witnessed transformations. A child grows up. A house is remodeled. Something is the same, yet different. This is the concept behind transforming Canvas objects.

Transforming objects allows you to create a new object based on the original. The new object can look very different from the original or only slightly changed. Transforming is a powerful tool because it creates change based on a small set of instructions.

Translating

I'm not talking about translating from English to French. Canvas translation means moving, or *translating*, the (0,0) point of the Canvas to a new position. A better word for translating Canvas positions might be *shifting*.

Figure 5-1 and Listing 5-1 demonstrate using translation to change the position on a Canvas for drawing a sequence of squares. The first (gray) square is drawn in the original (0,0) position in the upper-left corner of the Canvas. Each subsequent colored square is drawn by translating the Canvas to a new (0,0) position relative to the previous square. The translation is done by moving a specified amount horizontally and vertically.

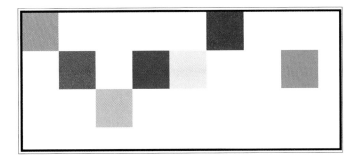

Figure 5-1: Translated Canvas positions.

Listing 5-1: Translating Canvas Positions

```
<!DOCTYPE HTML> <html> <head> <script>

// A. WINDOW LOAD function.
window.onload = function()
{
   // A1. CANVAS definition variables.
   canvas  = document.getElementById("canvasArea");
   context = canvas.getContext("2d");

   // A2. SIZE of square.
   var size = 35;

   // A3. DISPLAY squares.
   //         translateH  translateV  color
   //         ----------  ----------  --------
   drawSquare(        0,          0, "gray"  );
   drawSquare(     size,       size, "red"   );
   drawSquare(     size,       size, "orange");
   drawSquare(     size,      -size, "blue"  );
   drawSquare(     size,          0, "pink"  );
   drawSquare(     size,      -size, "purple");
   drawSquare(   2*size,       size, "green" );

   // B. DRAW SQUARE function.
   function drawSquare(translateH, translateV, color)
   {
      // B1. COLOR.
      context.fillStyle = color;

      // B2. TRANSLATE canvas.
      context.translate(translateH, translateV);

      // B3. SQUARE display.
```

```
        context.fillRect(0, 0, size, size);
    }
}
</script> </head> <body>
<div    style = "width:300px;  height:125px;  margin:0 auto; padding:5px;">
<canvas id   = "canvasArea"  width = "300"  height = "125"
        style = "border:2px solid black">
Your browser doesn't currently support HTML5 Canvas.
</canvas> </div> </body> </html>
```

To perform a translation, do the following:

1. **Define variables that will be used to calculate the translation.**

   For example, in A2 of Listing 5-1, a size variable is defined:

   ```
   var size = 35;
   ```

2. **Define a function that will include Canvas translation.**

   Often translation is included as part of a function that you define to draw objects. For example, in code section B of Listing 5-1, a function is defined that will draw a square at different positions on your Canvas based on parameters for horizontal position, vertical position, and color:

   ```
   function drawSquare(translateH, translateV, color)
       { . . . }
   ```

   Call this function and provide the appropriate parameters, such as size and color in code section A3:

   ```
   //          translateH  translateV  color
   //          ----------  ----------  --------
   drawSquare(        0,          0,  "gray");
   drawSquare(     size,       size,  "red" );
   ```

3. **Define a call to the `translate()` function.**

   Use the `translate()` function as shown in code B2 of Listing 5-1. This function has two parameters, the horizontal and vertical translation distances:

   ```
   context.translate(translateH, translateV);
   ```

   The `translate()` function is applied to the Canvas `context`. This means that any subsequent actions performed on the `context` will be oriented to the shifted (0,0) position.

4. **Draw your object using the translated position.**

   As in code B3, the `fillRect()` function uses the new (0,0) position as shown in the first two parameters representing the (x,y) coordinates of the new square:

   ```
   context.fillRect(0, 0, size, size);
   ```

Note that translation is performed from the *current* (0,0) position, *not* the original upper-left Canvas corner (0,0) position. Experiment with values in the example to see how they affect the placement of squares.

But wait, what if you want to perform a translation based on the original (0,0) position? You might not want the translations to build on each other. There's an easy solution, and it's up in the next section.

Saving Canvas States

Many methods of transforming objects work by changing the shape or position of the Canvas, such as in the translation example in Listing 5-1.

Imagine drawing a shape on the surface of a balloon. As you add more air to the balloon, the shape gets bigger. Let air out, and it gets smaller. This is similar to what takes place when you're transforming objects on a Canvas.

Because of this dynamic, any objects drawn after the Canvas is changed will reflect those shape changes. If multiple changes to the Canvas are made, they become additive. For example, the second change is added on top of the first, the third on top of the second, and so forth. This can lead to unpredictable and unwanted impacts on shapes drawn.

The solution to this potential problem is to save and then restore the Canvas context as you're drawing objects. To do so, follow these steps:

1. **Save the context.**

    Canvas contexts are saved in an array that is managed like a stack of dinner plates. When you save your context, like a dinner plate being put away, it is put on the top of the stack. You can save as many versions of your context as you like. Your stack of dinner plates doesn't have limits like the ones in your cabinet at home. To save your context, use this statement:

    ```
    context.save();
    ```

    Make sure that you use the correct context name in applications where you have more than one Canvas. It's easy to reference the wrong context and see very strange things happen on your Canvas. I've done it many times. So be careful with your context names.

2. **Restore the context.**

    Use the following statement to restore the Canvas context:

    ```
    context.restore();
    ```

    This removes the top plate, your Canvas, from the stack and restores those attributes.

You see an example of this practice in Listing 5-2 in the next section.

Scaling

Scaling allows you to change the dimensions of your Canvas. This is useful when you want to do things such as using the same sequence of code to draw objects with varying dimensions. Figure 5-2 and Listing 5-2 demonstrate scaling.

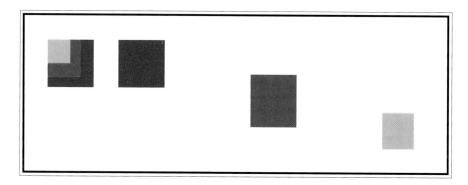

Figure 5-2: Scaled objects.

Listing 5-2:   Scaling Objects

```
<!DOCTYPE HTML> <html> <head> <script>

// A. WINDOW LOAD function.
window.onload = function()
{
    // A1. CANVAS definition variables.
    canvas  = document.getElementById("canvasArea");
    context = canvas.getContext("2d");

    // A2. DISPLAY squares.
    //         xPos  yPos scaleH scaleV color     save
    //         ----  ---- ------ ------ --------  -----
    drawSquare( 25,  25,  1.4,   1.4,   "purple", true );
    drawSquare( 25,  25,  1.0,   1.1,   "red",    true );
    drawSquare( 25,  25,  0.7,   0.7,   "orange", true );
    drawSquare(100,  25,  1.4,   1.4,   "purple", false);
    drawSquare(100,  25,  1.0,   1.1,   "red",    false);
    drawSquare(100,  25,  0.7,   0.7,   "orange", false);

    // B. DRAW SQUARE function.
```

(continued)

Listing 5-2 *(continued)*

```
function drawSquare(xPos, yPos, scaleH, scaleV, color, save)
{
   // B1. SAVE context.
   if (save) {context.save();}

   // B2. ATTRIBUTES & VARIABLES.
   context.fillStyle = color;     var size        = 35;

   // B3. TRANSLATE position.
   context.translate(xPos, yPos);

   // B4. SCALE canvas.
   context.scale(scaleH, scaleV);

   // B5. SQUARE display.
   context.fillRect(0, 0, size, size);

   // B6. RESTORE context.
   if (save) {context.restore();}
   }
}
</script> </head> <body>
<div    style = "width:450px;  height:160px;  margin:0 auto; padding:5px;">
<canvas id   = "canvasArea"  width = "450"  height = "160"
      style = "border:2px solid black">
Your browser doesn't currently support HTML5 Canvas.
</canvas> </div> </body> </html>
```

To draw objects on a scaled Canvas, follow these steps:

1. **Define a function that will include Canvas scaling.**

   Often scaling is included as part of a function that you define to draw objects. For example, in code section B of the example, a function is defined that will draw a square at different sizes and positions on your Canvas based on parameters for position, scaling factors, and color:

   ```
   function drawSquare(xPos, yPos, scaleH, scaleV, color, save)
   { . . . }
   ```

   Call this function and provide the appropriate parameters as in A2 of the example:

   ```
   //       xPos  yPos scaleH scaleV color      save
   //       ----  ---- ------ ------ --------   -----
   drawSquare( 25,  25,  1.4,   1.4,  "purple", true );
   drawSquare( 25,  25,  1.0,   1.1,  "red",    true );
   ```

2. Save and restore Canvas context states.

You'll likely want to use `context save()` and `restore()` when scaling a Canvas to change its dimensions. In the example, the leftmost set of three objects stacked one on top of the other were drawn using `save()` and `restore()`. The three objects to the right of those are the same objects drawn without using `save()` and `restore()`. The example uses a parameter to determine whether to use `save()` and `restore()` in code sections B1 and B6:

```
if (save) {context.save();}
.
.
.
if (save) {context.restore();}
```

3. Translate to the object on the Canvas.

Because the entire Canvas is being scaled, you need to translate the `(0,0)` position to the upper-left corner of the object you're scaling. If you don't do this, the result will be that the whole object is moved to a new position. Use the `translate()` function to reposition to the `(x,y)` coordinates of your object, as in this statement from B3 of Listing 5-2:

```
context.translate(xPos, yPos);
```

4. Scale objects with the `scale()` function.

Here's an example in B4 of Listing 5-2:

```
context.scale(scaleH, scaleV);
```

The `scaleH` and `scaleV` parameters provide numbers used to multiply against the horizontal and vertical dimension of an object. So, to decrease the horizontal dimension by 50 percent and double the vertical dimension, use the following statement:

```
context.scale(.5, 2.0);
```

5. Draw your object by using the appropriate function.

Here's B5 of the example:

```
context.fillRect(0, 0, size, size);
```

Mirroring

Mirroring objects allows you to create effects like reflected images. Figure 5-3 and Listing 5-3 demonstrate this. The silver ball has a reflected image on the surface below it. The background of blues and oranges is created using a gradient that enhances the reflected imagery.

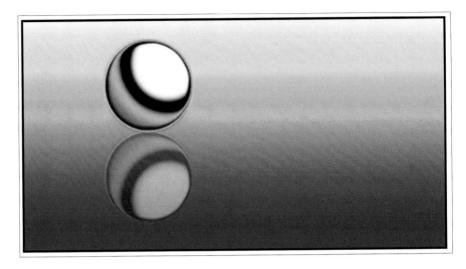

Figure 5-3: Mirrored object.

Listing 5-3:   Mirroring Objects

```
<!DOCTYPE HTML> <html> <head> <script>

// A. WINDOW LOAD function.
window.onload = function()
{
    // A1. CANVAS definition variables.
    canvas  = document.getElementById("canvasArea");
    context = canvas.getContext("2d");

    // A2. IMAGE variable and source.
    var ball = new Image();
    smallImage.src = "http://marketimpacts.com/storage/SilverBall100px.png";

    // A3. BALL variables.
    var ballXPos  = 75;   var ballYPos    = 15;
    var ballWidth = 90;   var ballHeight  = 90;

    // A4. REFLECTION variables.
    var reflectAdj   = 3.5;
    var reflectAlpha = .4;
    var reflectY     = (2*ballYPos) + (2*(ballHeight-reflectAdj));

    // A5. GRADIENT for surface.
    var gradLV = context.createLinearGradient(0, 0, 0, canvas.height);

    // B. LOAD image of ball.
```

```
ball.onload = function()
{
    // B1. COLORS for surface.
    gradLV.addColorStop( 0, "lightskyblue" );
    gradLV.addColorStop(.3, "orange"       );
    gradLV.addColorStop( 1, "blue"         );

    // B2. DRAW surface.
    context.fillStyle = gradLV;
    context.fillRect(0, 0, canvas.width, canvas.height);

    // B3. DRAW original image at specific size.
    context.drawImage(ball, ballXPos, ballYPos, ballWidth, ballHeight);

    // B4. TRANSLATE Y position to base of image.
    context.translate(0, reflectY);

    // B5. SCALE to create reflected image.
    context.scale(1,-1);

    // B6. TRANSPARENCY of reflected image.
    context.globalAlpha = reflectAlpha;

    // B7. DRAW reflected image.
    context.drawImage(ball, ballXPos, ballYPos, ballWidth, ballHeight);
    }
}
</script> </head> <body>
<div    style = "width:400px;  height:210px;  margin:0 auto; padding:5px;">
<canvas id    = "canvasArea"  width = "400"  height ="210"
        style = "border:2px solid black">
Your browser doesn't currently support HTML5 Canvas.
</canvas> </div> </body> </html>
```

To mirror an object over a background image, do the following:

1. **Load an image by creating a variable to hold the image and specifying the location of the source of the image.**

   See the example in A2 of Listing 5-3. Then create the function to be executed when the image is loaded, as in code section B:

   ```
   ball.onload = function()
   { . . . }
   ```

 The object you're mirroring doesn't have to be a loaded image as is used in the example. It could be a simple circle or rectangle. I use an image in the example to demonstrate how mirroring can add interest to Canvas images.

2. **Set image and reflection variables.**

   Set variables for the original and reflected objects, as in A3–4:

   ```
   var ballXPos   = 75;   var ballYPos    = 15;
   var ballWidth  = 90;   var ballHeight  = 90;
   var reflectAdj = 3.5;  var reflectAlpha = .4;
   var reflectY   = (2*ballYPos) + (2*(ballHeight-reflectAdj));
   ```

   - The `reflectAdj` variable adjusts for any distance between the bottom of the image object and the bottom edge of the image. For example, the image for the ball in Figure 5-3 is not fitted precisely against the edges of the loaded image. There is a small buffer space between the two. If this space isn't accounted for, the reflected image will not be positioned properly. Experiment with the `reflectAdj` value to see how the reflection changes position.

   - The `reflectY` variable sets the point at which the reflection is created based on the object position, height, and reflection adjustment.

   - The `reflectAlpha` variable sets the level of transparency for the reflected image.

   - The `ballXPos` and `ballYPos` variables set the position of the image on the Canvas.

   - The `ballWidth` and `ballHeight` parameters set the dimensions of the image.

3. **Create an optional gradient for the background using the `create LinearGradient()` function.**

   Here's an example from A5:

   ```
   var gradLV = context.createLinearGradient(0, 0, 0, canvas.height);
   ```

   The colors for the gradient are created by using the `addColorStop()` function, as in B1:

   ```
   gradLV.addColorStop(0,"lightskyblue");
   ```

4. **Using the gradient, fill a rectangle to create the background image.**

   This example is from B2:

   ```
   context.fillStyle = gradLV;
   context.fillRect(0, 0, canvas.width, canvas.height);
   ```

5. **Draw the image of the object to be reflected.**

   Here's an example from B3:

   ```
   context.drawImage(ball, ballXPos, ballYPos, ballWidth, ballHeight);
   ```

6. **Use the `translate()` function to adjust the (0,0) point of the Canvas vertically so that the reflected image will be drawn in the correct position.**

Here's an example in B4 of Listing 5-3:

```
context.translate(0,reflectY);
```

The horizontal *x* axis is left unadjusted because the reflection will be done only in the downward vertical direction.

7. **Use the `scale()` function to adjust the `(0,0)` point of the Canvas vertically so that the reflected image will be drawn in the correct position.**

Here's an example from B5 of Listing 5-3:

```
context.scale(1,-1);
```

The scale of the horizontal *x* axis is left unchanged because the reflection will be done only in the vertical direction. This statement is the heart of creating the reflection.

8. **Use the `globalAlpha` attribute to control the level of transparency for the reflected object.**

Here's B6 of the example:

```
context.globalAlpha = reflectAlpha;
```

The `reflectAlpha` variable in the example is set to .4, meaning that the reflected object will appear at 40 percent as opaque as the original.

9. **Draw the objects on the Canvas with the `drawImage()` function.**

Here are examples in B3 and B7:

```
context.drawImage(ball, ballXPos, ballYPos, ballWidth, ballHeight);
```

To create objects of a known height that can be used to calculate the reflection, the optional width and height parameters are used.

Even though the same set of parameters is used for the reflected image as the original image, when the reflected object is drawn, the `translate()` function, `scale()` function, and transparency setting will have changed the Canvas context, so the result of the `drawImage()` function is the reflected ball. Also note that other types of objects such as text, rectangles, and multi-sided shapes can also be used for mirroring. They require their own specific methods for drawing images.

Rotating

Rotating a Canvas facilitates drawing images and varying angles. It appears on the Canvas as though the object itself is rotating, when in fact, it is the Canvas on which the object is drawn that is rotating.

Rotating an object is demonstrated in Figure 5-4, which was produced by Listing 5-4. The pinwheel effect in the example is created by rotating a filled Bezier curve around a point at the center of the Canvas.

Figure 5-4: Rotating an object.

In addition to creating still images such as the one shown in Figure 5-4, the rotate() function can be used in conjunction with other functions to create animated motion (see Chapter 6).

At the heart of rotating an object is the rotate() function, as shown in B3 of Listing 5-4:

```
context.rotate(angleInRadians);
```

The Canvas context is rotated by the angle in radians. When the next object is drawn, it is placed in a new position.

Listing 5-4: Rotating Objects

```
<!DOCTYPE HTML> <html> <head> <script>

// A. WINDOW LOAD function.
window.onload = function()
{
    // A1. CANVAS definition variables.
    canvas  = document.getElementById("canvasArea");
    context = canvas.getContext("2d");

    // A2. ANGLE or rotation.
```

```
    var angle = 40;

    // A3. DRAW surface.
    context.fillStyle = "silver";
    context.fillRect(0, 0, canvas.width, canvas.height);

    // A4. TRANSLATE to rotation point.
    context.translate(canvas.width/2, canvas.height/2);

    // A5. DRAW curves.
    drawBezier(angle, "darkturquoise");     drawBezier(angle, "deeppink");
    drawBezier(angle, "gold");              drawBezier(angle, "mediumvioletred");
    drawBezier(angle, "yellow");            drawBezier(angle, "teal");
    drawBezier(angle, "chartreuse");        drawBezier(angle, "magenta");
    drawBezier(angle, "red");
}
// B. BEZIER curve drawing function.
function drawBezier(angle, color)
{
    // B1. ATTRIBUTES.
    context.fillStyle    = color;   context.lineWidth     = 7;
    context.shadowOffsetX = 3;       context.shadowOffsetY = 3;
    context.shadowBlur    = 5;       context.shadowColor   = "gray";

    // B2. SHAPE parameters.
    var xStart    = 0;    var yStart    = 0;
    var xControl1 = 90;   var yControl1 = 20;
    var xControl2 = -60;  var yControl2 = 60;
    var xEnd      = 60;   var yEnd      = 60;

    // B3. ROTATE.
    var angleInRadians = angle * Math.PI/180;
    context.rotate(angleInRadians);

    // B4. STARTING point.
    context.beginPath();
    context.moveTo(xStart, yStart);

    // B5. BEZIER curve.
    context.bezierCurveTo(xControl1, yControl1, xControl2, yControl2,
            xEnd, yEnd);
    // B6. DRAW curve.
    context.fill();
}
</script> </head> <body>
<div    style = "width:200px;  height:200px;  margin:0 auto; padding:5px;">
<canvas id    = "canvasArea"  width = "200"  height = "200"
        style = "border:2px solid black">
Your browser doesn't currently support HTML5 Canvas.
</canvas> </div> </body> </html>
```

To rotate a Canvas and draw images at new positions, do the following:

1. **Define a function that will include Canvas rotation.**

   Often rotation is included as part of a function that you define to draw objects. For example, in code section B of Listing 5-4, a function is defined that will draw a Bezier curve at different positions on your Canvas based on parameters for angle and color:

   ```
   function drawBezier(angle, color)
   { . . . }
   ```

   Call this function and provide the appropriate parameters, as in A5 of the example:

   ```
   drawBezier(angle, "darkturquoise");
   drawBezier(angle, "deeppink"    );
   ```

2. **Set the angle of rotation for each new curve drawn.**

   See A2 of the example:

   ```
   var angle = 40;
   ```

   Pass the angle to the drawing function as in B:

   ```
   function drawBezier(angle, color)
   ```

   Finally, convert the angle to radians as in B3:

   ```
   var angleInRadians = angle * Math.PI/180;
   ```

3. **Set the point on the Canvas around which you rotate the object.**

   In code section A4 of the example, the rotation point is set to the center of the Canvas:

   ```
   context.translate(canvas.width/2, canvas.height/2);
   ```

4. **Set parameters for the shape you will draw.**

   In the example, the object — a Bezier curve — is being rotated around the starting point of the curve. Because the point of rotation has been translated to the proper position on the Canvas context, the Bezier curve starts at the (0,0) position, as defined in B2:

   ```
   var xStart = 0;  var yStart = 0;
   ```

   How the parameters for a shape are set depends on the type of shape you rotate and where the center of rotation is placed. For example, to rotate a rectangle around its center, place the center of rotation in the middle of the rectangle and calculate the shape parameters from that position:

   ```
   var xStart = -rectWidth/2;   var yStart = -rectHeight/2;
   ```

5. **Rotate the Canvas context before drawing the object.**

   This is done in B3 in the example:

   ```
   context.rotate(angleInRadians);
   ```

6. **Use the `moveTo()` function to set the starting point for drawing your object.**

   See B4 of the example:

   ```
   context.moveTo(xStart, yStart);
   ```

   Note that the starting point in this example is the (0,0) point of the Canvas.

7. **Draw the object using the appropriate functions.**

   In the example code B5-6, a filled Bezier curve is used:

   ```
   context.bezierCurveTo(xControl1, yControl1,
                         xControl2, yControl2,
                         xEnd, yEnd);
   context.fill();
   ```

Applying a Transform Matrix

Canvas has a special function, `setTransform()`, that can be used to apply multiple effects to objects. The function uses a set of parameters, called the *transform matrix,* to calculate Canvas adjustments:

```
setTransform(scaleX, skewY, skewX, scaleY, translateX, translateY)
```

Look closely at these parameters. Does something look slightly off? It should. The matrix of parameters would make more sense if `skewY` and `scaleY` were interchanged. Nevertheless, this is the order of parameters that must be used. Now that you're aware of this slight confusion factor, hopefully it won't trip you up like it did me!

As the parameter names imply, they are change factors for the X (horizontal) and Y (vertical) dimensions of an object:

- **Scale:** Expands/contracts vertically/horizontally
- **Skew:** Shifts vertically/horizontally
- **Translate:** Moves vertically/horizontally

Figure 5-5 and Listing 5-5 demonstrate applying the `setTransform()` function. Each object in Figure 5-5 demonstrates a different combination of the parameters. Some combinations to note are

- **Scaling:** The scale of three of the rectangles was changed. (The aqua, orange, and pink rectangles.)
- **Skewing:** Five of the rectangles were skewed. (The green, red, yellow, orange, and pink rectangles.)
- **Translating:** All the rectangles used translating for placement on the Canvas.

Figure 5-5: Applying the setTransform() function.

Listing 5-5:   Applying the setTransform() Function

```
<!DOCTYPE HTML> <html> <head> <script>

// A. WINDOW LOAD function.
window.onload = function()
{
    // A1. CANVAS definition variables.
    canvas  = document.getElementById("canvasArea");
    context = canvas.getContext("2d");

    // A2. BACKGROUND.
    context.fillStyle = "silver";
    context.fillRect(0, 0, canvas.width, canvas.height);

    // A3. DRAW rectangles. Note abbreviations:
    //      sc:scale  sk:skew  tr:translate
```

```
//       X:horizontal axis  Y:vertical axis
//
//       scX  scY  skX  skY  trX  trY  color
//       ---  ---  ---  ---  ---  ---  --------
drawRect(1.0,  1.0,  0.0,  0.0,  25,   25,  "blue"  );
drawRect(1.0,  1.0,  0.2,  0.0,  125,  25,  "green" );
drawRect(1.0,  1.0,  0.0,  0.2,  225,  25,  "red"   );
drawRect(1.0,  1.0,  0.2,  0.2,  325,  25,  "yellow");
drawRect(1.2,  1.0,  0.0,  0.0,  25,   110, "purple");
drawRect(1.0,  1.2,  0.0,  0.0,  125,  110, "aqua"  );
drawRect(1.2,  1.2,  0.2,  0.2,  225,  110, "orange");
drawRect(1.3,  1.3,  -.2,  -.2,  325,  110, "pink"  );
}
// B. DRAW rectangle function.
function drawRect(scaleX, scaleY, skewX, skewY, translateX, translateY, color)
{
    // B1. ATTRIBUTES & VARIABLES.
    var width           = 60;      var height        = 40;
    context.shadowOffsetX = 4;       context.shadowOffsetY = 4;
    context.shadowBlur    = 5;       context.shadowColor   = "gray";
    context.fillStyle     = color;

    // B2. TRANSFORM matrix.
    context.setTransform(scaleX, skewY, skewX, scaleY, translateX, translateY);

    // B3. DISPLAY rectangle.
    context.fillRect(0, 0, width, height);
}
</script> </head> <body>
<div    style = "width:425px;  height:200px;  margin:0 auto; padding:5px;">
<canvas id      = "canvasArea"  width = "425"  height ="200"
        style = "border:2px solid black">
Your browser doesn't currently support HTML5 Canvas.
</canvas> </div> </body> </html>
```

To apply a transform matrix, use the following steps:

1. **Define a function that will include the transform matrix.**

   Often a transform matrix is included as part of a function that you define to draw objects. For example, in code section B of the example, a function is defined that will draw a rectangle using a transform matrix on your Canvas based on parameters for scale, skew, translation, and color:

   ```
   function drawRect(scaleX, scaleY, skewX, skewY, translateX, translateY,
                   color)
     {. . . }
   ```

Call this function and provide the appropriate parameters as in A3 of the example:

```
//      sc:scale  sk:skew  tr:translate
//      X:horizontal axis  Y:vertical axis
//
//      scX  scY  skX  skY  trX  trY  color
//      ---  ---  ---  ---  ---  ---  --------
drawRect(1.0, 1.0, 0.0, 0.0,  25,  25, "blue"  );
drawRect(1.0, 1.0, 0.2, 0.0, 125,  25, "green" );
```

2. **Apply the `setTransform()` function to the Canvas context.**

See B2 of the example:

```
context.setTransform(scaleX,      skewY,
                     skewX,       scaleY,
                     translateX, translateY);
```

3. **Draw your objects using the appropriate functions.**

In the example, a rectangle is drawn in B3:

```
context.fillRect(0, 0, width, height);
```

Scaling objects

To scale an object, use a positive or negative number for the `scaleX` and/or `scaleY` parameters. This number indicates a percentage of scaling of the dimension that will be applied. For example, the purple rectangle has a value of 1.2 for the `scaleX` parameter:

```
//      scX  scY  skX  skY  trX  trY  color
//      ---  ---  ---  ---  ---  ---  --------
drawRect(1.2, 1.0, 0.0, 0.0,  25, 110, "purple");
```

This value expands the X dimension of the rectangle to the right by 20 percent.

Skewing objects

To skew an object, use a positive or negative number for the `skewX` and/or `skewY` parameters. This number indicates a percentage of skewing of the dimension that will be applied. For example, the green rectangle has a value of 0.2 for the `skewX` parameter:

```
//      scX  scY  skX  skY  trX  trY  color
//      ---  ---  ---  ---  ---  ---  --------
drawRect(1.0, 1.0, 0.2, 0.0, 125,  25, "green" );
```

This value shifts the X dimension of the bottom of the rectangle to the right by 20 percent.

Translating objects

To translate an object, use a positive number for the `translateX` and/or `translateY` parameters. This number indicates a position on the Canvas. For example, the blue rectangle has a value of 25 for the `translateX` and `translateY` parameters:

```
//       scX  scY  skX  skY  trX  trY  color
//       ---  ---  ---  ---  ---  ---  --------
drawRect(1.0, 1.0, 0.0, 0.0,  25,  25, "blue" );
```

This places the upper-left corner of the rectangle on the Canvas at the (25,25) coordinate position.

6

Moving Objects

*T*he concept of moving an object can be deceptively simple. Just change the position from point A to point B. But ask a scientist how easy it is to move a rocket into orbit. It's much harder than just defining point A and point B. In the real world, objects have to contend with forces such as gravity, friction, and acceleration. In this chapter, you discover how to mimic these factors and integrate them with the basics of moving from one point to another.

The Basics of Movement

Even without considering factors such as gravity and friction, moving an object on a Canvas takes a bit of work. Figure 6-1 and Listing 6-1 demonstrate moving a circle linearly from the left of the Canvas to the right.

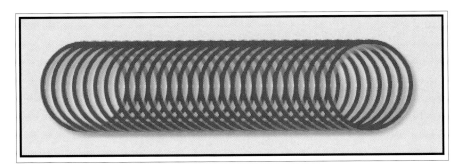

Figure 6-1: Moving circle.

Listing 6-1: Moving a Circle

```
<!DOCTYPE HTML> <html> <head> <script>

// A. WINDOW LOAD function.
window.onload = function()
{
    // A1. CANVAS definition variables.
    canvasC  = document.getElementById("canvasCircle");
    contextC = canvasC.getContext("2d");
    canvasBG  = document.getElementById("canvasBackground");
    contextBG = canvasBG.getContext("2d");

    // A2. PARAMETERS.
    var xPos     = 50;      var yPos       = canvasC.height/2;
    var radius   = 40;      var endXPos    = canvasC.width-75;
    var change   = 10;      var startAngle = (Math.PI/180)*0;
    var interval = 80;      var endAngle   = (Math.PI/180)*360;

    // A3. BACKGROUND canvas filled with color.
    contextBG.fillStyle = "silver";
    contextBG.fillRect(0,0,canvasBG.width,canvasBG.height);

    // A4. INTERVAL for drawing.
    var intervalID = setInterval(drawCircle,interval);

    // B. DRAW CIRCLE function.
    function drawCircle()
    {
        // B1. CLEAR Canvas for each image.
        //     Note: Comment out to see all images.
        //contextC.clearRect(0,0,canvasC.width,canvasC.height);

        // B2. ATTRIBUTES of the circle.
        contextC.strokeStyle   = "red";    contextC.lineWidth    = 4;
        contextC.shadowOffsetX = 3;        contextC.shadowOffsetY = 3;
        contextC.shadowBlur    = 5;        contextC.shadowColor   = "gray";

        // B3. POSITION change.
        xPos += change;

        // B4. STOP if reached end.
        if(xPos > endXPos) {clearInterval(intervalID)};

        // B5. DRAW circle.
        contextC.beginPath();
        contextC.arc(xPos, yPos, radius, startAngle, endAngle, true);
        contextC.stroke();
    }
```

```
}
</script> </head> <body> <div>

<!-- C. CANVAS ELEMENTS -->
<canvas id    = "canvasCircle"  width = "400"  height ="125"
        style = "border:2px solid black; position:absolute;
                 left:auto; top:auto; z-index: 2">
Your browser doesn't currently support HTML5 Canvas.
</canvas>
<canvas id    = "canvasBackground"  width = "400"  height ="125"
        style = "border:2px solid black; position:absolute;
                 left:auto; top:auto; z-index: 1">
Your browser doesn't currently support HTML5 Canvas.
</canvas>
</div> </body> </html>
```

To explain Listing 6-1, I cover three key aspects:

- Using multiple Canvas elements to create moving an object across a background

- Creating that background

- Using animation to draw the moving object

Using multiple Canvas elements

In most applications that involve movement, you'll be moving an object across a background. The background might be a simple color (refer to Listing 6-1), an image, or a collection of objects constructed by your application. If you use a single Canvas for the background and the moving object, you'll have to redraw the background every time the object moves, consuming valuable computing resources.

A much better approach is to use separate Canvas elements for the background and moving objects. You can change the content of the moving object Canvas independently of the background Canvas. You can change one without having to change the other.

This will become particularly important in more complex applications where you will use multiple Canvas elements to control backgrounds, moving objects, text displays, and other visual components.

To define multiple Canvas elements for your application, do the following:

1. **Define multiple Canvas tags.**

   Define multiple Canvas tags using unique IDs and z-index values, as shown in code section D of Listing 6-1:

   ```
   <canvas id    = "canvasCircle"  width = "400"  height ="125"
           style = "border:2px solid black; position:absolute;
                    left:auto; top:auto; z-index: 2">
   </canvas>
   <canvas id    = "canvasBackground"  width = "400"  height ="125"
           style = "border:2px solid black; position:absolute;
                    left:auto; top:auto; z-index: 1">
   </canvas>
   ```

   In this example, both Canvases are the same size. This will not always be the case. You might have smaller Canvases positioned in different locations above the background.

   The `z-index` parameter in the `style` attribute of the Canvas elements determines how the Canvases are layered. Canvases are "stacked" in ascending order. So in the example, `canvasCircle` is drawn on top of `canvasBackground`.

2. **Define multiple Canvas contexts.**

   To draw on these separate Canvas areas, define multiple Canvas contexts, as in A1 of the example:

   ```
   canvasC   = document.getElementById("canvasCircle");
   contextC  = canvasC.getContext("2d");
   canvasBG  = document.getElementById("canvasBackground");
   contextBG = canvasBG.getContext("2d");
   ```

Creating the background

A background Canvas can be anything from a simple color field to an area containing its own moving objects. In the example shown in A3 of Listing 6-1, a rectangle filled with a single color is used. To create this background, do the following:

1. **Set the attributes of the background.**

   In the example, a single color is used:

   ```
   contextBG.fillStyle = "silver";
   ```

2. **Draw the background with the appropriate function.**

   In the example, a rectangle the size of the Canvas is filled with the color defined in the `fillStyle`:

   ```
   contextBG.fillRect(0,0,canvasBG.width,canvasBG.height);
   ```

Drawing a moving object

On the top Canvas, referenced through `contextC`, draw the moving circle using the following steps:

1. **Set parameters for the moving object.**

   Set parameters such as those in A2 of Listing 6-1. Examples are the starting position, ending position, and radius of the object to be moved:

   ```
   var xPos   = 50;   var yPos   = canvasC.height/2;
   var radius = 40;   var endXPos = canvasC.width-75;
   ```

   Note that the Canvas context referenced is `canvasC`, the context for the moving circle.

2. **Set a time interval and function call.**

   Use the `setInterval()` function to do a number of things, as shown in A4:

   ```
   var intervalID = setInterval(drawCircle,interval);
   ```

   - `drawCircle`: Defines the function to be called after every `interval`. In this case, the function is `drawCircle()`, which will draw the red circle in Figure 6-1. This is termed a *callback* to the specified function.

   - `Interval`: Sets the number of milliseconds between calls to the `drawCircle()` function — that is, how often the image is moved and drawn.

     Setting the best interval for your moving object should be influenced by two important factors. The first is the power of device computing compared to the amount of drawing needed at each `interval`. If the `interval` is set too low, the device hardware may have difficulty keeping up and you will see sporadic delays in drawing the new images.

     The second factor is the fluidity of object movement. If the `interval` is set too high, the movement will appear halting and artificial.

   - `intervalID`: Defines the variable used in the `drawCircle()` function to terminate the `setInterval()` function at the end of the drawing sequence.

   There is another, similar function that creates only a single call to the specified function after the specified `interval`, the `setTimeout()` function. You can use this function if you're moving an object just once.

3. **Clear the Canvas used for drawing images if you want to see only a single image for each interval.**

   This option is coded in B1 of the example:

   ```
   contextC.clearRect(0,0,canvasC.width,canvasC.height);
   ```

   Normally, you'll want to clear the Canvas because you'll be animating the movement of an object across the Canvas.

4. **Set the attributes of the shape you're drawing.**

   For example, set the color and line width, as shown in B2:

   ```
   contextC.strokeStyle = "red";
   ```

5. **Change the position of the object on the Canvas using variables that control alterations to object coordinates.**

   In B3 of the example, the *x* coordinate is shifted by the variable `change`:

   ```
   xPos += change;
   ```

   The speed at which an object moves across the screen is determined by the combination of the `interval` and `change` parameters. For example, your object can move faster by doing either or both of the following:

   - Decreasing the `interval`
   - Increasing the `change`

6. **Stop the movement of your object when the limit of a variable has been reached.**

   In B4 of the example, the *x* coordinate position `xPos` is checked for reaching the limit specified in the variable `endXPos`:

   ```
   if(xPos > endXPos) {clearInterval(intervalID)};
   ```

   The mechanism for stopping calls to the drawing function is the `clear Interval()` function. As shown above, the `intervalID` created when the `setInterval()` function was called is passed to the `clear Interval()` function.

   Use different `intervalID`s to independently control multiple moving objects.

7. **Draw the object.**

   In B5 of the example, the object is a circle:

   ```
   contextC.beginPath();
   contextC.arc(xPos, yPos, radius, startAngle, endAngle, true);
   contextC.stroke();
   ```

Creating Circular Motion

Developing an application to create circular motion has a lot in common with creating linear motion. To avoid unnecessary repetition, this discussion of circular motion is divided into two sections, *basic* and *unique* aspects. Basic aspects are those that have already been explained and will be touched on lightly. Unique aspects are new topics and will be covered in more depth.

Figure 6-2 and Listing 6-2 demonstrate moving a ball in a circular motion around the center of the Canvas.

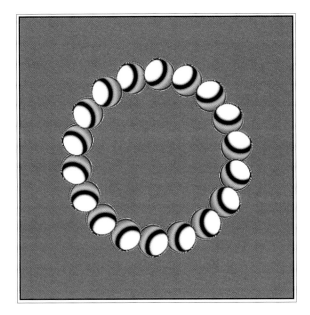

Figure 6-2: Circular motion.

Listing 6-2:   Creating Circular Motion

```
<!DOCTYPE HTML> <html> <head> <script>

// A. WINDOW LOAD function.
window.onload = function()
{
   // A1. CANVAS definition variables.
   canvasBall  = document.getElementById("canvasBall");
   contextBall = canvasBall.getContext("2d");
   canvasBG    = document.getElementById("canvasBackground");
```

(continued)

Listing 6-2 *(continued)*

```
contextBG    = canvasBG.getContext("2d");

// A2. PARAMETERS.
var xPos   = canvasBall.width/2;     var change   = 20;
var yPos   = canvasBall.height/2;    var interval = 50;
var count  = 0;                       var max      = 100;
var radius = 90;

// A3. BACKGROUND canvas filled with color.
contextBG.fillStyle = "deeppink";
contextBG.fillRect(0, 0, canvasBG.width, canvasBG.height);

// A4. BALL IMAGE loaded from website.
var ball = new Image();
ball.src = "http://marketimpacts.com/storage/SilverBall50px.png";

// B. LOAD IMAGE of ball.
ball.onload = function()
{
    // B1. CENTER rotation.
    contextBall.translate(xPos,yPos);

    // B2. INTERVAL for drawing.
    var intervalID = setInterval(drawBall,interval);

    // C. DRAW IMAGE function.
    function drawBall()
    {
        // C1. CLEAR Canvas for each ball image.
        //     Note: Comment out to see all images.
        contextBall.clearRect(-canvasBall.width/2, -canvasBall.height/2,
                              canvasBall.width,     canvasBall.height);

        // C2. STOP if reached end.
        count += 1;
        if(count > max) {clearInterval(intervalID)};

        // C3. ROTATE image.
        contextBall.rotate(((Math.PI)/180)*change);

        // C4. DRAW image.
        contextBall.drawImage(ball,radius,0);
    }
}
}
</script> </head> <body> <div>

<!-- D. CANVAS DEFINITIONS  -->
```

```
<canvas id    = "canvasBall"  width = "200"  height ="200"
        style = "border:2px solid black; position:absolute;
                 left:auto; top:auto; z-index: 2">
Your browser doesn't currently support HTML5 Canvas.
</canvas>
<canvas id    = "canvasBackground"  width = "200"  height ="200"
        style = "border:2px solid black; position:absolute;
                 left:auto;  top:auto;  z-index: 1">
Your browser doesn't currently support HTML5 Canvas.
</canvas>
</div> </body> </html>
```

Basic aspects

The basic aspects are common to many applications involving movement.
Use the following steps to cover these bases:

1. **Define multiple Canvas elements.**

   Define one Canvas for the background and another for the moving ball,
   as in D of Listing 6-2. Define Canvas contexts for each as in A1:

   ```
   canvasBall  = document.getElementById("canvasBall");
   contextBall = canvasBall.getContext("2d");
   ```

2. **Create the background.**

   Fill the background as in code section A3. The example uses a solid color:

   ```
   contextBG.fillStyle = "deeppink";
   contextBG.fillRect(0,0,canvasBG.width,canvasBG.height);
   ```

   Other background options are images and objects created by the
   application.

3. **Set the parameters for moving your object.**

   Here's the code from A2:

   ```
   var xPos  = canvasBall.width/2;  var change   = 20;
   var yPos  = canvasBall.height/2; var interval = 50;
   ```

4. **Set the time interval and function to call for creating the moving object.**

   See code section B2:

   ```
   var intervalID = setInterval(drawBall,interval);
   ```

5. **Clear the moving object Canvas if you want only each new image to
   appear.**

   Here's an example from C1:

   ```
   contextBall.clearRect(-canvasBall.width/2, -canvasBall.height/2,
                          canvasBall.width,     canvasBall.height);
   ```

6. **Define a variable and source for the image of the moving object.**

   See the code section A4. Define the function to be called when the image is loaded, as in code section B:

   ```
   var ball = new Image();
   ball.src = "http://marketimpacts.com/storage/SilverBall50px.png";

   ball.onload = function()  { . . . }
   ```

7. **Draw the object using the appropriate functions.**

   In the example, the image of a ball is used, as in C4:

   ```
   contextBall.drawImage(ball, radius, 0);
   ```

Unique aspects

Use the following steps to create rotation:

1. **Use the `translate()` function to move the `(0,0)` point of the Canvas to the center of rotation for the object.**

   Here's an example in B1 of Listing 6-2:

   ```
   contextBall.translate(xPos,yPos);
   ```

2. **Rotate the Canvas using the `rotate()` function.**

   The amount of rotation is determined by the variable change, as in C3:

   ```
   contextBall.rotate(((Math.PI)/180)*change);
   ```

3. **Stop the rotation based on a variable reaching a limit. See**

   See the example in code section C2:

   ```
   count += 1;
   if(count > max) {clearInterval(intervalID)};
   ```

   If you don't want to stop the rotation in your application, omit this code.

Creating Oscillation

Oscillation is a repetitive variation around a central value. In the real world, the entity oscillating can be an object, sound wave, electrical current, or even an economic factor. Common oscillations involve a clock pendulum, a bouncing spring, and the sound of the conversations we hear all around us.

The circularly rotating image from Figure 6-2 (in the preceding section) is a simple oscillation. The repetitive variation is the image movement around a central point, returning to the starting point once for every revolution.

Figure 6-3 and Listing 6-3 build on circular motion to create a simulation of a planet moving in an oscillating elliptical orbit around a sun.

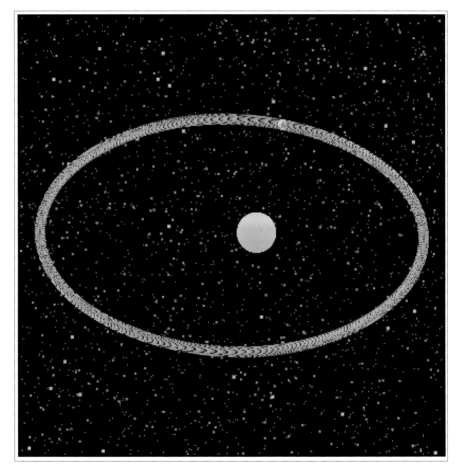

Figure 6-3: Oscillating elliptical motion.

Listing 6-3: Creating Oscillating Motion

```
<!DOCTYPE HTML> <html> <head> <script>

// A. WINDOW LOAD function.
window.onload = function()
{
    // A1. CANVAS contexts.
    canvasPlanet  = document.getElementById("canvasPlanet");
    contextPlanet = canvasPlanet.getContext("2d");
    canvasBG      = document.getElementById("canvasBackground");
    contextBG     = canvasBG.getContext("2d");

    // A2. PARAMETERS.
    var change    = .6;     var xPos      = canvasPlanet.width/2;
    var interval  = 33;     var yPos      = canvasPlanet.height/2;
    var radius    = 0;      var angle
    var radiusMin = 100;    var radiusMax = 175;
    var numStars1 = 2000;   var colorStar1 = "white";
    var numStars2 = 400;    var colorStar2 = "gray";
    var numStars3 = 30;     var colorStar3 = "darkgray";
    var planetSize = 12;    var sunSize   = 45;
    var imageCount = 0;     var imageQuant = 2;

    // A3. BACKGROUND Canvas color.
    contextBG.fillStyle = "black";
    contextBG.fillRect(0, 0, canvasBG.width, canvasBG.height);

    // A4. STARS drawing.
        for(var n=0; n<numStars1; n++)
        {
            var xStar = Math.random()*canvasBG.width;
            var yStar = Math.random()*canvasBG.height;
            contextBG.fillStyle = colorStar2;
            contextBG.fillRect(xStar, yStar, 1, 1);
        }
        for(var n=0; n<numStars2; n++)
        {
            var xStar = Math.random()*canvasBG.width;
            var yStar = Math.random()*canvasBG.height;
            contextBG.fillStyle = colorStar2;
            contextBG.fillRect(xStar, yStar, 2, 2);
        }
        for(var n=0; n<numStars3; n++)
        {
            var xStar = Math.random()*canvasBG.width;
            var yStar = Math.random()*canvasBG.height;
            contextBG.fillStyle = colorStar3;
            contextBG.fillRect(xStar, yStar, 3, 3);
        }
    // A5. IMAGE references.
    var planet = new Image();
```

```
planet.src = "http://marketimpacts.com/storage/Planet.png";
var sun    = new Image();
sun.src    = "http://marketimpacts.com/storage/Sun.png";

// B. SUN image load function.
sun.onload = function()
{
    // B1. DRAW image.
    contextBG.drawImage(sun, 200, 175, sunSize, sunSize);

    // B2. COUNT increment.
    imageCount ++;

    // B3. CHECK for all images loaded.
    if(imageCount == imageQuant)

        // B4. ANIMATION start.
        {var intervalID = setInterval(drawPlanet, interval)}
}
// C. PLANET image load function.
planet.onload = function()
{
    // C1. TRANSLATE to rotation point.
    contextPlanet.translate(xPos, yPos);

    // C2. COUNT increment.
    imageCount ++;

    // C3. CHECK for all images loaded.
    if(imageCount == imageQuant)

        // C4. ANIMATION start.
        {var intervalID = setInterval(drawPlanet, interval)}
 }
// D. DRAW IMAGE function.
function drawPlanet()
 {
    // D1. CLEAR Canvas for each image.
    //      Note: Comment out to see all images.
    contextPlanet.clearRect(-canvasPlanet.width/2, -canvasPlanet.height/2,
                             canvasPlanet.width,     canvasPlanet.height);
    // D2. RADIUS calculation
    var angleR = (Math.PI/180)*angle;
    var calcAS = radiusMax * Math.sin(angleR);
    var calcBC = radiusMin * Math.cos(angleR);
    radius     = (radiusMax * radiusMin) / Math.sqrt((calcAS*calcAS)+
                                                     (calcBC*calcBC));
    // D3. ROTATE image.
    contextPlanet.rotate(((Math.PI)/180)*-change);
    angle = angle + change;
```

(continued)

Listing 6-3 *(continued)*

```
    // D4. DRAW PLANET.
     contextPlanet.drawImage(planet, radius, 0, planetSize,planetSize);
   }
}
</script> </head> <body> <div>

<!-- E. CANVAS DEFINITIONS  -->
<canvas id   = "canvasPlanet"  width = "400"  height ="400"
       style = "border:2px solid black; position:absolute;
                  left:auto; top:auto;  z-index: 2">
</canvas>
<canvas id   = "canvasBackground" width = "400"  height ="400"
       style = "border:2px solid black; position:absolute;
                  left:auto; top:auto; z-index: 1">
Your browser doesn't currently support HTML5 Canvas.
</canvas>
</div> </body> </html>
```

Basic aspects

The basics of creating a moving object have been discussed in depth earlier in this chapter. I touch on them briefly here:

1. **Define multiple Canvas elements.**

   Define one Canvas for the background and another for the moving object, as in code section E of Listing 6-3. Define contexts for each Canvas as in A1:

   ```
   canvasPlanet  = document.getElementById("canvasPlanet");
   contextPlanet = canvasPlanet.getContext("2d");
   ```

2. **Set the parameters you want to use for moving and drawing your object.**

   Here's an example from code section A2:

   ```
   var change    = .6;    var xPos = canvasPlanet.width/2;
   var interval  = 33;    var yPos = canvasPlanet.height/2;
   ```

3. **Create the background.**

   Fill the background as in code section A3. The example uses a solid color:

   ```
   contextBG.fillStyle = "black";
   contextBG.fillRect(0, 0, canvasBG.width, canvasBG.height);
   ```

4. **Set the time interval and function to call for creating the moving object.**

   Here's an example from C4:

   ```
   intervalID = setInterval(drawPlanet, interval);
   ```

5. **Clear the moving object Canvas if you only want each new image to appear for each interval:**

    Here's an example from code section D1:

    ```
    contextBL.clearRect(0,0,canvasBL.width,canvasBL.height);
    ```

    If you want to see all the objects drawn, you can remove or comment out this statement, as was done earlier, to produce Figure 6-3.

6. **Draw your object using the appropriate functions.**

    The moving planet in the example is drawn using the `drawImage()` function:

    ```
    contextPlanet.drawImage(planet, radius, 0, planetSize, planetSize);
    ```

Unique aspects

A couple of aspects transform simple circular motion into an interesting simulation. One is aesthetic and the other scientific.

Creating an interesting background

The background could, of course, have been left black. But what fun would that be? To generate the sun and stars background in Listing 6-3, follow these steps:

1. **Create random star locations.**

    Listing 6-3 uses the technique of randomized position calculation to create a star field using the code in A4:

    ```
    var xStar = Math.random()*canvasBG.width;
    var yStar = Math.random()*canvasBG.height;
    ```

2. **Create a variety of star sizes and colors.**

    Three sizes of stars and a bit of color variation are used in A2 and A4 to generate the image of the vastness of space:

    ```
    var numStars1 = 2000;   var colorStar1 = "white";
    var numStars2 = 400;    var colorStar2 = "gray";
    var numStars3 = 30;     var colorStar3 = "darkgray";
    ```

3. **Create stars.**

    Fill a rectangle using the `fillRect()` function:

    ```
    contextBG.fillStyle = colorStar2;
    contextBG.fillRect(xStar, yStar, 1, 1);
    ```

Note that the stars are drawn as squares because of their extremely small size. It's simply not possible to draw a rounded-edge pixel. However, you have to look closely to see they are squares and not circles.

4. Create a sun.

And what sense would it make for a planet to be orbiting, well, nothing? So a sun is loaded in A5 and drawn in B:

```
var sun     = new Image();
sun.src     = "http://marketimpacts.com/storage/Sun.png";
sun.onload = function()
{contextBG.drawImage(sun, 200, 175, sunSize, sunSize)}
```

Loading multiple images

In the example in Listing 6-3, two images are used in creating the Canvas display. Both images — the sun and planet — must be loaded from the server before the animation can be started. This is a common aspect of Canvas animations. To ensure that all images are loaded and ready to go, follow the next set of steps.

If you don't count image loads using these techniques, the results are unpredictable. Depending on the speed with which the browser loads images, you may or may not see them on your Canvas.

1. Create an `onload` function for each image.

As in code sections B and C, define the function to be called when the image is loaded from the server:

```
sun.onload    = function() { . . . }
planet.onload = function() { . . . }
```

2. Take actions based on the particular image.

In the example, when the sun is loaded, it's drawn on the background Canvas, as in code section B1:

```
contextBG.drawImage(sun, 200, 175, sunSize, sunSize);
```

When the planet is loaded, the position on the planet Canvas is translated to the correct rotation point for simulated orbiting, as in code section C1:

```
contextPlanet.translate(xPos, yPos);
```

3. Increment the count of images.

Increment a counter as in B2 and C2:

```
imageCount ++;
```

4. When all images are loaded, start the animation.

Check the image count, and when the images are loaded, call the `setInterval()` function, as in B3-4 and C3-4:

```
if(imageCount == imageQuant)
   {var intervalID = setInterval(drawPlanet, interval)}
```

Drawing the oscillating object

In Listing 6-3, a planet is drawn orbiting the sun. To create this motion, use the following steps:

1. **Calculate the radius of rotation.**

   This is the heart of creating the oscillation pattern you see earlier, in Figure 6-3. Changing a circular motion into an elliptical motion requires recalculating the radius before drawing every image. The formula for calculating a radius based on an angle of rotation in radians is

   ```
   radius = ( radiusMax * radiusMin )   / √ x
   ```

   where

   ```
   x = ( radiusMax  *  sin(angleInRadians) ) ² +
         ( radiusMin  * cos(angleInRadians) ) ²
   ```

   Use this code to calculate the radius based on this formula:

   ```
   var angleR = (Math.PI/180)*angle;
   var calcAS = radiusMax * Math.sin(angleR);
   var calcBC = radiusMin * Math.cos(angleR);
   radius     = (radiusMax * radiusMin) / Math.sqrt((calcAS*calcAS) +
                (calcBC*calcBC));
   ```

2. **Rotate the image.**

   Rotate the image of the planet based on the `change` parameter and increment the angle for the next rotation:

   ```
   contextPlanet.rotate(((Math.PI)/180) * -change);
   angle = angle + change;
   ```

 Experiment with the code in Listing 6-3 to see the effect of changing the `radiusMax` and `radiusMin` values. You'll see the ellipse change its oblong shape, becoming alternately thinner and fatter. You can also vary the speed of oscillation using variables in A2:

   ✔ `interval`: The time in milliseconds between drawing the planet images

   ✔ `change`: The distance between each planet image

Adjusting Movement for Acceleration, Gravity, Friction, and Bounce

In this section, you find out how to model the real-world forces of acceleration, gravity, friction, and bounce. Most Canvas applications don't need to achieve high degrees of accuracy in mimicking these forces. You can construct them to have the appearance of the real world.

It *is* possible to incorporate formulas and techniques to create the very accurate models that might be required for scientific applications. This section touches on these topics, but their full treatment is outside the scope of this book.

Figure 6-4 and Listing 6-4 demonstrate the impact of real-world forces on a metal ball moving across a wooden table with rubber bumper sides. This is something you might find in applications modeling pool tables or pinball machines. The application includes parameters that you can modify to change the effect of these forces.

Figure 6-4: Modeling momentum, acceleration, gravity, friction, and bounce.

Listing 6-4:   Adjusting Movement for Acceleration, Gravity, Friction, and Bounce

```
<!DOCTYPE HTML> <html> <head> <script>

// A. WINDOW LOAD function.
window.onload = function()
{
    // A1. CANVAS definition variables.
    canvasBL  = document.getElementById("canvasBall");
    contextBL = canvasBL.getContext("2d");
    canvasBG  = document.getElementById("canvasBackground");

    contextBG = canvasBG.getContext("2d");

    // A2. PARAMETERS.
    var xVector      = -15;      var yVector     = -30;
    var yVectorMin   = -20;      var yVectorMax  = -30;
    var ballX        = 300;      var ballY       = 450;
    var interval     = 30;       var radius      = 15;
    var frictionL    = .01;      var frictionC   = 0;
    var gravityL     = 0;        var gravityC    = 0;
    var accelerL     = .008;     var accelerC    = .001;
    var damping      = .03;      var incline     = .25;
    var imageCount   = 0;        var imageQuant  = 2;
    var feetPerPixel = .01;      var ballImage;

    // A3. ATTRIBUTES of ball.
    contextBL.shadowOffsetX = -2;
    contextBL.shadowOffsetY = 3;
    contextBL.shadowBlur    = 5;
    contextBL.shadowColor   = "black";

    // A4. IMAGE sources.
    var wood       = new Image();
    wood.src       = "http://marketimpacts.com/storage/Wood.jpg";
    var silverBall = new Image();
    silverBall.src = "http://marketimpacts.com/storage/SilverBall50px.png";

    // A5. GRAVITY calculation.
    gravityL = .0322*(interval/feetPerPixel);

    // B. BALL image load function.
    silverBall.onload = function()
    {
        // B1. BALL variable setting.
        ballImage = silverBall;

        // B2. COUNT increment.
        imageCount ++;

        // B3. CHECK for all images loaded.
```

(continued)

Listing 6-4 *(continued)*

```
    if(imageCount == imageQuant)

        // B4. ANIMATION start.
        {var intervalID = setInterval(drawBall, interval)}
    }
// C. BACKGROUND image load function.
wood.onload = function()
{
    // C1. BACKGROUND fill.
    contextBG.drawImage(wood, 0, 0, canvasBG.width, canvasBG.height);

    // C2. GRAVITY adjustment for incline.
    gravityL *= Math.sin(incline*(Math.PI/180));

    // C3. Y VECTOR random value.
    yVector = yVectorMin + (Math.random()*(yVectorMax-yVectorMin));

    // C4. COUNT increment.
    imageCount ++;

    // C5. CHECK for all images loaded.
    if(imageCount == imageQuant)

        // C6. ANIMATION start.
        {var intervalID = setInterval(drawBall, interval)}
    }
// D. DRAW BALL function.
function drawBall()
{
    // D1. MOVE ball.
    moveBall();

    // D2. CLEAR Canvas to show only moving ball.
    contextBL.clearRect(0,0,canvasBL.width, canvasBL.height);

    // D3. DRAW ball.
    contextBL.drawImage(silverBall, ballX-radius, ballY-radius,
                                 2*radius,    2*radius);
    // D4. SIDE BOUNCE.
    if (ballX < radius || ballX > canvasBL.width-radius)

            // D5. REVERSE x vector.
            {xVector *= -1*(1-damping)}

    // D6. CEILING & FLOOR BOUNCE.
    if (ballY < radius || ballY > canvasBL.height-radius)
    {
        // D7. REVERSE y vector.
```

```
        yVector *= -1*(1-damping);


        // D8. FLOOR bounce check.
        if((yVector < 0) && (yVector < -gravityL))


            // D9. GRAVITY reduction.
            {yVector += gravityL}
    }
}
// E. MOVE BALL function.
function moveBall()
{
    // E1. FRICTION adjustment.
    frictionL = frictionL - frictionC;
    if(frictionL < 0) {frictionL = 0}

    // E2. ACCELERATION adjustment.
    accelerL = accelerL - accelerC;
    if(accelerL < 0) {accelerL = 0}

    // E3. GRAVITY adjustment.
    gravityL = gravityL - gravityC;
    if(gravityL < 0) {gravityL = 0}

    // E4. FRICTION/ACCELERATION factor.
    faFactor = (1-frictionL)*(1+accelerL);

    // E5. X VECTOR change.
    xVector  = xVector*faFactor;

    // E6. X POSITION change.
    ballX   += xVector;

    // E7. Y vector & coordinate change
    //     if ball is above floor.
    if((ballY+radius)<(canvasBL.height))
    {
        // E8. GRAVITY adjustment.
        var adjGravityL = Math.min(gravityL, (canvasBL.height-ballY));

        // E9. Y VECTOR change.
        yVector = (yVector*faFactor) + adjGravityL;
    }
    // E10. Y POSITION change.
    ballY += yVector;

    // E11. BOUNDS check & adjustment.
    if((ballX+(radius-1)) > canvasBL.width)
        {ballX=(canvasBL.width-(radius-1))}
```

(continued)

Listing 6-4 *(continued)*

```
        if((ballX-(radius-1)) < 0)
            {ballX=(radius-1)}
        if((ballY+(radius-1)) > canvasBL.height)
            {ballY=(canvasBL.height-(radius-1))
             if(yVector < (gravityL+radius))
                {gravityL = .9*gravityL}}
        if((ballY-(radius-1)) < 0)
            {ballY=(radius-1)}
    }
}
</script> </head> <body> <div>

<!-- F. CANVAS DEFINITIONS  -->
<canvas id    = "canvasBall"  width = "350"  height ="500"
        style = "border:6px solid black;  position:absolute;
                 left:auto; top:auto;  z-index: 2">
</canvas>
<canvas id    = "canvasBackground"  width = "350"  height ="500"
        style = "border:6px solid black;  position:absolute;
                 left:auto; top:auto;  z-index: 1">
Your browser doesn't currently support HTML5 Canvas.
</canvas>
</div> </body> </html>
```

Basic aspects

The basics of creating and moving an object have been discussed in depth in previous sections. Follow these steps to address them:

1. **Define multiple Canvas elements, one for the background and one for the moving object.**

   Define one Canvas for the background and another for the moving ball, as in F of Listing 6-4. Define variables for each Canvas as in A1:

   ```
   canvasBL  = document.getElementById("canvasBall");
   contextBL = canvasBL.getContext("2d");
   ```

2. **Create the background.**

   Fill the background as in code section C1:

   ```
   contextBG.drawImage(wood, 0, 0, canvasBG.width,
                                   canvasBG.height);
   ```

3. **Set the parameters and attributes for moving and drawing the object.**

   Here are examples from A2–3:

   ```
   contextBL.shadowOffsetX = -2;
   contextBL.shadowOffsetY = 3;
   ```

4. Load images for the object and background.

Load images from your website as in A4:

```
var wood = new Image();
wood.src = "http://marketimpacts.com/storage/Wood.jpg";
```

5. Set the time interval and function to call for creating the moving object.

When all images have been loaded, use the `setInterval()` function to start the animation. Here's an example from B4:

```
intervalID = setInterval(drawBall, interval);
```

6. Clear the moving object Canvas if you want only each new image to appear.

Here's the code from D2:

```
contextBL.clearRect(0, 0, canvasBL.width, canvasBL.height);
```

If you want to see all the objects drawn, you can remove or comment out this statement.

7. Draw your object using the appropriate functions.

The moving circle in the example is drawn using the `arc()` function in D3:

```
contextBL.drawImage(silverBall, ballX-radius, ballY-radius,
                          2*radius,      2*radius);
```

Unique aspects

You need to deal with a number of new aspects when introducing real-world forces on your moving object, as discussed in the following sections.

Using a vector for object motion

A *vector* is a quantity possessing both *magnitude* and *direction*. This is an essential concept in moving an object around a space. Every time you move an object, you need to provide information on which direction and how far the object will go.

To use a vector to move an object, follow these steps:

1. Define *x* and *y* vector variables.

In the example, the vectors are defined with their initial values in A2:

```
var xVector = -15;   var yVector = -30;
```

2. **Define *x* and *y* position variables.**

The current *x* and *y* position coordinates are defined with their initial values:

```
var ballX = 300;     var ballY = 450;
```

3. **Change the object position with vector values.**

To move an object in your two-dimensional Canvas space, calculate new *x* and *y* coordinates using a vector value for each coordinate, as shown in Figure 6-5.

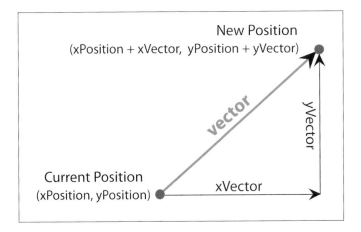

Figure 6-5: Using a vector to change position.

To move the ball from the current to next position, add the vector values to the current position values, as in E6 and E10:

```
ballX += xVector;
ballY += yVector;
```

Handling bounces

To bounce an object off a vertical or horizontal surface, which is depicted in Figure 6-6, implement the following steps:

1. **Detect touching a surface.**

To detect the surface, check the position of the ball *x* coordinate for a wall touch and the ball *y* coordinates for a floor/ceiling touch.

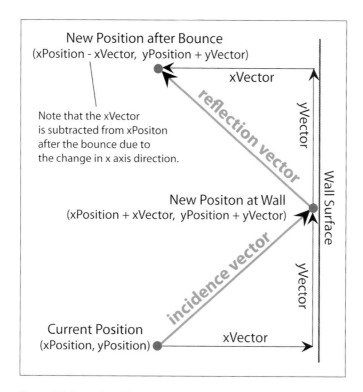

Figure 6-6: Bouncing off a vertical surface.

Check for a touch at a distance of the `radius` of the ball so that the ball will appear to bounce when the *surface* of the ball touches the edge of the Canvas.

This is demonstrated in D4 and D6 of the example:

```
if (ballX < radius || ballX > canvasBL.width-radius)
if (ballY < radius || ballY > canvasBL.height-radius)
```

Note that the < expressions check for touching the left/top of the Canvas and the > expressions check for touching the right/bottom of the Canvas.

2. **Change direction if the object touches a surface.**

If a touch of a surface occurs, change the direction of the ball by reversing the direction of the *x* vector if there's a touch of the *x* coordinate, and the *y* vector if there's a touch of the *y* coordinate.

Change the vector direction by multiplying the vector by –1. This works for vertical and horizontal surfaces. For angled surfaces, calculation of the angle of bounce is more complex.

While changing direction, apply a `damping` factor to account for the loss of energy from the bounce. The `damping` factor is defined (in A2 of the example) as a variable between 0 and 1:

```
var damping = .03;
```

Damping simulates the loss of energy that takes place when an object bounces off a surface. Think of the bounce of a tennis ball. When the ball is new, it bounces higher than after it's been used for a while. Expressed in terms of damping, the tennis ball has a higher damping factor as it ages.

Change in direction is demonstrated in D5 and D7 of the example:

```
xVector *= -1 * (1-damping);
yVector *= -1 * (1-damping);
```

The force of gravity for objects near the surface of Earth

Gravity is the force between two objects that pulls them together. We think of gravity as pulling down because of our position on Earth. Objects out in the universe can be pulled in any direction by gravitational interaction with other objects.

The formula for the force of gravity is

$$F = G\,(m_1 \times m_2)\,/\,r^2$$

where:

G = Gravitational Constant $\approx 6.674 \times 10^{-11}$

m_1 = mass of the object 1

m_2 = mass of the object 2

r = distance between the objects

Because the size of Earth dwarfs the size of objects on the planet, only the mass of Earth is meaningful in the gravity formula. This is why when two balls of different sizes are dropped from the same height, they fall at the same speed and reach the ground at the same time. (If they have very different shapes, friction from air might affect their speed.)

For objects near the surface of Earth, the distance between Earth and the object is insignificant in the calculation. The size of Earth is huge relative to other objects. If you're simulating a rocket moving far enough from Earth's surface, you would need to account for decreases in gravity. For objects staying near the surface, distance doesn't matter.

Therefore, the force of gravity can be approximated as a constant for your Canvas applications. This calculation comes out to an increase in speed of falling objects every second of approximately 32.2 feet/second.

Calculating gravity for your application

When simulating gravity for earthbound objects in your Canvas application, adjust the object's *y* coordinate in each drawing interval. In Listing 6-4, this is every time the `drawBall()` function is called in A10 by the `setInterval()` function. Gravity "pulls" to *increase* the *y* coordinate. So to account for gravity, increase the *y* coordinate by the necessary number of pixels.

You can take one of two approaches, or a combination approach, to setting gravity for an application:

✏ **Scientific:** Based on calculations, as explained in this section.

✏ **Aesthetic:** Based on how the result looks. Unless you're trying to simulate movement with scientific accuracy, what's truly important is how the user perceives movement and reacts to your simulation. So, you can adjust the gravity factor to fine-tune its effect.

For the sample application in Listing 6-4, I used a scientific approach and this formula, as shown in code section A5:

```
gravityL = .0322*(interval/feetPerPixel);
```

To determine the number of gravity adjustment pixels in a scientific manner, use the following steps:

1. **Decide how many feet a single pixel on your Canvas represents.**

   The feet per pixel (FPP) ratio you choose can vary widely. For a "close-up" scene, a pixel might represent only a fraction of a single foot. For a "distance" scene, a pixel might represent many feet. It all depends on what you're simulating.

   In the Listing 6-4 example, a ball is rolling on a simulated wooden surface five feet high. The Canvas is 500 pixels in height. Therefore, you can calculate the feet per pixel dimension of your Canvas this way:

   FPP = height in feet / height in pixels

        = 5 feet / 500 pixels

        = .01 feet/pixel

2. **Calculate gravity in pixels per second (PPS).**

   Gravity pulls down on your ball at 32.2 feet/sec^2. (See the earlier sidebar on calculating gravity for objects near the surface of Earth.) This means that the speed of the ball increases by 32.2 feet/sec every second. So after 2 seconds, the speed would be increased by 64.2 feet/sec. Also, in the first second, the 32.2 feet/sec is not reached until the end of that second. Given these factors, I used 32.2 feet/sec as an approximation.

Use the following formula to calculate the pixels per second (PPS) increase in the *y* coordinate of your ball that's necessary to account for gravity:

$$PPS = 32.2 \text{ feet/sec} / \text{FPP}$$

$$= 32.2 \text{ feet/sec} / .01 \text{ feet/pixel}$$

$$= 3220 \text{ pixels/sec}$$

3. **Translate pixels per second into pixels per frame.**

Now translate PPS into pixels per frame (PPF) of your animation to determine how many pixels to add to the *y* coordinate of your ball in every animation frame. Let's say your animation frame interval (FI) equals 30 milliseconds. That is, you're moving your ball every 30 milli-seconds. Next calculate your frame rate (FR) using the formula:

$$FR = 1,000 \text{ milliseconds/second} / \text{FI}$$

$$= 1,000 \text{ milliseconds/second} / 30 \text{ milliseconds/frame}$$

$$= 33.3 \text{ frames/second}$$

Now calculate pixels per frame (PPF) using the following formula:

$$PPF = PPS / FR$$

$$= 3220 \text{ pixels/sec} / 33.33 \text{ frames/sec}$$

$$= 96.6 \text{ pixels per frame}$$

4. **Combine formulas for a simplified calculation.**

Good news. Here's a handy way to combine these formulas to create a simplified formula for Earth gravity for your application:

$$PPF = PPS / FR$$

$$= (32.2/\text{FPP}) / (1000/\text{FI})$$

$$= (32.2/\text{FPP}) \times (\text{FI}/1000)$$

$$= (32.2/1000) \times (\text{FI}/\text{FPP})$$

$$= .0322 \times (\text{FI}/\text{FPP})$$

Where:

FI = Frame Interval (in milliseconds)

FPP = Feet per Pixel

For this example of simulating a bouncing ball in front of a house, Earth gravity pixels per frame calculate as follows:

$$PPF = .0322 \times (\text{FI}/\text{FPP})$$

$$= .0322 \times (30/.01)$$

$$= 96.6$$

Estimating friction for your objects

Friction is a force that resists the motion of one material against another. Those materials can be solids, liquids, or gases. In your Canvas application, friction pushes against your *x* and *y* vectors slowing motion.

Precisely modeling the friction of one object against another is beyond the scope of this book. Each set of object combinations requires its own, complex, analysis. For example:

- Rubber covered baseball against air
- Flat plastic hockey puck against frozen water
- Glass marble against a concrete sidewalk
- Smooth stone falling through water

Fortunately, for most Canvas applications, it's sufficient to use an estimate of friction in the form of a percent reduction in the movement of an object. This is referred to as the *coefficient of friction.*

To develop the coefficient of friction for your objects, follow these steps:

1. **Guess at an initial value.**

   Most often, friction will reduce movement by a small number of percentage points. Start with an estimate in the range of 1 percent to 2 percent unless you're simulating moving relatively rough surfaces against one another. In Listing 6-4, this value is set in code section A2:

   ```
   var frictionL = .01
   ```

2. **Observe the behavior of real-world objects.**

   Observe real-world objects similar to those you're modeling. Watch how they move in real life so that you can compare them to your Canvas simulation.

3. **Apply friction to the object vector.**

   Apply the coefficient of friction to the *x* and *y* vectors for your object. In Listing 6-4, friction is combined with acceleration and then applied to the vectors, as in code sections E4, E5, and E9:

   ```
   faFactor = (1-frictionL)*(1+accelerL);
   xVector  =  xVector*faFactor;
   yVector  = (yVector*faFactor)+adjGravityL;
   ```

4. **Adjust the value to reflect the reality you're simulating.**

   Experiment with different values for the coefficient of friction, `frictionL`, in your working application. Observe the results and modify the coefficient to help produce the results you want.

You might decide you don't want to model reality precisely. Don't get hung up on what's "real" unless you're developing a scientific application that needs to model natural forces as closely as possible. Most Canvas applications are as much art as they are science.

Estimating acceleration for your objects

Acceleration is the rate at which the velocity of your object changes over time. Precisely modeling acceleration is beyond the scope of this book. Like friction, each type of acceleration requires its own complex analysis. For example, acceleration of:

- A baseball off a bat
- A rocket burning fuel
- A sailboat pushed by the wind

Fortunately, for most Canvas applications, it's sufficient to use an estimate of acceleration in the form of a percent increase in the movement of an object. To develop an acceleration factor for your objects, follow these steps:

1. **Guess at an initial value.**

   Start with an estimate in the range of 1 percent to 5 percent unless you're simulating a rapidly accelerating object like a rocket. In Listing 6-4, this value is set in code section A2:

   ```
   var accelerL = .008;
   ```

2. **Observe the behavior of real-world objects.**

   Observe real-world objects like those you're modeling. Watch how they move in real life and compare them to your Canvas simulation.

3. **Set the object's starting vector values.**

   The initial values you set for the x and y vectors for your object will determine its initial velocity. Velocity is the speed of an object in a given direction. This is, in effect, an instant acceleration to a starting velocity.

   In the Listing 6-4 code A2, the starting x vector is set as a fixed value:

   ```
   var xVector = -15;
   ```

   The y vector is set as a random value between a minimum and maximum in order to create variation in the path of the ball — just to add a bit of fun. The minimum and maximum values are set in A2:

   ```
   var yVectorMin = -20;    var yVectorMax = -30;
   ```

The *y* vector itself is calculated in C3:

```
yVector = yVectorMin + (Math.random() * (yVectorMax-yVectorMin));
```

4. **Apply acceleration to the object vector.**

   Apply the acceleration factor to the *x* and *y* vectors for your object. In the example, acceleration is combined with friction and then applied to the vectors, as in code sections E4, E5, and E9:

```
faFactor = (1-frictionL)*(1+accelerL);
xVector  =  xVector*faFactor;
yVector  = (yVector*faFactor)+adjGravityL;
```

5. **Adjust the value to model the reality you want to simulate.**

   Experiment with different values for acceleration in your working application. Observe the results and modify the coefficient to help produce the results you want.

Modeling the combined natural forces

As shown in Figure 6-7, a number of forces act on a moving object. Momentum and acceleration act to move the object in the vector direction it's already pointed. Friction pushes back against the vector, trying to decrease both the `xVector` and `yVector` components. Gravity pulls down against only the `yVector`.

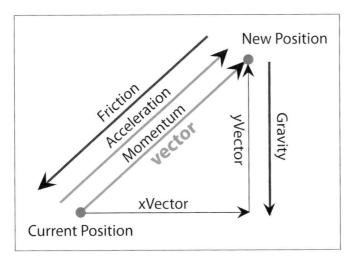

Figure 6-7: The forces of momentum, friction, acceleration, and gravity.

To model the combined effect of these forces, use the following steps:

1. **Define variables for force levels and change factors.**

   Here's code section A2 of Listing 6-4:

   ```
   var frictionL  = .01;    var frictionC = 0;
   var gravityL   = 0;      var gravityC  = 0;
   var accelerL   = .008;   var accelerC = .001;
   ```

   The change factors variables (those ending in C) are modeled to reduce the level of the factor (those variables ending in L) over time. For example, if you were modeling a rocket moving into outer space, the effects of gravity and friction would decrease as the rocket moves farther away from Earth.

2. **Calculate gravity.**

   Use the 32 feet/sec approximation to calculate the force of gravity based on the animation interval and feet per pixel scale of the animation image, as in code section A5:

   ```
   gravityL = .0322*(interval/feetPerPixel);
   ```

3. **Adjust gravity for the incline.**

   Adjust the level of gravity for the incline of the table on which the ball moves. The adjustment is based on the sine of the angle of incline. This is shown in C2:

   ```
   gravityL *= Math.sin(incline*(Math.PI/180))
   ```

4. **Change force levels as the simulation progresses, with a check to prevent the factor from dropping below zero.**

   This is modeled in Listing 6-4 in E1–3. Here is the example for friction:

   ```
   frictionL = frictionL - frictionC;
   if(frictionL < 0) {frictionL = 0}
   ```

   This modeling can be made more complex if moving your application objects requires adjustments for additional influences. In the example of modeling a rocket, you might model friction and gravity as a function of distance from Earth.

5. **Combine friction and acceleration.**

   For convenience, combine the forces of friction and acceleration, because these affect both the *x* and *y* vectors. Acceleration is a positive force, and friction a negative force. In the example, this is done in E4:

   ```
   faFactor = (1-frictionL)*(1+accelerL);
   ```

6. **Change the `xVector` of the object using the friction/acceleration factor.**

   Here's an example in E5:

   ```
   xVector = xVector*faFactor;
   ```

7. **Add the *x* vector to the position of the object.**

   Here's an example in E6:

   ```
   ballX += xVector;
   ```

8. **Before updating the `yVector`, check to see whether the object is on the floor.**

   If this check isn't applied, the ball continues sinking out of sight. Yikes! If the ball is on the floor, don't update the *y* vector.

   To detect an "on floor" condition, test to see whether the edge of the ball touches the edge of the Canvas, as in E7:

   ```
   if((ballY+radius) < canvasBL.height)
   {
    . . . update y vector . . .
   }4
   ```

9. **Adjust gravity for near floor condition. That is:**

   As the object approaches the floor, decrease gravity to prevent the object from being pushed through the floor by gravity.

   This can happen if the value for gravity is large relative to the speed of the object. Adjust gravity to the minimum of the gravity level and the distance between the object and the floor, as in E8 of the example:

   ```
   var adjGravityL = Math.min(gravityL, (canvasBL.height-ballY));
   ```

10. **Update the *y* vector using the friction/acceleration factor and adjusted gravity.**

    Here's an example in E9:

    ```
    yVector = (yVector*faFactor) + adjGravityL;
    ```

11. **Add the *y* vector to the position of the object.**

    Here's an example in E10:

    ```
    ballY += yVector;
    ```

12. **Check for out -of -bounds conditions and move the object inside the Canvas, if necessary.**

    At high object speeds, it's possible that after the object has moved, its new position will be outside the bounds of the Canvas. Here's how the right edge condition is handled in E11:

    ```
    if((ballX+(radius-1)) > canvasBL.width)
       {ballX=(canvasBL.width-(radius-1))}
    ```

    The adjustment of −1 pixel is necessary to keep the ball from being trapped against a Canvas edge.

Part III
Breathing Life into Your Canvas

The 5th Wave   By Rich Tennant

RURAL WEB DESIGN

"What you want to do, is balance the image of the pick-up truck sittin' behind your home page, with a busted washing machine in the foreground."

In this part . . .

In Part III, I show you how to breathe life into your Canvas. I demonstrate how to use Canvas composition and color. You also discover how to have your application interact with the user. I show you techniques for creating lifelike movement and how to use multimedia such as audio.

7

Mastering the Art of Canvas

reating a work of art is a challenging task. It takes a combination of technique, artistic vision, persistence, and a bit of courage. I happen to believe that we all have an inner artist that just needs a little encouragement to find its way out into the world.

Whether something is a work of art or just another image can be a subjective judgment. What's beautiful art to one person can be mundane and boring to another. However, many paintings, sculptures, and other objects are widely recognized as art. Possibly the most famous is Leonardo da Vinci's *Mona Lisa*. This painting, and many others, have been admired, analyzed, and praised by experts and ordinary viewers around the world.

In this chapter, you discover techniques for layout, composition, and the use of color that will help you create artful Canvas spaces and objects to fill them. As any good artist would, use these techniques as guidelines and apply your own creativity and self-expression to develop Canvas masterpieces.

Creating Appealing Canvas Spaces

When beginning a Canvas project, you're faced with the first fundamental design decision: what width and height to choose for your Canvas space. Additionally, you need to decide where to place your shapes and designs on the Canvas to create a visually appealing layout. You can find out more about how to make these decisions in the following sections.

Choosing the size and proportions of your Canvas

Almost any size and proportioned Canvas can be made artful. Some Canvases might have to be functional and fit into a specific space on a web page. Others might be the defining aspect of a web page and drive the placement of other elements. Still others might be more functional in nature, such as many of the Canvases used in this book, which were sized to fit as compactly as possible on a page with text.

The proportions of your Canvas — its relative width and height — influence other aspects such as object placement. So take some time to consider these elements:

- The **purpose** of the Canvas. It might be to
  - Attract attention
  - Provide a game
  - Explain something
  - Enhance the web page
- The **characteristics of the objects** you'll place on the Canvas:
  - Quantity
  - Size
  - Movement and interaction
- The Canvas **orientation:**
  - Portrait (vertical)
  - Landscape (horizontal)
  - Square

If you're unsure where to begin with your dimensions, consider using a rect-angle, as shown in Figure 7-1, that has the relative proportions 13 x 8 (or 8 x 13 for a portrait orientation). These dimensions are called the *divine propor-tion.* They create a space for very balanced and appealing images.

Resizing and rescaling your Canvas

After choosing your starting dimensions and as you progress through your development, you can alter the size and shape of your Canvas. Figure 7-2 and Listing 7-1 demonstrate resizing and rescaling. (This code is based on Listing 4-9, which draws randomized circles. See Chapter 4 for a discussion of this listing and the randomizing code.)

Figure 7-1: Divine proportion rectangular Canvas.

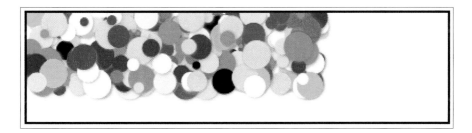

Figure 7-2: Resized and rescaled Canvas.

Listing 7-1:   Resizing and Rescaling a Canvas

```
<!DOCTYPE HTML> <html> <head> <script>

// A. WINDOW LOAD function.
window.onload = function()
{
    // A1. CANVAS definition standard variables.
    canvas  = document.getElementById("canvasArea");
    context = canvas.getContext("2d");

    // A2. PARAMETERS for circles.
    var numCircles = 300;
    var maxRadius  = 20;    var minRadius  = 3;
    var colors     =
    ["aqua", "black", "blue", "fuchsia", "green", "cyan", "lime",
```

(continued)

Listing 7-1 *(continued)*

```
    "maroon", "navy", "olive", "purple", "red", "silver", "teal",
    "yellow", "azure", "gold", "bisque", "pink", "orange"];
  var numColors = colors.length;

  // A3. RESIZE & RESCALE Canvas.
  canvas.width = 400;    canvas.height = 100;
  context.scale(.7, .7);

  // A4. CREATE circles.
  for(var n=0; n<numCircles; n++)
  {
    // A5. RANDOM values for circle characteristics.
    var xPos       = Math.random()*canvas.width;
    var yPos       = Math.random()*canvas.height;
    var radius     = minRadius+(Math.random()* (maxRadius-minRadius));
    var colorIndex = Math.random()*(numColors-1);
    colorIndex     = Math.round(colorIndex);
    var color      = colors[colorIndex];

    // A6. DRAW circle.
    drawCircle(context, xPos, yPos, radius, color);
  }
};
// B. CIRCLE drawing function.
function drawCircle(context, xPos, yPos, radius, color)
{
  //B1. PARAMETERS for shadow and angles.
  var startAngle        = (Math.PI/180)*0;
  var endAngle          = (Math.PI/180)*360;
  context.shadowColor   = "gray";
  context.shadowOffsetX = 1;
  context.shadowOffsetY = 1;
  context.shadowBlur    = 5;

  //B2. DRAW CIRCLE
  context.beginPath();
  context.arc(xPos, yPos, radius, startAngle, endAngle, false);
  context.fillStyle = color;
  context.fill();
}
</script> </head> <body>

<!-- C. CANVAS definition -->
<div    style = "width:200px; height:200px; margin:0 auto; padding:5px;">
<canvas id    = "canvasArea" width = "200" height = "200"
        style = "border:2px solid black">
Your browser doesn't currently support HTML5 Canvas.
```

You can change the size and dimensions of your Canvas in two ways: resize and rescale.

Resizing

Resizing changes the width and/or height dimensions of the Canvas space. This can be done by using HTML code or Java code.

✔ **Change the characteristics in HTML code.** Alter element characteristics defining the width and height in HTML tags. For example, to change the Canvas dimensions to 400 x 100, you can change the code in C of Listing 7-1 to this:

```
<div    style = "width:400px; height:100px; margin:0 auto; padding:5px;">
<canvas id    = "canvasArea"  width = "200"  height = "200"
        style = "border:2px solid black">
Your browser doesn't currently support HTML5 Canvas.
</canvas> </div>
```

✔ **Change the characteristics in Java code.** Alter the width and height characteristics of the Canvas using a reference to the Canvas in Java code, as in A3 of the example:

```
canvas.width = 400;    canvas.height = 100;
```

You should understand the order in which HTML code parameters and JavaScript parameters are applied. JavaScript code is executed after the browser has used HTML to configure the web page. Therefore, JavaScript resizing trumps HTML resizing. Rescaling via JavaScript, discussed in the following section, is based on the HTML parameters (instead of on replacing them). So JavaScript rescaling doesn't trump HTML rescaling — it uses the HTML scale as a base to work from.

Rescaling

Rescaling changes the dimensions of the objects within the Canvas in addition to the overall dimensions of the Canvas space.

To rescale your Canvas, use the `scale()` function (described in Chapter 5), as in A3 of Listing 7-1:

```
context.scale(.7, .7);
```

Note that if you use different scaling factors for the *x* and *y* coordinates of the `scale()` function, your objects will be distorted from their original shape.

Experiment with the code in Listing 7-1 to see the effects from different scaling values. If you try using the parameters `(.7, .3)`, you see oval shapes instead of circles. If you want ovals, great. If not, look out!

Dividing your Canvas with the rule of thirds

After you've decided on a starting size and dimensions for your Canvas, what comes next?

One way to proceed is to segment your Canvas into virtual sub-spaces that you can use to guide your placement of shapes and designs. A popular segmentation strategy is termed the *rule of thirds.* Divide your Canvas into three sections vertically and horizontally, as shown in Figure 7-3.

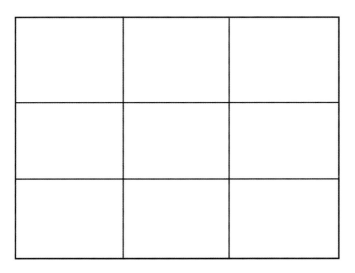

Figure 7-3: Subdividing a Canvas using the rule of thirds.

The design idea behind the rule of thirds is to place interesting elements along the lines and line intersections of the sub-divided space. An example of this is shown in Figure 7-4. Note how prominent features like the bicycle tires are placed at line intersections or near the lines themselves.

You don't have to actually draw the dividing lines on your Canvas. You can imagine their rough placement in your mind and let them be one guide when drawing your Canvas objects. A *Canvas* is a space with width and height pixel dimensions. Because all elements are located precisely where your code specifies, you should have at least an idea of your design before you start coding. Of course, changes and adjustments can be made as you code, but you should have a starting point for your design.

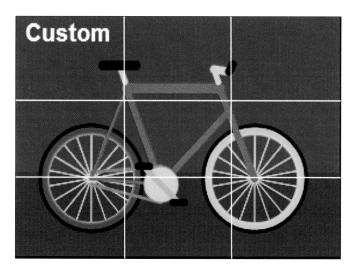

Figure 7-4: Example of using the rule of thirds.

If you're developing an application that involves significant object movement, the rule of thirds can be helpful for designing the background image and the placement of any stationary objects.

The rule of thirds works for several reasons:

- **The magic number 3:** In mathematics and the arts, three is considered to be a very balanced and harmonious number. Two and four are probably very jealous.

- **Manageable number of sub-spaces:** The horizontal and vertical subdivision by three creates a very manageable number of nine sub-spaces. Not too many, not too few.

- **Reasonable distances from the edges:** Objects squashed up against the Canvas edges can look crowded and out of place. The subdivision lines and intersections tend to pull objects away from the edges.

- **Pleasing placement:** The lines and intersections are at pleasing distances from one another.

Using the golden ratio in your design

How can you resist trying something named the *golden ratio?* This relationship between two numbers has been in use for at least 2,400 years, dating back to Pythagoras and Euclid in ancient Greece.

Figure 7-5 demonstrates the golden ratio with a pair of adjacent rectangles where the ratio of sides a to b is the same as the ratio of sides a+b to a, or about 1.61:

a/b = (a+b)/a = 1.61803…

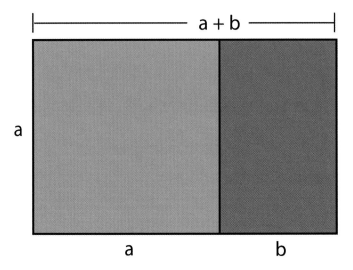

Figure 7-5: The golden ratio.

The golden ratio can be applied repeatedly to create a grid structure, as shown in Figure 7-6. Each smaller rectangle is divided into approximate golden ratio relationships. The dimensions also follow the Fibonacci sequence where each number is the sum of the previous two:

0, 1, 1, 2, 3, 5, 8, 13 …

The Fibonacci sequence has been used to help explain numerical relationships in science, nature, financial markets, and many other domains.

One example from nature is the nautilus shell, shown in Figure 7-7. There is controversy over the extent to which shapes like the nautilus shell conform to the ratio. For example, I had to adjust the overall dimensions of the nautilus image in Figure 7-7 slightly to fit it onto the grid.

For the purposes of designing Canvas spaces, the main point is that the golden ratio is another tool for creating pleasing layouts and spatial relationships.

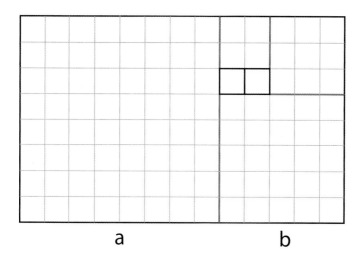

a   b

Figure 7-6: The golden ratio grid.

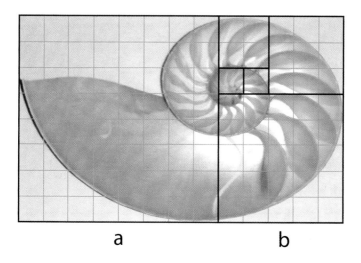

a   b

Figure 7-7: The golden ratio is applied.

Creating Complex Shapes and Images

After you've chosen your Canvas dimensions and possibly a grid structure to
guide your layout, it's time to populate your Canvas with objects and images.

Most applications will use complex objects to generate a more interesting result than can be achieved with simple objects such as single lines, rectangles, and circles. Figure 7-8 and Listing 7-2 demonstrate building complex shapes and organizing them into an appealing image.

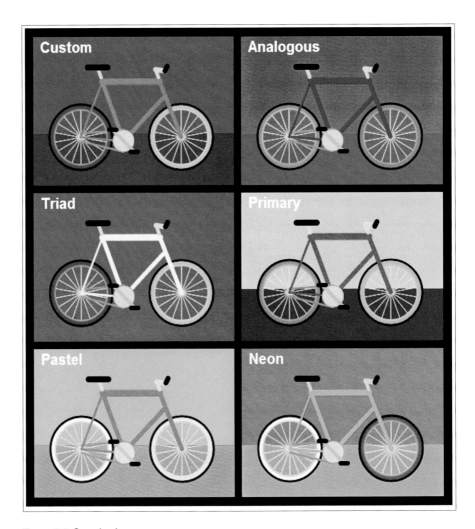

Figure 7-8: Complex images.

Listing 7-2:   Creating Complex Images

```
<!DOCTYPE HTML> <html> <head> <script>

// A. WINDOW LOAD function.
window.onload = function()
{
    // A1. CANVAS contexts.
    canvasBike  = document.getElementById("canvasBike");
    contextBike = canvasBike.getContext("2d");
    canvasBG    = document.getElementById("canvasBackground");
    contextBG   = canvasBG.getContext("2d");

    // A2. PARAMETERS.
    var width        = 280;         var height       = 200;
    var gap          = 10;          var hubRadius     = 5;
    var pedalRadius  = 15;          var tireWidth     = 3;
    var rimRadius    = 40;          var rimWidth      = 8;
    var spokeWidth   = 1;           var spokeNum      = 50;
    var spokeInterval = 20;         var spokeColor    = "silver";
    var wheelFOffsetX = 80;         var wheelFOffsetY = -5;
    var wheelROffsetX = -60;        var wheelROffsetY = -5;
    var strutFOffsetX = 50;         var strutFOffsetY = -80;
    var strutROffsetX = -30;        var strutROffsetY = -80;
    var braceFOffsetX = 55;         var braceFOffsetY = -58;
    var handleOffsetX = 49;         var handleOffsetY = -79;
    var bikeX        = (width/2)-13;
    var bikeY        = (height/2)+40;
    var startAngle   = (Math.PI/180)*0;
    var endAngle     = (Math.PI/180)*360;

    // A3. BACKGROUND color.
    contextBG.fillStyle = "black";
    contextBG.fillRect(0, 0, canvasBG.width, canvasBG.height);

    // A4. DRAW BIKES.
    //     row col floor     wall      chassis   backRim   frontRim  type
    //     --- --- --------- --------- --------- --------- --------- -----------
    drawBike(1, 1,"#4B0082","#2F4F4F","#FF1493","#0000FF","#7FFF00","Custom"   );
    drawBike(1, 2,"#8C0CE8","#E8160C","#1000FF","#FF5C0D","#FF00CC","Analogous");
    drawBike(2, 1,"#B2159E","#4C2DFF","#FFDE50","#0000FF","#7FFF00","Triad"    );
    drawBike(2, 2,"#050099","#FFBD00","#CC0200","#CC5800","#40FF00","Primary"  );
    drawBike(3, 1,"#FF6571","#57CC4D","#BC3BFF","#FFEE4D","#73FFF9","Pastel"   );
    drawBike(3, 2,"#FF9000","#F600FF","#04CC00","#FFEB00","#CC0100","Neon"     );

    // B. DRAW BIKE function.
    function drawBike(row,col,floor,wall,chassis,backRim,frontRim,colorScheme)
    {
```

(continued)

Listing 7-2 *(continued)*

```
// B1. TRANSLATE to corner of drawing area.
contextBG.save();
contextBG.translate  (((col*gap)+((col-1)*width)),
                      ((row*gap)+((row-1)*height)));
contextBike.save();
contextBike.translate(((col*gap)+((col-1)*width)),
                      ((row*gap)+((row-1)*height)));
// B2. FLOOR.
contextBG.fillStyle = floor;
contextBG.fillRect(0, height/2, width, height/2);


// B3. WALL.
contextBG.fillStyle = wall;
contextBG.fillRect(0, 0, width, height*.65);


// B4. COLOR SCHEME ID.
contextBG.font        = "bold 15pt arial";
contextBG.fillStyle   = "white";
contextBG.strokeStyle = "white";
contextBG.textAlign   = "left";
contextBG.fillText(colorScheme, 10, 21);


// B5. TRANSLATE to center of pedals.
contextBike.translate(bikeX, bikeY);


// B6. WHEELS.
wheel(wheelFOffsetX, wheelFOffsetY, frontRim);
wheel(wheelROffsetX, wheelROffsetY, backRim );


// B7. CHASSIS.
chassisPart(0, 0, wheelROffsetX, wheelROffsetY, 3, chassis);
chassisPart(0, 0, strutROffsetX, strutROffsetY, 6, chassis);
chassisPart(strutROffsetX, strutROffsetY, strutFOffsetX, strutFOffsetY,
                                          9, chassis);
chassisPart(strutFOffsetX, strutFOffsetY, wheelFOffsetX, wheelFOffsetY,
                                          6, chassis);
chassisPart(0, 0, braceFOffsetX, braceFOffsetY, 6, chassis);


// B8. CHAIN
chassisPart(0, -pedalRadius, wheelROffsetX, wheelROffsetY-hubRadius,
                                          3, "gray");
chassisPart(0, pedalRadius, wheelROffsetX, wheelROffsetY+hubRadius,
                                          3, "gray");
chassisPart(wheelROffsetX, wheelROffsetY, strutROffsetX, strutROffsetY,
                                          3, chassis);
// B9. SEAT.
chassisPart(strutROffsetX-1,  strutROffsetY-5,
            strutROffsetX-5,  strutROffsetY-16, 5, "silver");
```

```
chassisPart(strutROffsetX-20, strutROffsetY-19,
            strutROffsetX+8,  strutROffsetY-19, 8, "black" );

// B10. HANDLE BAR.
chassisPart(strutFOffsetX-1,  strutFOffsetY-5,
            strutFOffsetX-5,  strutFOffsetY-16, 5, "silver");
chassisPart(strutFOffsetX-5,  strutFOffsetY-16,
            strutFOffsetX+8,  strutFOffsetY-14, 7, "silver");
chassisPart(strutFOffsetX+8,  strutFOffsetY-14,
            strutFOffsetX+11, strutFOffsetY-20, 7, "black" );

// B11. PEDAL HUB.
contextBike.beginPath();
contextBike.arc(0, 0, pedalRadius, startAngle, endAngle, false);
contextBike.fillStyle   = "silver";
contextBike.strokeStyle = "gray";
contextBike.lineWidth   = 1;
contextBike.fill();
contextBike.stroke();

// B12. PEDALS.
chassisPart(-15, -15, +15, +15, 5, "darkgray");
chassisPart(-20, -15, -10, -15, 6, "black"  );
chassisPart(+20, +15, +10, +15, 6, "black"  );

// B13. RESTORE CONTEXTS.
contextBG.restore();
contextBike.restore();

// C. WHEEL function.
function wheel(xPos, yPos, color)
{
   // C1. TRANSLATE to center of the wheel.
   contextBike.save();
   contextBike.translate(xPos, yPos);

   // C2. GRADIENT.
   var grad = contextBike.createRadialGradient(0, 0, rimRadius-rimWidth,
                                               0, 0, rimRadius);
   grad.addColorStop(.5, "darkgray");
   grad.addColorStop( 1, color     );

   // C3. SPOKES.
   contextBike.save();
   for(s=0; s<=spokeNum; s++)
      {
      contextBike.rotate(((Math.PI)/180)*spokeInterval);
      contextBike.strokeStyle = spokeColor;
      contextBike.lineWidth   = spokeWidth;
```

(continued)

Listing 7-2 *(continued)*

```
            contextBike.beginPath();
            contextBike.moveTo(0, 0);
            contextBike.lineTo(0, rimRadius);
            contextBike.stroke();
            }
        contextBike.restore();

        // C4. RIM.
        contextBike.fillStyle = grad;
        contextBike.beginPath();
        contextBike.arc(0,0,rimRadius,startAngle,endAngle,false);
        contextBike.strokeStyle = grad;
        contextBike.lineWidth    = rimWidth;
        contextBike.stroke();

        // C5. TIRE.
        contextBike.beginPath();
        contextBike.arc(0,0,rimRadius+(rimWidth/2),startAngle,endAngle,false);
        contextBike.strokeStyle = "black";
        contextBike.lineWidth    = tireWidth;
        contextBike.stroke();

        // C6. RESTORE context.
        contextBike.restore();
    }
    // D. CHASSIS PART function.
    function chassisPart(xStart, yStart, xEnd, yEnd, width, color)
    {
        contextBike.strokeStyle = color;
        contextBike.lineWidth    = width;
        contextBike.lineCap      = "round";
        contextBike.beginPath();
        contextBike.moveTo(xStart, yStart);
        contextBike.lineTo(xEnd,    yEnd);
        contextBike.stroke();
    }
  }
}
</script> </head> <body> <div>

<!-- E. CANVAS DEFINITIONS  -->
<canvas id    = "canvasBike"  width = "590"  height ="640"
        style = "border:2px solid black; position:absolute;
                 left:auto; top:auto; z-index: 2">
</canvas>
<canvas id    = "canvasBackground"  width = "590"  height ="640"
        style = "border:2px solid black; position:absolute;
                 left:auto; top:auto; z-index: 1">
Your browser doesn't currently support HTML5 Canvas.
</canvas>
</div> </body> </html>
```

To build composite images, follow the steps in the next few sections.

Basic aspects

The basics of creating objects have been discussed in depth in previous sections, including defining Canvas elements, creating a background, setting parameters and drawing basic objects. To address them, follow these steps:

1. **Define multiple Canvas elements. Define one Canvas for the background and another for the main image.**

   See the example in code block E of Listing 7-2. Define contexts for each Canvas as in this example from code section A1:

   ```
   canvasBike  = document.getElementById("canvasBike");
   contextBike = canvasBike.getContext("2d");
   ```

2. **Create the background.**

   Fill the background as in code section A3. The example uses a solid color:

   ```
   contextBG.fillStyle = "black";
   contextBG.fillRect(0, 0 ,canvasBG.width, canvasBG.height);
   ```

3. **Set parameters and attributes you want to use for drawing your objects.**

   See the example in A2:

   ```
   var width = 280;   var height  = 200;
   var gap   = 10;    var hubRadius = 5;
   ```

4. **Draw your object using the appropriate function.**

   For example:

   - *Lines:* As in code C3 & D of Listing 7-2
   - *Rectangles:* As in code B2–3
   - *Text:* As in code B4
   - *Circles:* As in code C4–5

Key aspects

A number of aspects that are not new to drawing complex objects take on special significance. These include creating layered Canvases, using the `translate()` function and drawing complex objects. To address them, follow these steps:

1. **Create layered Canvas spaces.**

   As is the case in Listing 7-2, drawing composite objects often requires manipulating the Canvas context, such as using translation (described in Chapter 5) to move to a new position or using rotation to draw new objects. It's helpful to organize objects into separate groups, each using its own Canvas for drawing.

   The code in Listing 7-2 separates Canvas layers as follows:

   - *Background* (`canvasBG`, `contextBG`): Black framing, walls, floors
   - *Bike* (`canvasBike`, `contextBike`): Bicycles, text

2. **To help simplify drawing a complex object, choose a focal point for the object, and translate the Canvas context to that point.**

   In Listing 7-2, translation is used to:

   - Move to the corner of the individual bicycle section frame (code section B1). From this point, the text, wall, floor, and bicycle are drawn.
   - Move to the center of the pedal circle of the bicycle image (code section B5). From this point, the individual parts of the bicycle are drawn, including the wheels, chassis, chain, seat, and handlebar.
   - Move to the center of the wheel (code section C1). From this point, the spokes, rim, and tire are drawn.

   Before each translation, save the Canvas context, as in B1 and C1, and then restore the context after the drawing is finished, as in B13. If you don't do this, you might get some truly wild results. If you see objects being drawn in radically wrong places, it's often because you haven't saved and restored the Canvas context properly.

3. **After your position on a Canvas is shifted using translation, use relative positioning from the new (0,0) point to draw your objects.**

   An example is C3 from Listing 7-2. To draw each wheel spoke, `contextBike` is rotated around the center of the wheel:

   ```
   contextBike.save();
   for(s=0; s<=spokeNum; s++)
      {
      contextBike.rotate(((Math.PI)/180)*spokeInterval);
      contextBike.strokeStyle = spokeColor;
      contextBike.lineWidth   = spokeWidth;
      contextBike.beginPath();
      contextBike.moveTo(0,0);
      contextBike.lineTo(0, rimRadius);
      contextBike.stroke();
      }
   contextBike.restore();
   ```

   Note that `contextBike` is saved before the rotations begin and restored after they are complete.

4. Organize your object drawing into appropriate functions.

For example, in Listing 7-2:

- drawBike() in code section B calls the wheel() and chassisPart() functions to create a bicycle.

- wheel() in code section C draws circles and spoke lines.

- chassisPart() in code section D draws lines.

Without creating these kinds of functions, you might see your code size and complexity get out of hand. Always be alert to the possibility of creating a new function for specialized object types.

Getting the Most Out of Color

Your options for color selection and combination are vast. There are millions of different colors when you include all the variations of hue, saturation, and lightness. One approach to creating your color palette is trial and error. If you have a good color sense, this might work quite well for you. Pick a starting base color and go from there. Another option is to use tools such as websites and books dedicated to exploring and combining colors.

Using online color tools

One of the most popular and useful color tools is the kuler.adobe.com website, at kuler.adobe.com/#create/formacolor. Figure 7-9 shows the kuler web page for creating your own combination of colors. Also on the website are color themes created by an active community of designers who contribute their ideas.

Using kuler, you can easily experiment with different colors and color combinations. The web page is divided into two main areas, a color wheel centered at the top and a series of five color sample squares and values across the bottom. As you move the controls for the color wheel (the little circles) and samples (the little triangles), you'll see your colors change as well as their numeric values:

- **HSV:** Hue, Saturation, Value (lightness). Specifies the color, amount of color, and amount of black/white.

- **RGB:** Red, Green, Blue proportions.

- **CMYK:** Cyan, Magenta, Yellow, Black proportions.

- **LAB:** Lightness and a/b color space.

- **HEX:** The six-digit hexadecimal number specifying the color, including hue, saturation, and value.

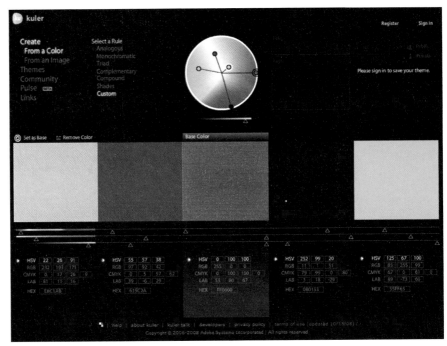

Figure 7-9: The Adobe kuler color tool.

Hue

Hue is determined by position in the color wheel. For example, in Figure 7-9, the red square base color in the center relates to the double circle at the 3 o'clock position on the color wheel. The blue square to the right of the red square relates to the filled-in circle at the 5 o'clock position, and so forth.

Saturation

Saturation is determined by the amount of color. For example, the red color in Figure 7-9 is fully saturated, as indicated by the middle number 100 in the HSV row just below the color square. The pink color to the far left has very little saturation, as indicated by the number 26 as its HSV saturation value.

Lightness (value)

Lightness (value) is determined by the amount of white in the color. The blue color to the right of the red in Figure 7-9 has very little white, as indicated by the 20 value number in its HSV row.

Combining colors

Earlier in this chapter, Figure 7-8 and Listing 7-2 demonstrate combining colors in different ways.

Analogous

Analogous colors come from the same region of the color wheel. In Figure 7-8, the colors are all on the same half of the wheel as red, from 12 o'clock to 6 o'clock.

Triad

Triad colors come from three regions that are equally spaced one from another. In Figure 7-8, purple, yellow, and blue/green.

Primary

From a technical perspective, primary colors are those that can be combined to make a useful group of other colors. Some examples are

- Red, green, blue
- Red, yellow, blue
- Cyan, magenta, yellow, black

Artists often combine these to create images (such as the one in the example) that have a basic color feel. Usually the colors have a high level of saturation and lightness.

Pastel

Pastel colors have higher levels of lightness and lower levels of saturation. You might refer to this as "less color."

Neon

Neon color combinations are aggressive color combinations with high color saturation.

Custom

The custom example is included to emphasize that you are free to experiment and create your own combinations. The example uses a background of low lightness with the bicycle in more saturated tones.

Creating Textures

Textures are generated by using repeated patterns. The patterns can vary from simple squares or rectangles that are repeated in a grid to sophisticated patterns generated by algorithms.

Figure 7-10 and Listing 7-3 demonstrate creating a texture from a small Canvas repeated as a pattern.

Figure 7-10: Texture.

Listing 7-3:   Creating Texture

```
<!DOCTYPE HTML> <html> <head> <script>

// A. WINDOW LOAD function.
window.onload = function()
{
   // A1. CANVAS contexts.
   canvasObjects= document.getElementById("canvasObjects");
   contextObjects = canvasObjects.getContext("2d");
   canvasTexture  = document.getElementById("canvasTexture");
   contextTexture = canvasTexture.getContext("2d");

   // A2. TEXTURE creation.
   //                       color                x  y  w  h
   //                       ------------         -  -  -  -
   contextTexture.fillStyle = "grey";      contextTexture.fillRect(0, 0, 1, 1);
   contextTexture.fillStyle = "grey";      contextTexture.fillRect(0, 1, 1, 1);
   contextTexture.fillStyle = "lightgrey"; contextTexture.fillRect(0, 2, 1, 1);
   contextTexture.fillStyle = "lightgrey"; contextTexture.fillRect(1, 0, 1, 1);
   contextTexture.fillStyle = "grey";      contextTexture.fillRect(1, 1, 1, 1);
   contextTexture.fillStyle = "grey";      contextTexture.fillRect(1, 2, 1, 1);
   contextTexture.fillStyle = "darkgrey";  contextTexture.fillRect(2, 0, 1, 1);
   contextTexture.fillStyle = "darkgrey";  contextTexture.fillRect(2, 1, 1, 1);
   contextTexture.fillStyle = "grey";      contextTexture.fillRect(2, 2, 1, 1);
```

```
// A3. PATTERN set to texture Canvas.
var pattern = contextObjects.createPattern(canvasTexture, "repeat");

// A4. FILLSTYLE set to pattern.
contextObjects.fillStyle = pattern;

// A5. OBJECTS filled with fillStyle pattern.
contextObjects.fillRect(0, 0, canvasObjects.width, canvasObjects.height);
}
</script> </head> <body> <div>

<!-- B. CANVAS DEFINITIONS  -->
<canvas id    = "canvasObjects"  width = "400"  height ="100"
        style = "border:2px solid black; position:absolute;
                  left:auto; top:auto; z-index: 2">
</canvas>
<canvas id    = "canvasTexture"  width = "3"  height ="3"
        style = "position:absolute; left:auto; top:auto; z-index: 1">
Your browser doesn't currently support HTML5 Canvas.
</canvas>
</div> </body> </html>
```

To create a texture, follow these steps:

1. **Define multiple Canvas elements. Define one Canvas for the texture and another for the main image.**

   See the example in section B of Listing 7-3:

   ```
   <canvas id    = "canvasObjects"  width = "400"  height ="100"
           style = "border:2px solid black; position:absolute;
                     left:auto; top:auto; z-index: 2">
   </canvas>
   <canvas id    = "canvasTexture"  width = "3"  height ="3"
           style = "position:absolute; left:auto; top:auto; z-index: 1">
   Your browser doesn't currently support HTML5 Canvas.
   </canvas>
   ```

   Here are some aspects to note about texture Canvases:

   • The texture Canvas is very small in this example, only a 3-pixel square. You can make it any size and dimension you want. The larger the texture Canvas, the larger the repeated texture image.

   • Don't include a border in the texture Canvas style unless you want it to show as part of the texture.

   • If you're using multiple textures, define multiple Canvas elements, one for each texture.

Next, define contexts for each Canvas, as in A1:

```
canvasObjects =document.getElementById("canvasObjects");
contextObjects=canvasObjects.getContext("2d");
canvasTexture =document.getElementById("canvasTexture");
contextTexture=canvasTexture.getContext("2d");
```

2. **Create a bit sequence of colors by filling each pixel in the texture Canvas.**

   In the example in A2, this is accomplished using the `fillStyle()` function to set a color and the `fillRect()` function a width and height of 1 to color each pixel:

```
//                          color                    x  y  w  h
//                          -----------              -  -  -  -
contextTexture.fillStyle="grey";      contextTexture.fillRect(0, 0, 1, 1);
contextTexture.fillStyle="grey";      contextTexture.fillRect(0, 1, 1, 1);
contextTexture.fillStyle="lightgrey"; contextTexture.fillRect(0, 2, 1, 1);
contextTexture.fillStyle="lightgrey"; contextTexture.fillRect(0, 2, 1, 1);
```

For larger texture Canvas areas, consider developing code to create your bit sequence using loops and algorithms.

3. **Create a pattern using the `createPattern()` function with the `canvasTexture` and `repeat` parameters.**

   Here's an example from A3:

```
var pattern = contextObjects.createPattern(canvasTexture, "repeat");
```

   The `repeat` parameter will cause the `canvasTexture` to be repeated to completely fill an object.

4. **Create a fill style using the pattern.**

   Set the `fillStyle` to the `pattern` created for the context containing the objects to be filled as in A4:

```
contextObjects.fillStyle = pattern;
```

5. **Fill your objects using the appropriate function.**

   See the example for `fillRect()` in A5:

```
contextObjects.fillRect(0, 0, canvasObjects.width, canvasObjects.height);
```

Other types of objects, such as lines, circles, and multi-sided objects, can be filled with a pattern using their associated functions. See Chapter 3 for more on patterns.

8

Introducing User Interaction

*A*dding user interaction to your application contributes a vital element to bringing your Canvas alive. People naturally want to be involved. They would rather have a conversation with someone than be lectured to. They would rather learn by doing than by just listening. They would rather be part of something than just standing to the side and observing.

HTML5 Canvas gives you the tools you need to prompt and detect user actions to help pull those users into the virtual world you've created. And the more interaction your application has with a user, the more likely it is to accomplish its purpose.

Responding to User Events

A *user event* occurs when someone presses a key on the keyboard, uses the mouse, or touches the screen (if it's touch sensitive). The device's operating system notifies the browser of the event, and the browser then calls any application functions that you have designated to handle that event. The sequence is illustrated in Figure 8-1.

To make this all work, you have to tell the browser which application functions to invoke for each type of event you want to respond to.

Figure 8-2 and Listing 8-1 demonstrate this mechanism with an application that lets the user experiment with the effect of simulated real-world forces such as gravity and friction on a bouncing ball. The application responds to mouse clicks, mouse movement, and a number of key presses, as explained by the legend in Figure 8-2 and code section K in Listing 8-1.

Browser
- Process Interaction
- Invoke Callback Functions
Canvas Application
- Callback Functions
- React to Interaction
Operating System
- Recognize Interaction
- Interface with Browser
User
- Key Press
- Mouse Use
- Screen Touch

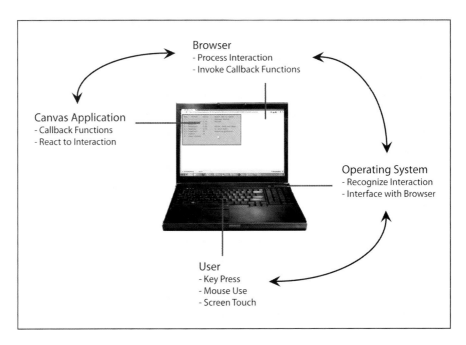

Figure 8-1: User interaction processing.

Try the application yourself. You should feel yourself being drawn in to the experience. How will the application react to this change? What will happen if I do this? How close can I get the ball to act like it would in the real world? The interaction becomes like a small game that encourages the user to continue.

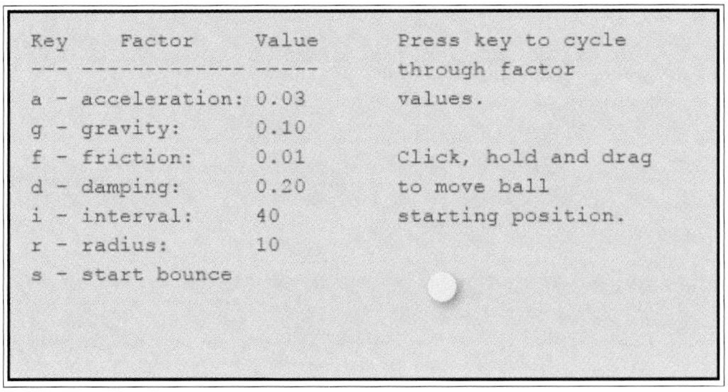

Key Factor Value
--- ------------- -----
a - acceleration: 0.03
g - gravity: 0.10
f - friction: 0.01
d - damping: 0.20
i - interval: 40
r - radius: 10
s - start bounce
Press key to cycle through factor values.
Click, hold and drag to move ball starting position.

Figure 8-2: User interaction.

Listing 8-1:   Responding to User Interaction

```
<!DOCTYPE HTML> <html> <head> <script>

// A. PARAMETERS.
   var interval   = 40;       var intervalT  = 70;
   var intervalI  = 5;        var intervalB  = 5;
   var radius     = 10;       var radiusT    = 25;
   var radiusI    = 5;        var radiusB    = 5;
   var frictionS  = .01;      var frictionB  = 0;
   var frictionL  = 0;        var frictionC  = 0;
   var frictionI  = .01;      var frictionT  = .05;
   var gravityS   = .1;       var gravityB   = .0;
   var gravityL   = 0;        var gravityC   = 0;
   var gravityI   = .01;      var gravityT   = .2;
   var accelerS   = .03;      var accelerB   = .01;
   var accelerL   = 0;        var accelerC   = .001;
   var accelerI   = .01;      var accelerT   = .1;
   var damping    = .20;      var dampingT   = .50;
   var dampingI   = .10;      var dampingB   = 0;
   var xVectorCur = 25;       var yVectorCur = 10;
   var ballXCur   = 20;       var ballYCur   = 20;
   var intervalID = 0;
   var startAngle = (Math.PI/180)*0;
   var endAngle   = (Math.PI/180)*360;
   var dragMouse  = 0;

// B. WINDOW LOAD function.
window.onload = function()
{
   // B1. CANVAS contexts.
   canvasBL  = document.getElementById("canvasBall");
   contextBL = canvasBL.getContext("2d");
   canvasBG  = document.getElementById("canvasBackground");
   contextBG = canvasBG.getContext("2d");

   // B2. MOUSE listeners.
   canvasBL.addEventListener("mousedown", mouseDown, false);
   canvasBL.addEventListener("mousemove", mouseMove, false);
   canvasBL.addEventListener("mouseup",   mouseUp,   false);

   // B3. BOUNCE BALL.
   bouncingBall(ballXCur, ballYCur, xVectorCur, yVectorCur);
}
// C. KEY functions.
document.onkeydown = function(event)
{
   // C1. KEY code.
   var key = event.keyCode;
```

(continued)

Listing 8-1 *(continued)*

```
// C2. RESTART using s key.
if (key == 83) {clearInterval(intervalID);
    bouncingBall(ballXCur, ballYCur, xVectorCur, yVectorCur);
    }
// C3. ACCELERATION change using the a key.
if (key == 65) {accelerS += accelerI;
    if (accelerS > accelerT) {accelerS = accelerB};
    clearInterval(intervalID);
    bouncingBall(ballXCur, ballYCur, xVectorCur, yVectorCur);
    }
// C4. GRAVITY change using the g key.
if (key == 71) {gravityS += gravityI;
    if (gravityS > gravityT) {gravityS = gravityB};
    clearInterval(intervalID);
    bouncingBall(ballXCur, ballYCur, xVectorCur, yVectorCur);
    }
// C5. FRICTION change using the f key.
if (key == 70) {frictionS += frictionI;
    if (frictionS > frictionT) {frictionS = frictionB};
    clearInterval(intervalID);
    bouncingBall(ballXCur, ballYCur, xVectorCur, yVectorCur);
    }
// C6. DAMPING change using the d key.
if (key == 68) {damping += dampingI;
    if (damping > dampingT) {damping = dampingB};
    clearInterval(intervalID);
    bouncingBall(ballXCur, ballYCur, xVectorCur, yVectorCur);
    }
// C7. INTERVAL change using the i key.
if (key == 73) {interval += intervalI;
    if (interval > intervalT) {interval = intervalB};
    clearInterval(intervalID);
    bouncingBall(ballXCur, ballYCur, xVectorCur, yVectorCur);
    }
// C8. RADIUS change using the r key.
if (key == 82) {radius += radiusI;
    if (radius > radiusT) {radius = radiusB};
    clearInterval(intervalID);
    bouncingBall(ballXCur, ballYCur, xVectorCur, yVectorCur);
    }
}
// D. MOUSE DOWN.
function mouseDown(event)
{
    // D1. MOUSE event.
    mouseEvent(event);

    // D2. DRAGGING on.
    dragMouse = 1;
```

```
    // D3. CLEAR canvas to show only moving ball.
    contextBL.clearRect(0, 0, canvasBL.width, canvasBL.height);
    clearInterval(intervalID);

    // D4. DRAW ball.
    contextBL.beginPath();
    contextBL.arc(ballXCur, ballYCur, radius, startAngle, endAngle, true);
    contextBL.closePath();
    contextBL.fill();
}
// E. MOUSE MOVE.
function mouseMove(event)
{
    // E1. DRAG check.
    if (dragMouse == 1)
    {
        // E2. MOUSE event.
        mouseEvent(event);

        // E3. CLEAR canvas to show only moving ball.
        contextBL.clearRect(0, 0, canvasBL.width, canvasBL.height);
        clearInterval(intervalID);

        // E4. DRAW ball.
        contextBL.beginPath();
        contextBL.arc(ballXCur, ballYCur, radius, startAngle, endAngle, true);
        contextBL.closePath();
        contextBL.fill();
    }
}
// F. MOUSE UP.
function mouseUp(event)
{
    // F1. MOUSE event.
    mouseEvent(event);

    // F2. DRAGGING off.
    dragMouse = 0;

    // F3. BOUNCE bal.
    clearInterval(intervalID);
    bouncingBall(ballXCur, ballYCur, xVectorCur, yVectorCur);
}
// G. MOUSE EVENT.
function mouseEvent(event)
{
    // G1. BROWSERS except Firefox.
    if (event.x != undefined && event.y != undefined)
```

(continued)

Listing 8-1 *(continued)*

```
   {
      ballXCur = event.x;
      ballYCur = event.y;
   }
   // G2. FIREFOX.
   else
   {
      ballXCur = event.clientX + document.body.scrollLeft +
                  document.documentElement.scrollLeft;
      ballYCur = event.clientY + document.body.scrollTop +
                  document.documentElement.scrollTop;
   }
   // G3. CURSOR position.
   ballXCur -= canvasBL.offsetLeft;
   ballYCur -= canvasBL.offsetTop;
}
// H. BOUNCING BALL function.
function bouncingBall(ballX, ballY, xVector, yVector)
{
   // H1. RESET VARIABLES.
   frictionL = frictionS;
   gravityL  = gravityS;
   accelerL  = accelerS;

   // H2. ATTRIBUTES of ball.
   contextBL.shadowOffsetX = 3;        contextBL.shadowOffsetY = 3;
   contextBL.shadowBlur    = 5;        contextBL.shadowColor    = "gray";
   contextBL.fillStyle     = "gold";

   // H3. BACKGROUND Canvas with text.
   background();

   // H4. START DRAWING balls.
   intervalID = setInterval(drawBall,interval);

   // I. DRAW BALL function.
   function drawBall()
   {
      // I1. MOVE ball.
      moveBall();

      // I2. CLEAR Canvas to show only moving ball.
      contextBL.clearRect(0, 0, canvasBL.width, canvasBL.height);

      // I3. DRAW ball.
      contextBL.beginPath();
      contextBL.arc(ballX, ballY, radius, startAngle, endAngle, true);
      contextBL.closePath();
      contextBL.fill();
```

```
    // I4. SIDE BOUNCE.
    if (ballX < radius || ballX > canvasBL.width-radius)

        // I5. REVERSE x vector.
        {xVector *= -1*(1-damping)}

    // I6. CEILING & FLOOR BOUNCE.
    if (ballY < radius || ballY > canvasBL.height-radius)
    {
        // I7. REVERSE y vector.
        yVector *= -1*(1-damping);

        // I8. FLOOR bounce check.
        if((yVector < 0) && (yVector < -gravityL))

            // I9. GRAVITY reduction.
            {yVector += gravityL}
    }
}
// J. MOVE BALL function.
function moveBall()
{
    // J1. FRICTION adjustment.
    frictionL = frictionL - frictionC;
    if(frictionL < 0) {frictionL = 0}

    // J2. ACCELERATION adjustment.
    accelerL = accelerL - accelerC;
    if(accelerL < 0) {accelerL = 0}

    // J3. GRAVITY adjustments.
    gravityL = gravityL - gravityC;
    if(gravityL < 0) {gravityL = 0}

    // J4. FRICTION & ACCELERATION factor.
    faFactor = (1-frictionL) * (1+accelerL);

    // J5. X VECTOR change.
    xVector  =  xVector * faFactor;

    // J6. X POSITION change.
    ballX    += xVector;

    // J7. Y vector & coordinate change if ball is above floor.
    if((ballY+radius) < canvasBL.height)
    {
        // J8. GRAVITY adjustment.
        var adjGravityL = Math.min(gravityL, (canvasBL.height-ballY));
```

(continued)

Listing 8-1 *(continued)*

```
    // J9. Y VECTOR change.

    yVector = (yVector*faFactor) + adjGravityL;
}
// J10. Y POSITION change.
ballY += yVector;

// J11. BOUNDS check & adjustment.
if((ballX+(radius-1))>canvasBL.width) {ballX=(canvasBL.width-(radius-1))}
if((ballX-(radius-1))<0)              {ballX=(radius-1)}
if((ballY+(radius-1))>canvasBL.height){ballY=(canvasBL.height-(radius-1))
    if(yVector < (gravityL+radius))   {gravityL=.9*gravityL}}
if((ballY-(radius-1))<0)              {ballY=(radius-1)}
}
// K. BACKGROUND.
function background()
{
    // K1. ATTRIBUTES.
    contextBG.font        = "11pt courier";
    contextBG.textAlign    = "left";
    contextBG.textBaseline = "middle";

    // K2. VARIABLES.
    var xPos1 = 15;   var xPos2 = 175;   var xPos3 = 275;
    var yPos  = 20;

    // K3. COLOR FILL.
    contextBG.fillStyle = "silver";
    contextBG.fillRect(0, 0, canvasBG.width, canvasBG.height);

    // K4. FIX decimal points.
    accelerL = accelerL.toFixed(2);     gravityL  = gravityL.toFixed(2);
    frictionL = frictionL.toFixed(2);    dampingL  = damping;
    dampingL  = dampingL.toFixed(2);

    // K5. TEXT.
    contextBG.fillStyle  = "darkslategrey";
    contextBG.fillText("Key    Factor",       xPos1, yPos*1);
    contextBG.fillText("Value",               xPos2, yPos*1);
    contextBG.fillText("--- ------------",     xPos1, yPos*2);
    contextBG.fillText("-----",               xPos2, yPos*2);
    contextBG.fillText("a - acceleration:",    xPos1, yPos*3);
    contextBG.fillText(accelerL,               xPos2, yPos*3);
    contextBG.fillText("g - gravity:",         xPos1, yPos*4);
    contextBG.fillText(gravityL,               xPos2, yPos*4);
    contextBG.fillText("f - friction:",        xPos1, yPos*5);
    contextBG.fillText(frictionL,              xPos2, yPos*5);
    contextBG.fillText("d - damping:",         xPos1, yPos*6);
```

```
      contextBG.fillText(dampingL,               xPos2, yPos*6);
      contextBG.fillText("i - interval:",        xPos1, yPos*7);
      contextBG.fillText(interval,               xPos2, yPos*7);
      contextBG.fillText("r - radius:",          xPos1, yPos*8);
      contextBG.fillText(radius,                 xPos2, yPos*8);
      contextBG.fillText("s - start bounce",     xPos1, yPos*9);
      contextBG.fillText("Press key to cycle",   xPos3, yPos*1);
      contextBG.fillText("through factor",       xPos3, yPos*2);
      contextBG.fillText("values.",              xPos3, yPos*3);
      contextBG.fillText("Click, hold and drag", xPos3, yPos*5);
      contextBG.fillText("to move ball",         xPos3, yPos*6);
      contextBG.fillText("starting position.",   xPos3, yPos*7);
   }
 }
</script> </head> <body> <div>

<!-- L. CANVAS DEFINITIONS  -->
<canvas id    = "canvasBall"  width = "500"  height ="250"
        style = "border:2px solid black;  position:absolute;
                 left:auto; top:auto;  z-index: 2">
</canvas>
<canvas id    = "canvasBackground"  width = "500"  height ="250"
        style = "border:2px solid black;  position:absolute;
                 left:auto; top:auto;  z-index: 1">
Your browser doesn't currently support HTML5 Canvas.
</canvas> </div> </body> </html>
```

The application in Listing 8-1 is an adaptation of the code in Listing 6-4, from Chapter 6. The discussion in this chapter focuses on the code added to handle user interaction. For details about the code that moves the ball and bounces it off the Canvas edges, refer to Chapter 6.

To include these ball-bounce functions in your application, follow these steps:

1. **Define parameters that will be used in the application.**

   See the parameters defined in code section A of Listing 8-1:

   ```
   var interval  = 40;      var intervalT = 70;
   var intervalI = 5;       var intervalB = 5;
   var radius    = 10;      var radiusT   = 25;
   ```

2. **Define a function that is called to handle the setup of your animation.**

   See the function defined in code section H of Listing 8-1:

   ```
   function bouncingBall(ballX, ballY, xVector, yVector)
   { . . . }
   ```

3. **At the appropriate places in your application, call the animation setup function.**

   See the calls to the animation setup function in B3 and F3:

   ```
   bouncingBall(ballXCur, ballYCur, xVectorCur, yVectorCur);
   ```

4. **Define a function that will be invoked for each animation frame.**

   Take a look at the animation function defined in code section I:

   ```
   function drawBall() { . . . }
   ```

5. **Use the `setInterval()` function to generate calls to your animation function at your specified time interval.**

   Here's an example in code H4:

   ```
   intervalID = setInterval(drawBall,interval);
   ```

   See Chapter 6 for more on the `setInterval` function.

6. **Define functions that are called from the animation function.**

   For example, define the function to move a ball, as in code section J:

   ```
   function moveBall() { . . . }
   ```

The Document Object Model (DOM), event listeners, and callbacks

The *Document Object Model (DOM)* is a standard for interacting with objects in HTML documents. Your Canvas is one of those objects.

The term *document* comes from the history of the World Wide Web, which at its inception in the late 1980s was focused on creating a structure of linked hypertext documents. Today, we think more in terms of web pages. The term document stuck and eventually contributed to the name Document Object Model when the concept was developed in the mid-1990s.

When a browser reads the HTML code defining your web page and Canvas, it creates a DOM tree structure in memory, as shown in Figure 8-3. The DOM is then used by the

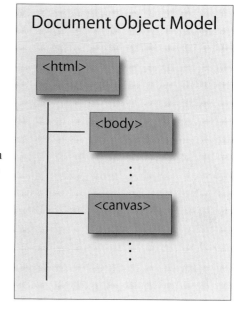

Figure 8-3: Document Object Model.

web browser as the place in which to store information about handling user events.

To configure your code to respond to user events, do the following:

1. **Register event listeners to inform the browser about which functions should be called back (thus the term *callback*) when specified event types occur.**

   By registering an event listener for the "mousedown" event, you're telling the browser to notify you, by calling the callback function `mouseDown`, when the mouse button is pressed.

   In Listing 8-1, listeners for mouse events are registered in code section B2:

   ```
   canvasBL.addEventListener("mousedown", mouseDown, false);
   ```

   A listener function for key events is registered in code section C:

   ```
   document.onkeydown = function(event) { . . . }
   ```

   Notice that the JavaScript form of how functions are specified for mouse and key events is different. Mouse events are registered as separate functions for individual actions, such as `mousedown` and `mouseup`. The mouse events are being associated with the Canvas area, as opposed to the full browser window. The `key` event is registered as associated with the browser window (see Figure 8-4, in the following section.) A single function is used to handle all key events in which the `event keycode` is used to determine which key has been pressed. This function is defined as an anonymous function as a convenient way to define code passed as a callback function. This is a JavaScript coding preference.

2. **Define functions in your application that will be called by the browser when the events occur. (These are the *callback functions*.)**

   In Listing 8-1, callback functions are defined in code sections C, D, E, and F. For example, here is the function that is called when the user clicks the mouse button:

   ```
   function mouseDown(event) { . . . }
   ```

Confused? Try this simple analogy. Event listeners and callbacks function similarly to leaving a message in someone's voice mail. Your message resembles a callback function. You tell the person you're calling what you want them to do. They're always listening for notifications that they have messages. When they hear the voice-mail notification tone, they pick up your message and, of course, do exactly as you requested.

Event listener response areas

You can register event listeners to respond to actions associated with your Canvas area or the browser window area, as shown in Figure 8-4. Which you use for a given event type depends on how you want your application to interact with the user. The application in Listing 8-1 uses Canvas area event listeners for mouse events and browser window event listeners for keyboard events.

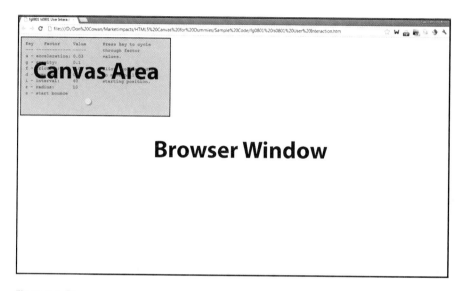

Figure 8-4: Response areas.

One factor to consider in deciding which type of event listener to use is how the user would intuitively expect the application to respond. In the application in Listing 8-1, because the purpose of clicking the mouse is to have the ball react, it makes sense that the mouse pointer should be somewhere on the Canvas. The user might, however, want a pressed key to work no matter where the pointer is located on the browser window.

Here's a summary of the two options:

✔ **Event listeners registered for the Canvas** will cause the associated function to be called when focus is on the Canvas, such as when the mouse pointer is positioned over the Canvas.

✔ **Event listeners registered for the browser window** will cause the associated function to be called when focus is on the window, such as when the mouse pointer is positioned anywhere over the window, not necessarily over the Canvas.

You can test this distinction using the application in Listing 8-1. If you position the mouse cursor on the browser window outside the Canvas and press the S key, you see the Canvas display react. However, if you click with your mouse, nothing happens. To get the application to react to the mouse, the pointer has to be positioned inside the Canvas. After you move the pointer and then click the mouse, you see the application react as the ball moves to the pointer position.

DOM event definitions

There are a large number of event types to which your application can respond using event listeners and callback functions. A full description of all event types is beyond the scope of this book. This chapter focuses on a select group of events to demonstrate the event listener and callback mechanisms. The full list and details of DOM events are controlled by the international standards organization World Wide Web Consortium (W3C). For more information, see:

```
www.w3.org/TR/DOM-Level-3-Events/#event-definitions
```

Canvas event listeners

Common Canvas events that are targeted for interaction include these:

click	dblclick	focus	focusin
focusout	keydown	keypress	keyup
mousedown	mouseenter	mousemove	mouseover
mouseup	mousewheel	pause	scroll
touchend	touchmove	touchstart	volumechange

This chapter focuses on mousedown, mousemove, and mouseup to demonstrate handling user events.

To define an event listener for a Canvas event, follow these steps:

1. **Define an event listener using the `addEventListener()` function to associate the listener with a Canvas.**

   This function has the following format:

   ```
   addEventListener(eventType, eventFunction, false)
   ```

   When an eventType takes place, the eventFunction is called. The third parameter, shown here as false, is no longer used by newer browser releases but is required in older releases, so it's best to include it.

Listing 8-1 defines three listeners for mouse events on `canvasBL` in code section B2:

```
canvasBL.addEventListener("mousedown",mouseDown,false);
canvasBL.addEventListener("mousemove",mouseMove,false);
canvasBL.addEventListener("mouseup"  ,mouseUp ,false);
```

 2. **Define the callback functions associated with the event listeners.**

Define a function for each event listener callback. For example, the `mouseDown()` function is defined in code section D:

```
function mouseDown(event)
{
 Code to handle the mouse down event goes here.
 }
```

Browser window event listeners

Common browser window events that are targeted for interaction include:

altKey	click	ctrlKey	dblclick
keydown	keypress	keyup	mousedown
mousemove	mouseout	mouseover	mouseup
shiftkey			

To define an event listener for a browser window event, follow these steps:

 1. **Define a browser window document reference by using the appropriate event type.**

For example, see the code in section C of Listing 8-1:

```
document.onkeydown = function(event)
```

 2. **Define the code to be executed when the callback is initiated.**

For example, when the `keydown` event is detected, the browser executes this code in code section C:

```
{
 Code for response to the keydown event.
 }
```

Handling Key Events

Key events are generated when users press any key on their keyboard. In most applications, actions taken after a key is pressed depend on the specific key used.

Discovering key codes

Each key is assigned a `keyCode` that's passed to the application function via the key `event`. Table 8-1 lists the codes for keyboard keys.

Key	Code	Key	Code	Key	Code
		Table 8-1		**Key Codes**	
Key	*Code*	*Key*	*Code*	*Key*	*Code*
a	65	0	48	Backspace	8
b	66	1	49	Pause/Break	19
c	67	2	50	Caps Lock	20
d	68	3	51	Esc	27
e	69	4	52	Page Up	33
f	70	5	53	Page Down	34
g	71	6	54	End	35
h	72	7	55	Home	36
i	73	8	56	←	37
j	74	9	57	↑	38
k	75	F1	112	→	38
l	76	F2	113	↓	40
m	77	F3	114	Insert	45
n	78	F4	115	Delete	46
o	79	F5	116	Left Windows key	91
p	80	F6	117	Right Windows key	92
q	81	F7	118	Select[1] key	93
r	82	F8	119	; (semicolon)	186
s	83	F9	120	= (equal sign)	187
t	84	F10	121	, (comma)	188
u	85	F11	122	– (dash)	189
v	86	F12	123	. (period)	190
w	87	0 (numpad)	96	* (multiply)	106
x	88	1 (numpad)	97	+ (add)	107
y	89	2 (numpad)	98	– (subtract, on numpad)	109
z	90	3 (numpad)	99	. (decimal point on numpad)	110

(continued)

Table 8-1 *(continued)*

Key	Code	Key	Code	Key	Code
Tab	9	4 (numpad)	100	/ (divide)	111
Enter	13	5 (numpad)	101	Num Lock	144
Shift	16	6 (numpad)	102	Scroll Lock	145
Ctrl	17	7 (numpad)	103	/ (forward slash)	191
Alt	18	8 (numpad)	104	\ (back slash)	220
		9 (numpad)	105	[(open bracket)	219
				] (close bracket)	221
				' (single quote)	222

[1]*See* www.ehow.com/facts_7392123_select-key-computer-keyboard.html

Handling a key press

Your application can respond to as many keys as you want — one or dozens. In Listing 8-1, code section C takes actions based on seven different keys: s, a, g, f, d, i, and r.

To respond to key presses in your application, follow these steps:

1. **Define a callback function to respond to *any* key press.**

   In Listing 8-1, this function is defined in section C:

   ```
   document.onkeydown = function(event){ . . . }
   ```

2. **Within that function, first access the `event` and `keycode`.**

   See section C1 of the example:

   ```
   var key = event.keyCode;
   ```

3. **Test for specific key presses by using the codes in Table 8-1.**

   In the example from code section C3, the letter *a* key press (code 65) triggers a change in acceleration of the bouncing ball:

   ```
   if (key == 65) { . . . }
   ```

4. **For each key you want your application to respond to, define the actions to be taken.**

In Listing 8-1, for the *a* key, acceleration is increased and checked for terminal value, and the bouncing ball re-initiated:

```
// Increase acceleration by accelerI.
accelerS += accelerI;

// Check for terminal acceleration.
if (accelerS > accelerT)

    // If over terminal maximum, set to minimum base.
    {accelerS = accelerB};

// Stop current bouncing ball.
clearInterval(intervalID);

// Start new bouncing ball.
bouncingBall(ballXCur, ballYCur, xVectorCur, yVectorCur);}
```

Handling Mouse Events

Mouse events — such as presses, releases, and movements — can be used for a variety of application functions, including

- Dragging and dropping objects
- Drawing shapes
- Painting object colors
- Clicking on objects such as buttons and shapes

In Listing 8-1, code sections D–F use mouse events to drag and drop a ball.

To respond to mouse events, follow these steps:

1. **Define a callback function for each type of mouse event your application will respond to.**

   In Listing 8-1, these functions are defined in section B2, for example:

   ```
   canvasBL.addEventListener("mousedown",mouseDown,false);
   ```

   When the mouse button is clicked, control is passed to the callback function:

   ```
   function mouseDown(event) { … }
   ```

   See the next section, "Dragging and Dropping Objects," for an example of using mouse events.

2. **Define a function to determine the position of the mouse pointer on the Canvas.**

   In Listing 8-1, the `mouseEvent()` function is defined for this in code section G.

   As of this writing, as shown in the following chunk of code, the Firefox browser must be handled a bit differently than other browsers. In JavaScript, the undefined property indicates that no value has been assigned to a variable. Because `event.x` and `event.y` are undefined by Firefox, the following chunk of code causes execution in the `else{}` statement a method of finding the *x* and *y* coordinates that works for Firefox:

```
function mouseEvent(event)
{
    // Find cursor position in browsers except Firefox.
    if (event.x != undefined && event.y != undefined)
    {
        ballXCur = event.x;
        ballYCur = event.y;
    }
    // Find cursor position in Firefox browser.
    else
    {
        ballXCur = event.clientX + document.body.scrollLeft +
                document.documentElement.scrollLeft;
        ballYCur = event.clientY + document.body.scrollTop +
                document.documentElement.scrollTop;
    }
    // Set cursor position within Canvas.
    ballXCur -= canvasBL.offsetLeft;
    ballYCur -= canvasBL.offsetTop;
}
```

3. **In each of your mouse handling callback functions, define the actions to take in response to the mouse activity.**

   For example, drag and drop objects, as explained in the next section.

Dragging and Dropping Objects

Dragging and dropping objects involves coordinating three types of mouse events:

- **Mouse down:** Select the object.
- **Mouse move:** Move the object.
- **Mouse up:** Release the object.

In Listing 8-1, code sections D–F define these functions.

Mouse down events

A *mouse down event* is typically used to select an object or position on a Canvas. In code section D of Listing 8-1, a click of the mouse moves the ball to the position of the mouse pointer. To use a mouse down event to initiate dragging and dropping, follow these steps:

1. **Define an event listener for the Canvas that you want to detect the mouse down condition.**

   See code section B2 of Listing 8-1:

   ```
   canvasBL.addEventListener("mousedown", mouseDown, false);
   ```

2. **Define a function that will contain the code to be executed when the mouse is clicked.**

   See code section D of the example:

   ```
   function mouseDown(event) { . . . }
   ```

3. **Within the `mouseDown()` function, use your mouse event function (see code section G) to determine the position of the mouse on your Canvas.**

   See code section D1 in Listing 8-1:

   ```
   mouseEvent(event);
   ```

4. **Turn on an indicator that will tell other code sections that a drag-and-drop operation is in progress.**

   This is shown in D2 of the example:

   ```
   dragMouse = 1;
   ```

5. **Clear the Canvas.**

   Clear the Canvas so that only the ball at the new position is drawn, as in D3:

   ```
   contextBL.clearRect(0,0,canvasBL.width,canvasBL.height);
   ```

6. **Stop the animation that is currently in progress so that you can start a new animation when the object is released.**

   In code section D3, this is done using the `clearInterval()` function and the `intervalID` of the animation:

   ```
   clearInterval(intervalID);
   ```

7. **Draw the object at the mouse position.**

   In the example, this has the effect of moving the ball to the cursor position as shown in code D4:

   ```
   contextBL.beginPath();
   contextBL.arc(ballXCur, ballYCur, radius, startAngle, endAngle, true);
   contextBL.closePath();
   contextBL.fill();
   ```

Mouse move events

A *mouse move event* is typically used to move an object or draw a line or color. In code section E in Listing 8-1, if the dragging indicator is on, the ball is redrawn at the new position. Follow these steps to handle a mouse move event:

1. **Define an event listener for the Canvas that you want to detect the mouse move condition.**

   See code section B2 of Listing 8-1:

   ```
   canvasBL.addEventListener("mousemove", mouseMove, false);
   ```

2. **Define a function that will contain the code to be executed when the mouse is moved.**

   See code section D of the example:

   ```
   function mouseMove(event) { . . . }
   ```

3. **Check the dragging indicator for the on condition.**

   If the dragging indicator is on, continue with the steps below. This is shown in E1 of the example:

   ```
   if (dragMouse == 1)
   ```

4. **Within the `mouseMove()` function, use your mouse event function (code section G) to determine the position of the mouse on your Canvas.**

   See code section E2:

   ```
   mouseEvent(event);
   ```

5. **Clear the Canvas.**

   Clear the Canvas so that only the ball at the new position is drawn, as in E3:

   ```
   contextBL.clearRect(0,0,canvasBL.width,canvasBL.height);
   ```

6. **Stop the animation that is currently in progress so that you can start a new animation when the object is released.**

   In code E3, this is done using the `clearInterval()` function and the `intervalID` of the animation:

   ```
   clearInterval(intervalID);
   ```

7. **Draw the object at the mouse position.**

   In the example, this has the effect of moving the ball to the cursor position as shown in code E4:

```
contextBL.beginPath();
contextBL.arc(ballXCur, ballYCur, radius, startAngle, endAngle, true);
contextBL.closePath();
contextBL.fill();
```

Mouse up events

A *mouse up event* is typically used to drop an object and restart any paused animations. In code section F of Listing 8-1, the dragging indicator is turned off, and the bouncing ball is restarted:

1. **Define a listener for the Canvas that you want to detect the mouse down condition.**

   See code section B2 of Listing 8-1:

   ```
   canvasBL.addEventListener("mouseup", mouseUp, false);
   ```

2. **Define a function that will contain the code to be executed when the mouse is released.**

   See code section F of the example:

   ```
   function mouseUp(event) { . . . }
   ```

3. **Determine the mouse position.**

   Within the `mouseUp()` function, use your mouse event function (code section G) to determine the position of the mouse on your Canvas, as shown in F1:

   ```
   mouseEvent(event);
   ```

4. **Turn on an indicator that will tell other code sections that a drag and drop operation is in progress.**

   This is shown in F2 of the example:

   ```
   dragMouse = 0;
   ```

5. **Stop the animation that is currently in progress so that you can start a new animation when the object is released.**

   In code F3, this is done using the `clearInterval()` function and the `intervalID` of the animation:

   ```
   clearInterval(intervalID);
   ```

6. **Restart the animation.**

   Draw the object at the mouse position. In the example, this has the effect of moving the ball to the cursor position as shown in code F3:

   ```
   bouncingBall(ballXCur, ballYCur, xVectorCur, yVectorCur);
   ```

Displaying Information for the User

One important way to interact with your application user is through text that conveys information about the application and assists in the user/application feedback loop. Figure 8-2 (earlier in this chapter) shows the text used by the sample application to display information about how to use the bouncing ball application and the current values of key application parameters.

To display Canvas application information, follow these steps:

1. **Define a Canvas to display your text.**

   Define a Canvas using the HTML Canvas tag as in code section L of Listing 8-1:

   ```
   <canvas id     = "canvasBackground"  width = "500"  height ="250"
           style = "border:2px solid black; position:absolute;
                    left:auto; top:auto; z-index: 1">
   Your browser doesn't currently support HTML5 Canvas.
   </canvas>
   ```

2. **Define a context for your text display Canvas.**

   As in code section B1, define a context for references to the text display Canvas:

   ```
   canvasBG  = document.getElementById("canvasBackground");
   contextBG = canvasBG.getContext("2d");
   ```

3. **Separate the code that will display your text into a function that is called from other areas of your application.**

   In Listing 8-1, this function is defined in code section K:

   ```
   function background() { . . . }
   ```

4. **Call the background function when you want to update the text.**

   See code section H3 of the sample:

   ```
   background();
   ```

5. **Set the attributes of the text, such as font and alignment.**

   Within the background display function, as in code section K1 of the example, set attributes:

   ```
   contextBG.font         = "11pt courier";
   contextBG.textAlign    = "left";
   contextBG.textBaseline = "middle";
   ```

6. **Set any variables needed to position the text.**

   See code section K2:

   ```
   var xPos1 = 15;   var xPos2 = 175;   var xPos3 = 275;   var yPos  = 20;
   ```

7. **Fill the background color.**

   If you're not using other Canvases to create a background for the text, fill a rectangle with a color, as in code section K3:

   ```
   contextBG.fillStyle = "silver";
   contextBG.fillRect(0, 0, canvasBG.width, canvasBG.height);
   ```

8. **If you want to make sure that fractional numbers are limited to a fixed number of decimal places, use the `toFixed()` function.**

   See code section K4 where variables are limited to 2 decimal places:

   ```
   accelerL = accelerL.toFixed(2);
   gravityL = gravityL.toFixed(2);
   ```

9. **Use the `fillStyle` attribute to set the color of your text.**

   See code section K5:

   ```
   contextBG.fillStyle = "darkslategrey";
   ```

10. **Use the `fillText()` function to display the text.**

    See code section K5 of Listing 8-1:

    ```
    contextBG.fillText("g - gravity:",  xPos1, yPos*4);
    contextBG.fillText(gravityL,        xPos2, yPos*4);
    contextBG.fillText("f - friction:", xPos1, yPos*5);
    contextBG.fillText(frictionL,       xPos2, yPos*5);
    ```

9

Creating Engaging Imagery and Motion

In This Chapter

Designing imagery and movement to fit your objectives

Encouraging users to interact with your application

Creating moving background images

Creating an application to test browser performance

The speed and precision of browser rendering of Canvas images is increasing rapidly. Newer browser versions are being developed with a strong emphasis on graphics capabilities. Browsers are leveraging graphics processing unit acceleration and the use of multiple CPU cores.

However, simply achieving greater speed and resolution of your Canvas images isn't normally sufficient to create a compelling and successful application. In the final analysis, what really matters is how users react to your application. In this chapter, you discover techniques for creating engaging imagery and motion that fits and enhances your Canvas application objectives.

Developing an Application Look and Feel

A Canvas application is a mixture of art and science, presenting both opportunities and challenges. The images, shapes, colors, and movements that you use in your application are important. Figure 9-1 and Listing 9-1 demonstrate a background scene intended to be relaxing and fun to watch. Clouds drift by, changing shape, transparency, and position. It's almost a game all by itself. Watch the clouds and see what comes next. Chill out.

In the following sections, I show you how to design and manage the components for a successful look and feel to your application.

Figure 9-1: Clouds moving across a landscape.

Listing 9-1:   Drawing Clouds Moving across a Landscape

```
<!DOCTYPE HTML> <html> <head> <script>

// A. ANIMATION variables.
   var animType = 1;  var interval = 16;  var moveAdj = 1;  var lastTime = 0;

// B. CLOUDS variables.
   var clouds      = new Array();
   var cloudsSpace = 1.8;   var cloudsCount = 5;    var cloudsLoad  = 0;
   var cloudsWidth = 200;   var cloudsTop   = -10;  var cloudsWMin  = 150;
   var cloudsWMax  = 350;   var cloudsHMin  = 40;   var cloudsHMax  = 180;
   var cloudsAMin  = .3;    var cloudsAMax  = .8;   var cloudsMMin  = .004;
   var cloudsMMax  = .05;

// C. FRAME RATE variables.
   var fpsCounter  = 0;     var fpsDisplay  = 50;   var fpsDisplayX = 60;
   var fpsDisplayY = 340;   var fpsPromptX  = 249;  var fpsPromptY  = 340;
   var fpsExplX    = 65;    var fpsExplY    = 100;  var fpsExplYD1  = 6;
   var fpsExplYD2  = 2;     var fpsOffset   = 95;   var fps         = 0;
```

```
    var fpsMultMax  = 20;   var fpsWidthL  = 1;    var fpsScreen  = -1;
    var fpsAlphaL   = .5;    var fpsAlphaE  = .8;   var fpsLineCt  = 5;
    var fpsLineSp   = 18;
    var fpsColor    = "white";
    var fpsColorE   = "darkblue";
    var fpsColorL   = "blue";
    var fpsFont     = "12pt arial";
    var fpsFontE    = "11pt arial";
    var fpsTitle    = "Frame Rate:";
    var fpsPrompt1  = "Click or touch for more information."
    var fpsPrompt2  = "Click or touch for less information."
    var fpsLine1    = "This is an HTML5 Canvas demonstration of moving"
    var fpsLine2    = "clouds of random sizes, shapes, transparencies"
    var fpsLine3    = "and speeds across a background image."
    var fpsLine4    = "The Frame Rate displayed below tracks the"
    var fpsLine5    = "number of animation frames per second."

// D. WINDOW LOAD function.
window.onload = function()
{
    // D1. CANVAS contexts.
    canvasBG  = document.getElementById("canvasBackground");
    contextBG = canvasBG.getContext("2d");
    canvasFR  = document.getElementById("canvasFrameRate");
    contextFR = canvasFR.getContext("2d");
    canvasCL  = document.getElementById("canvasClouds");
    contextCL = canvasCL.getContext("2d");

    // D2. IMAGE definitions.
    var sky    = new Image();
    sky.src    = "http://marketimpacts.com/storage/RiverScene2.jpg";
    var cloud0 = new Image();
    cloud0.src = "http://marketimpacts.com/storage/Cloud0.gif";
    var cloud1 = new Image();
    cloud1.src = "http://marketimpacts.com/storage/Cloud1.gif";
    var cloud2 = new Image();
    cloud2.src = "http://marketimpacts.com/storage/Cloud2.gif";
    var cloud3 = new Image();
    cloud3.src = "http://marketimpacts.com/storage/Cloud3.gif";
    var cloud4 = new Image();
    cloud4.src = "http://marketimpacts.com/storage/Cloud4.gif";

    // D3. CLOUD image load functions.
    cloud0.onload = function(){createCloud(0, cloud0); cloudsLoad++;}
    cloud1.onload = function(){createCloud(1, cloud1); cloudsLoad++;}
    cloud2.onload = function(){createCloud(2, cloud2); cloudsLoad++;}
    cloud3.onload = function(){createCloud(3, cloud3); cloudsLoad++;}
    cloud4.onload = function(){createCloud(4, cloud4); cloudsLoad++;}
```

(continued)

Listing 9-1 *(continued)*

```
// D4. EVENT listeners.
canvasFR.addEventListener("mousedown", screenChange, false);
canvasFR.addEventListener("touchstart",screenChange, false);
canvasFR.addEventListener("touchmove", screenChange, false);
canvasFR.addEventListener("touchend", screenChange, false);

// D5. SCREEN CHANGE event.
function screenChange(event) {fpsScreen = -fpsScreen;}

// E. SKY image load function.
sky.onload = function()
{
    // E1. DRAW background image.
    contextBG.drawImage(sky, 0, 0, canvasBG.width, canvasBG.height);
    // E2. START moving cloud scene.
    cloudScene();
}
}
// F. CREATE CLOUD function.
function createCloud(number, image)
{
    clouds[number]        = {};
    clouds[number].xPos   = number*cloudsWidth;
    clouds[number].yPos   = cloudsTop;
    clouds[number].width  = cloudsWMin+(Math.random()*(cloudsWMax-cloudsWMin));
    clouds[number].height = cloudsHMin+(Math.random()*(cloudsHMax-cloudsHMin));
    clouds[number].alpha  = cloudsAMin+(Math.random()*(cloudsAMax-cloudsAMin));
    clouds[number].move   = cloudsMMin+(Math.random()*(cloudsMMax-cloudsMMin));
    clouds[number].image  = image;
}
// G. CLOUD SCENE function.
function cloudScene()
{
    // G1. START animation clouds using setInterval.
    if(animType == 0)
        {intervalID = setInterval(drawClouds,interval);}

    // G2. START animation clouds using requestAnimationFrame.
    if(animType == 1)
    {
        // G3. ANIMATION loop.
        (function animLoop()
        {
            // G4. REQUEST ANIMATION FRAME
            requestAnimFrame(animLoop);

            // G5. DRAW clouds.
            drawClouds();
        }
        ) ();
    }
```

```
// H. DRAW CLOUDS function.
function drawClouds()
{
   // H1. FRAME RATE calculation.
   var date     = new Date();
   var time     = date.getTime();
   var timeDiff = time - lastTime;
   fps          = 1000/Math.max(timeDiff, 1);
   lastTime     = time;

   // H2. FRAME COUNTER increment.
   fpsCounter++;

   // H3. FRAME RATE display.
   if((fpsCounter > fpsDisplay) && (timeDiff > 1))
   {
      // H4. COUNTER reset.
      fpsCounter = 0;

      // H5. DISPLAY frame rate and click prompt.
      frameRateDisplay();
   }
   // H6. FRAME RATE adjustment calculation.
   var fpsTarget  = 1000/interval;
   var fpsDiff    = fpsTarget - fps;
   var fpsMult    = fpsDiff/Math.max(fps, 1);
   var fpsAdjust  = Math.min(fpsMult, fpsMultMax);

   // H7. CLEAR canvas.
   contextCL.clearRect(0,0, canvasCL.width, canvasCL.height);

   // H8. LOOP through clouds.
   for(var c=0; c<(clouds.length); c++)
   {
      // H9. CLOUDS LOAD check.
      if(cloudsLoad >= cloudsCount)
      {
         // H10. ADJUSTMENT calculation.
         var moveAdjust = fpsAdjust * clouds[c].move * moveAdj;

         // H11. CHANGE x position.
         clouds[c].xPos += (clouds[c].move + moveAdjust);

         // H12. OFF CANVAS condition check.
         if(clouds[c].xPos > canvasCL.width)
         {
            // H13. CREATE cloud.
            createCloud(c, clouds[c].image);

            // H14. STAGE cloud for canvas entry.
            clouds[c].xPos = -cloudsWidth * cloudsSpace;
         }
```

(continued)

Listing 9-1 *(continued)*

```
        // H15. TRANSPARENCY setting.
        contextCL.globalAlpha = clouds[c].alpha;

        // H16. DRAW cloud image.
        contextCL.drawImage(clouds[c].image, clouds[c].xPos, clouds[c].yPos,
                            clouds[c].width, clouds[c].height);

    }
}
// I. FRAME RATE DISPLAY function.
function frameRateDisplay()
{
    // I1. CLEAR frame speed canvas.
    contextFR.clearRect(0, 0, canvasFR.width, canvasFR.height);

    // I2. MORE INFO prompt.
    if(fpsScreen == -1)
    {
        // I3. ATTRIBUTES of text.
        contextFR.font = fpsFont;   contextFR.fillStyle = fpsColor;

        // I4. DISPLAY text.
        contextFR.fillText(fpsPrompt1, fpsPromptX, fpsPromptY );
    }
    // I5. EXPLANATION text.
    if(fpsScreen == 1)
    {
        // I6. ATTRIBUTES of counter.
        contextFR.font = fpsFont;    contextFR.fillStyle = fpsColor;

        // I7. FIX precision of fps.
        fps = fps.toFixed(0);

        // I8. COUNTER text.
        contextFR.fillText(fpsTitle, fpsDisplayX,              fpsDisplayY);
        contextFR.fillText(fps,      fpsDisplayX + fpsOffset, fpsDisplayY);

        // I9. LESS info prompt.
        contextFR.fillText(fpsPrompt2,fpsPromptX, fpsPromptY );
        // I10. LINE drawing.
        contextFR.strokeStyle = fpsColorL;
        contextFR.globalAlpha = fpsAlphaL;
        contextFR.lineWidth   = fpsWidthL;
        contextFR.beginPath();
        contextFR.moveTo(fpsExplX-10, fpsExplY + fpsExplYD1);
        contextFR.lineTo(fpsExplX-10, fpsExplY + fpsExplYD2 +
                        (fpsLineCt * fpsLineSp));
        contextFR.stroke();
```

```
        // I11. TEXT display.
        explanationText(fpsLine1, 1);    explanationText(fpsLine2, 2);
        explanationText(fpsLine3, 3);    explanationText(fpsLine4, 4);
        explanationText(fpsLine5, 5);
      }
    }
    // J. EXPLANATION TEXT function.
    function explanationText(text, lineNumber)
    {
        // J1. SPACING of line.
        var lineSpace = lineNumber * fpsLineSp;

        // J2. ATTRIBUTES of text.
        contextFR.globalAlpha = fpsAlphaE;   contextFR.font = fpsFontE;
        contextFR.fillStyle   = fpsColorE;

        // J3. DISPLAY text.
        contextFR.fillText(text, fpsExplX, fpsExplY + lineSpace);
      }
    }
}
// K. REQUEST ANIMATION FRAME function.
   window.requestAnimFrame = (function()
   {
       // K1. RETURN function available.
       return window.requestAnimationFrame       ||
              window.webkitRequestAnimationFrame ||
              window.mozRequestAnimationFrame    ||
              window.oRequestAnimationFrame      ||
              window.msRequestAnimationFrame     ||

       // K2. FALLBACK setTimeout function.
       function(callback) {window.setTimeout(callback, interval);};
   })();
</script> </head> <body> <div>

<!-- L. CANVAS DEFINITIONS  -->
<canvas id    = "canvasClouds"  width = "500"  height ="350"
        style = "border:2px solid black; position:absolute;
                 left:auto; top:auto; z-index: 2">
</canvas>
<canvas id    = "canvasFrameRate"  width = "500"  height ="350"
        style = "border:2px solid black; position:absolute;
                 left:auto; top:auto; z-index: 3">
</canvas>
<canvas id    = "canvasBackground"  width = "500"  height ="350"
        style = "border:2px solid black; position:absolute;
                 left:auto; top:auto; z-index: 1">
Your browser doesn't currently support HTML5 Canvas.
</canvas> </div> </body> </html>
```

Defining dimensions of appearance and motion

The look and feel of an application can be hard to quantify. To tackle this tricky topic, I've devised four dimensions to help you define the look and feel of your application:

- ✔ Abstract ↔ Realistic
- ✔ Muted ↔ Colorful
- ✔ Simple ↔ Complex
- ✔ Relaxing ↔ Active

You can use these dimensions to set objectives for your design. For example, you might want to develop a particle movement demonstration that's

> Abstract, Colorful, Simple, Relaxing

Or an adventure game that is

> Realistic, Muted, Complex, Active

These decisions will drive your choices of imagery and motion.

There aren't right and wrong answers to the questions of where to fit in these dimensions. It's simply a technique for helping you think about key aspects of your application and make conscious choices for your design. You can make your Canvas application virtual world anything you want.

Defining the visual dimensions of your application

Figure 9-2 provides a series of images for reference in defining visual dimensions. They're versions of the background image that's used in the Listing 9-1 sample application. I created this group of images by using image processing tools in Adobe Photoshop. Each image is rated on a scale of 1 to 10 for each of the four dimensions described in the preceding section.

Figure 9-3 shows how the Listing 9-1 example can be plotted on a scale of 1 to 10 for each of the four visual dimensions. To define the dimensions of appearance and motion for your application, follow these steps:

1. **Choose and/or define the dimensions of appearance and motion.**

   Keep in mind that the four dimensions I defined in the preceding section and in Figure 9-3 may not work for your application. For example, you might be developing an application that's all buttons, selectors, and other types of control. If you need different dimensions, create your own by using the four I've included as a starting point.

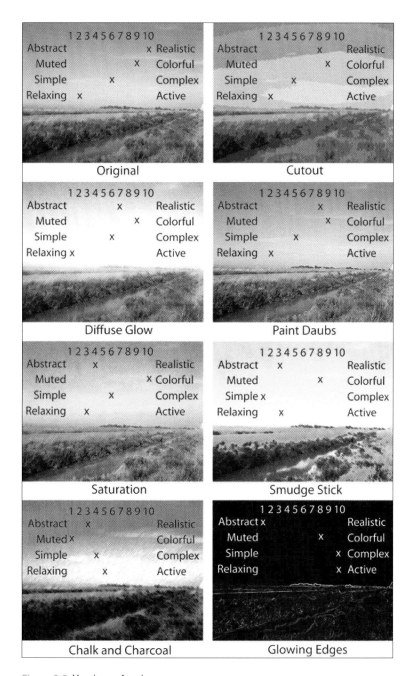

Figure 9-2: Versions of an image.

2. **Choose a point on the abstract/realistic scale.**

   In Figure 9-2, the range of the 1-to-10 scale is represented by the abstract Glowing Edges image at one end of the scale and the realistic Original photograph at the other end of the scale. I chose to be at an 8. I used a Paint Daubs filter to take the edge off pure realism.

3. **Choose a point on the muted/colorful scale.**

   The range of this scale is represented by the muted Chalk and Charcoal image at a 1 and the high color Saturation image at a 10. I chose a level of 9. I saturated the colors in the image but not to the full extent possible.

4. **Choose a point on the simple/complex scale.**

   The range of this scale is represented by the simple Smudge Stick image at a 1 and the highly detailed Glowing Edges image at a 10. I chose a level of 5. Using Paint Daubs, I cut back on some of the detail to give the scene a bit of a dreamy quality.

5. **Choose a point on the relaxing/active scale.**

   The range of this scale is represented by the Diffuse Glow image at a 1 and the Glowing Edges images at a 10. I used the relaxing Paint Daubs image.

Figure 9-3 summarizes the dimensions of the sample application in Listing 9-1.

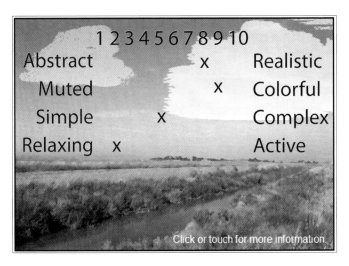

Figure 9-3: Visual dimensions of the moving clouds application in Listing 9-1.

Using an image as a background

One tool for defining the appearance of your application is the use of a background image. You can use a photograph, an image you create with a drawing program, or a mixture of the two.

Use these steps to draw a static image as part of your application background:

1. **Use a tool such as Adobe Photoshop or Adobe Illustrator to create your background image.**

2. **Upload the image to a server.**

   Typically, you use the server hosting the website containing your Canvas application.

3. **Define a Canvas to hold the image.**

   As shown in code section L of Listing 9-1, define a Canvas:

   ```
   <canvas id    = "canvasBackground"  width = "500"  height ="350"
          style = "border:2px solid black; position:absolute;
                    left:auto; top:auto; z-index: 1">
   Your browser doesn't currently support HTML5 Canvas.
   </canvas>
   ```

4. **Define a Canvas variable and context.**

   As shown in code section D1 of Listing 9-1, define a Canvas variable and context:

   ```
   canvasBG  = document.getElementById("canvasBackground");
   contextBG = canvasBG.getContext("2d");
   ```

5. **Define the image variable and source for the image.**

   See code section D2:

   ```
   var sky = new Image();
   sky.src = "http://marketimpacts.com/storage/RiverScene2.jpg";
   ```

6. **Define a function that will draw the image after it's loaded from the source server.**

   See code section E:

   ```
   sky.onload = function()
   {
      contextBG.drawImage(sky, 0, 0, canvasBG.width, canvasBG.height);
   }
   ```

Prompting User Interaction

An important aspect of engaging users is getting them to interact with your application. If you can entice users to click on or touch your Canvas, you'll improve your chances of retaining their interest and achieving the goals of your application. Figure 9-4 shows the screen that's displayed if someone clicks or touches the Canvas created by Listing 9-1.

In the following sections, I show you how to generate user interaction.

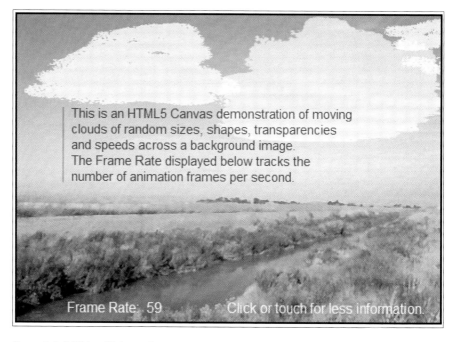

This is an HTML5 Canvas demonstration of moving clouds of random sizes, shapes, transparencies and speeds across a background image. The Frame Rate displayed below tracks the number of animation frames per second.

Frame Rate: 59   Click or touch for less information.

Figure 9-4: Additional information displayed after click or touch by user.

Using motion to attract attention

Canvas applications have a powerful tool for attracting attention — motion. A well-designed animation can be an effective way to start interacting with users.

Animations on web pages are not new. Unfortunately, animations are often mishandled and create annoying, distracting movement. This can cause web page visitors to move on instead of engaging in interaction. The opposite of what you want.

Responding to interaction

If your Canvas application captures the attention of a user who then clicks on the screen or presses a key, you should make something happen. In the example in Listing 8-1 (in Chapter 8), you see interaction using the mouse and keyboard. In Listing 9-1, when the user touches or clicks on the Canvas area, additional explanatory text is alternately displayed and removed.

To change text displays on a Canvas in response to user interaction, follow these steps:

1. **Define a variable that will keep track of which screen version is being displayed.**

   Listing 9-1 has only two screen versions:

   - *Initial screen prompt:* See Figure 9-1; `fpsScreen = -1`.
   - *Additional information screen:* See Figure 9-4; `fpsScreen = 1`.

   The variable is defined in code section C:

   ```
   var fpsScreen = -1;
   ```

2. **Define a Canvas to contain display information.**

   See code section L in Listing 9-1:

   ```
   <canvas id    = "canvasFrameRate"  width = "500"  height ="350"
           style = "border:2px solid black; position:absolute;
                    left:auto; top:auto; z-index: 3">
   </canvas>
   ```

3. **Define a Canvas variable and context for reference by your code.**

   See code section D1:

   ```
   canvasFR  = document.getElementById("canvasFrameRate");
   contextFR = canvasFR.getContext("2d");
   ```

4. **Define event listeners for mouse and touch events.**

   Event listeners define the user actions that will trigger calls to a speci-fied function, as in code section D4 for mouse and touch events:

   ```
   canvasFR.addEventListener("mousedown",  screenChange, false);
   canvasFR.addEventListener("touchstart", screenChange, false);
   canvasFR.addEventListener("touchmove",  screenChange, false);
   canvasFR.addEventListener("touchend",   screenChange, false);
   ```

5. **Define the function that will be called when a user event takes place.**

   See code section D5:

   ```
   function screenChange(event) {fpsScreen = -fpsScreen;}
   ```

Because Listing 9-1 has only two versions of the screen display, this function is straightforward. It toggles the `fpsScreen` variable between its two values.

6. **Test the variable used to track the status of interaction with the user and take the appropriate actions for each status type.**

See code sections I2 and I5 of the example:

```
if(fpsScreen == -1)
{ . . . code responding to this screen status}
    .
    .
    .
if(fpsScreen == 1)
{ . . . code responding to this screen status}
```

Managing Animations

As your applications become more sophisticated, you'll need better control over object movement. In the following sections, you find out how to move objects at controlled speeds with fluid motion. Figure 9-1 and Listing 9-1 demonstrate moving clouds across a background image and are used for examples in the following sections.

Animation frame rates

The number of Canvas frames per second (fps) that your application draws is referred to as the *frame rate.* The human brain retains an image the eye sees for about one-fifteenth of a second, or about 66 milliseconds (ms). If the next image in an animation sequence is shown in less than 66 ms (a frame rate of 15 fps), the brain blends the images, and the illusion of motion is created. In the following sections, you see how to create optimal frame rate performance to create smooth-looking animations.

The minimum effective frame rate

The minimum useful frame rate is the rate needed so that motion will be perceived as smooth and natural. At 15 fps, although motion is perceived, it's seen as choppy and unnatural. Early silent films had this frame rate, and the motion was choppy.

Through experimentation and development in film and television, it was determined that in order for our brains to perceive fluid motion, the minimum frame rate required is 24 frames per second (an interval of 41 ms.).

The maximum useful frame rate

The maximum useful frame rate is tied to the refresh rate of displays. The *refresh rate* is the number of times per second the display is changed. The normal refresh rate for LCD displays is 60 cycles per second. This equates to an interval between display changes of 16.66 ms. Therefore, a frame rate of over 60 (or a frame interval of less than 16.66 ms) will be "wasted." Your application can redraw a Canvas more than 60 frames per second, but not all of the redraws will appear on the screen.

The desired frame rate

Because 60 fps will be fully used by LCD displays and produces the most fluid motion, it is seen at the best frame rate for Canvas applications. So use 60 fps as the frame rate for your application if you can. If you have to go below this rate, keep your animation frame rate above 24 fps. To summarize:

- **60 fps/16 ms interval:** Maximum useful and most desirable frame rate.

- **24 fps/41 ms interval:** Minimum effective frame rate.

In designing your animation drawing functions, keep in mind that you have between 16 and 41 ms to draw a single frame on your Canvas. How much your application can do within this time interval depends on the speed of the computing device running the browser. This limitation may not be much of a factor for simpler Canvas applications where 16–41 ms is plenty of time to draw your images. As your applications increase in complexity, however, you may need to improve the efficiency of your code to keep the frame rate at optimal levels.

Defining your animation control function

You find out about basic animation sequences in Chapter 6 and how to use the setInterval() function to generate callbacks to your animation code at specified time intervals. Now you build on that knowledge with more-sophisticated animation timing. You see how to let the browser call your animation code at optimized intervals and how to create motion at a controlled speed regardless of the length of the animation interval.

Using the requestAnimationFrame () function

The requestAnimationFrame() function tells the browser to call a designated function in your application at optimal time intervals determined by system activity. Most browsers use 60 fps as the target frame rate. The actual frame rate will vary from about 50 to 70, depending on system activity.

There are a number of advantages to using `requestAnimationFrame()` instead of `setInterval()`:

- **Consistent optimum frame rate:** As discussed in the preceding section, 60 fps is the optimum frame rate based on today's display technology.

- **Callback efficiency:** If you use `setInterval()` with a specific callback interval, not all of your callbacks will be executed — because of interference from other processes. When using `requestAnimationFrame()`, 100 percent of your callbacks will be executed.

- **CPU efficiency:** Because the browser is determining the optimum callback interval and you're not wasting any callback requests, `request AnimationFrame()` uses fewer CPU cycles than `setInterval()`.

- **Power consumption:** Better CPU efficiency means lower power consumption. This is an especially important factor for battery-powered devices.

- **Background activity eliminated:** When a window using `request AnimationFrame()` is minimized, the browser stops executing callbacks. This results in zero CPU cycles used by your application in a minimized window. When you're using `setInterval()`, your application will continue to request callbacks even when minimized.

- **Smoother animation:** Because of the greater efficiency of `request AnimationFrame()`, your application animations should appear smoother.

The `requestAnimationFrame()` function is experimental and still in development. The W3C web page for timing control of script-based animations contains the latest status of the feature and suggested code for calling the function at `www.w3.org/TR/animation-timing`.

Although `requestAnimationFrame()` is still in development, all the major browsers have implemented it in their latest releases. Because of the advantages I just discussed, I recommend using it by following these steps:

1. **(Optional) Define a variable to turn on `requestAnimationFrame()` code.**

   This step is optional. The purpose is to give your application the flexibility of using either `requestAnimationFrame()` or `setInterval()`. As in code section A of Listing 9-1, define your variable:

   ```
   var animType = 1;
   ```

   If the variable is set to 1, your code will use `requestAnimation Frame()`. If it is set to 0, your code will use `setInterval()`.

2. **Define a timing interval in milliseconds that will be used if the `requestAnimationFrame()` function is not available on a browser.**

   Here's an example in code section A:

   ```
   interval = 16;
   ```

3. **Define an animation loop by using `requestAnimationFrame()`.**

   If `animType` is set to 1, execute an animation loop as in code sections G2–G5:

   ```
   if(animType == 1)
   {
      (function animLoop()
      {
         requestAnimFrame(animLoop);
         drawClouds();
      }
      ) ();
   }
   ```

   This is essentially a recursive function that calls itself via the browser. The `animLoop()` function will be called by the browser in the range of 60 times per second (once every 16 ms). Within the `animLoop()` function, call the function you're using to draw your animation scene. In Listing 9-1, that is the `drawClouds()` function.

4. **Define an implementation of the `requestAnimationFrame()` function.**

   This step is necessary because of the temporary, experimental nature of `requestAnimationFrame()`. When the official definition of `requestAnimationFrame()` settles down and the major browsers develop a uniform version of the function, this step will not be needed. For now, use the following code as in section K of the example:

   ```
   window.requestAnimFrame = (function()
   {
      return window.requestAnimationFrame       ||
             window.webkitRequestAnimationFrame ||
             window.mozRequestAnimationFrame    ||
             window.oRequestAnimationFrame      ||
             window.msRequestAnimationFrame     ||

      function(callback)
             {window.setTimeout(callback, interval)};
   })();
   ```

   This code will use the individual browser implementations of `requestAnimationFrame()` and, if none is supported by the browser, revert to a `setTimeout()` function by using the interval defined in your application. The code is based on an implementation by Paul Irish.

5. **Define your main animation drawing function.**

   This is the function that is called from your animation loop in Step 3 and carries out your animation drawing as in code section H of the example:

   ```
   function drawClouds()
       { . . . }
   ```

Using the setInterval () function

In addition to implementing the requestAnimationFrame() approach to animation, you can include code with setInterval() by following these steps:

1. **(Optional) Define a variable to turn on setInterval() code.**

   This step is optional. The purpose is to give your application the flexibility of using either requestAnimationFrame() or setInterval(). As in code section A of Listing 9-1, define your variable:

   ```
   var animType = 0;
   ```

   If the variable is set to 1, your code will use requestAnimation Frame(). If it's set to 0, your code will use setInterval().

2. **Define a timing interval in milliseconds that will be used by the setInterval() function.**

   Here's an example in code section A:

   ```
   interval = 16;
   ```

3. **Define code to invoke the setInterval() function.**

   If animType is set to 0, execute the setInterval() function as in code section G1:

   ```
   if(animType == 0)
       {intervalID = setInterval(drawClouds, interval);}
   ```

   The setInterval() function will call the drawClouds() function as close as possible to every interval milliseconds. Due to other activities within a user's browser and computer, not every call to setInterval() will be satisfied. The intervalID is returned by the setInterval() function and can be used to terminate the callbacks.

4. **Define your main animation drawing function.**

   This is the function that is called from the setInterval() function in Step 3 and carries out your animation drawing as in code section H of Listing 9-1:

   ```
   function drawClouds()
       { . . . }
   ```

Defining your main animation drawing function

Your main animation drawing code is invoked as a callback function by the
`setInterval()`, `setTimeout()`, or `requestAnimationFrame()` function,
as described in the preceding section. Within the main animation function,
your application draws a single frame for display on your Canvas or canvases. You can call as many other functions from within this main function
as you like. In Listing 9-1, the main animation drawing function is `draw`
`Clouds()` in code section H:

```
function drawClouds()
  { . . . }
```

Calculating and displaying the animation frame rate

Displaying the frame rate of your application is useful for gaining a sense of
how efficiently your application is performing and whether you're staying
in the 24–60 fps optimum frame rate range. To display the frame rate, follow
these steps:

1. **Define a Canvas for displaying the frame rate.**

   It's useful to implement a separate Canvas for displaying the frame rate.
   You can layer it anywhere you like in relation to the other canvases in your
   application by using the `z-index` attribute. This lets you adjust for the
   best visibility and prevent it from interfering with other images or animations. In the sample application, this Canvas is defined in code section L:

   ```
   <canvas id    = "canvasFrameRate"  width = "500"  height ="350"
           style = "border:2px solid black; position:absolute;
                    left:auto; top:auto; z-index: 2">
   </canvas>
   ```

2. **Define a variable and context that you'll use for referencing the
   Canvas in your code.**

   See section D1:

   ```
   canvasFR  = document.getElementById("canvasFrameRate");
   contextFR = canvasFR.getContext("2d");
   ```

3. **Calculate the frame rate in frames per second (fps) by using the
   `Date()` and `getTime()` functions.**

   See code section H1:

   ```
   var date     = new Date();
   var time     = date.getTime();
   var timeDiff = time - lastTime;
   fps          = 1000/Math.max(timeDiff, 1);
   lastTime     = time;
   ```

The `Math.max(timeDiff, 1)` function is used to prevent division by zero when `timeDiff = 0`.

4. **Use a counter and time difference to control the frame rate display frequency.**

   If you display the frame rate at every frame interval, you'll see the number changing so often that it will be difficult to understand what's taking place. To avoid this, use a counter to limit how often the frame rate display is changed, as in code section C and H2–H5 of the example:

   ```
   var fpsCounter = 0;
     .
     .
     .
   fpsCounter++;
      if((fpsCounter > fpsDisplay) && (timeDiff > 1))
      {
         fpsCounter = 0;
         frameRateDisplay;
      }
   ```

5. **Display the frame rate.**

   As in code section I, display the frame rate:

   ```
   function frameRateDisplay()
   { . . . }
   ```

6. **Display the frame rate explanatory text.**

   There is no built-in function to display multi-line text. It's helpful to implement your own support function as is done in code section J of the example:

   ```
   function explanationText(text, lineNumber)
   { . . . }
   ```

Moving objects at controlled speeds

The timing of callbacks from the browser to your main animation drawing function will vary depending on activity on the host browser and computer. In many applications, you move objects at a set speed regardless of the variation in callback intervals. To do this, adjust the distance you move an object based on the variation of the actual frame rate from your targeted frame rate.

Use the following steps to make these adjustments:

1. **If you want to be able to turn your adjustment code on and off, include a variable that will be used during object moves.**

In Listing 9-1, this variable is defined in code section A:

```
var moveAdj = 1;
```

2. **Define a target drawing interval in milliseconds.**

See code section A:

```
var interval = 16;
```

3. **Define variables for frames per second and time tracking.**

Define variables as in code sections A and C:

```
var lastTime = 0;
var fps      = 0;
```

4. **Define a variable to limit the fps adjustment.**

If your animation is paused and then restarted, this can cause a very large difference between animation frame times. If you calculate an adjustment based on this difference, you can see large and disruptive movements in your objects. To eliminate these disruptions, define a variable that will be used as a cutoff for adjustments. This variable is defined in code section C:

```
var fpsMultMax = 20;
```

5. **Calculate an adjustment factor for object movement.**

Based on the previous variables, calculate the factor by which you'll adjust object movement, as in code section H6:

```
var fpsTarget = 1000/interval;
var fpsDiff   = fpsTarget - fps;
var fpsMult   = fpsDiff/Math.max(fps, 1);
var fpsAdjust = Math.min(fpsMult, fpsMultMax);
```

The `Math.max(fps, 1)` function is used to prevent division by zero.

6. **When changing the position of an object, apply the adjustment factor.**

See code sections H10 and H11 in Listing 9-1:

```
var moveAdjust = fpsAdjust * clouds[c].move * moveAdj;
clouds[c].xPos += (clouds[c].move + moveAdjust);
```

Note that if the variable `moveAdj` is set to 0, no adjustment will be made.

Defining and storing image sequences

One technique for adding interest to an application is to move images across a background image. The Listing 9-1 application uses this technique to move clouds across a landscape.

This moving imagery is based on a set of images you create and store on a server. To define and store a series of images, follow these steps:

1. **Use a tool such as Adobe Illustrator to create images with a transparent background and save them as .gif files.**

   Figure 9-5 shows the images created for use in Listing 9-1.

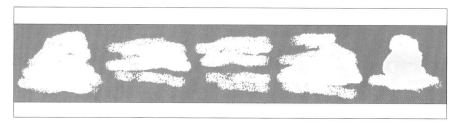

Figure 9-5: Images for moving clouds.

2. **Upload the .gif images to a server.**

   Normally the images you download to your Canvas application will be stored on the server hosting the website containing the application. Upload your images to a folder on the server.

3. **Define an array to hold the images in your application.**

   Define an images array as in code section B:

   ```
   var clouds = new Array();
   ```

4. **Define variables that will be used to characterize each image.**

   In code section B, this includes a number of minimum (Min) and maximum (Max) variables that will be used to create random characteristics in Step 7:

   ```
   var clouds      = new Array();
   var cloudsSpace = 1.8;
   var cloudsCount = 5;     var cloudsLoad = 0;
   var cloudsWidth = 200;   var cloudsTop  = -10;
   var cloudsWMin  = 150;   var cloudsWMax = 350;
   var cloudsHMin  = 40;    var cloudsHMax = 180;
   var cloudsAMin  = .3;    var cloudsAMax = .8;
   var cloudsMMin  = .004;  var cloudsMMax = .05;
   ```

5. **Define a variable and source for each image.**

As in code section D2, define a variable and server location for each image. One example is

```
var cloud0 = new Image();
cloud0.src = "http://marketimpacts.com/storage/Cloud0.gif";
```

6. **Define a function that will be called for each image after it's successfully loaded from the server.**

   Here's one example from code section D3 in Listing 9-1:

```
cloud0.onload = function() {createCloud(0, cloud0);}
```

   In the example, this function calls the image definition function described in Step 7.

7. **Define a function that will place an image in an array and generate image characteristics that will be used when drawing the image on your Canvas.**

   In code section F of Listing 9-1, the `Math.random()` function is used to generate random characteristics for the width, height, alpha (transparency), and move distance:

```
function createCloud(number, image)
{
    clouds[number]          =  {};
    clouds[number].xPos     =  number*cloudsWidth;
    clouds[number].yPos     =  cloudsTop;
    clouds[number].width    =  cloudsWMin+(Math.random()*
                               (cloudsWMax-cloudsWMin));
    clouds[number].height   =  cloudsHMin+(Math.random()*
                               (cloudsHMax-cloudsHMin));
    clouds[number].alpha    =  cloudsAMin+(Math.random()*
                               (cloudsAMax-cloudsAMin));
    clouds[number].move     =  cloudsMMin+(Math.random()*
                               (cloudsMMax-cloudsMMin));
    clouds[number].image    =  image;
}
```

   Using random characteristics is a powerful way to generate interesting scenes based on a limited number of images.

Moving images across a background

During each animation cycle, change the position of each image and draw it on the Canvas. In the Listing 9-1 example, clouds are drawn moving across the background image of a sky. As illustrated in Figure 9-6, the images are recycled with changed and randomized characteristics.

Figure 9-6: Moving recycled images across a background.

To create your moving images animation, follow these steps:

1. **Using the `clearRect()` function, clear the Canvas you're using to draw your images.**

   See code section H7 of Listing 9-1:

   ```
   contextCL.clearRect(0,0, canvasCL.width, canvasCL.height);
   ```

2. **Loop through the images in your array.**

   Loop through the entire array as in code section H8:

   ```
   for(var c = 0; c < (clouds.length); c++)    { . . . }
   ```

3. **Change the position of each image.**

   Change the coordinate(s) of each image. In code section H11 of Listing 9-1, clouds are being moved only horizontally, so there is only an *x* coordinate, `clouds[c].xPos`, to adjust. There is no vertical movement and thus no *y* coordinate to change. The base move distance is stored in the `clouds` array as `clouds[c].move`. The `move` distance is adjusted by the frames per second adjustment factor `fpsAdjust` if the `moveAdj` variable is set to 1. As explained earlier, this creates a consistent cloud speed under varying frame rates in code sections H10 and H11:

   ```
   var moveAdjust  = fpsAdjust * clouds[c].move * moveAdj;
   clouds[c].xPos += (clouds[c].move + moveAdjust);
   ```

4. **Check to see whether objects have moved past the width of the Canvas.**

   See code section H12 in Listing 9-1:

   ```
   if(clouds[c].xPos > canvasC1.width)
   ```

5. Create a new object.

After an object has moved off the Canvas, it can be recycled. That is, its position in the object array can be filled with a new object. In the sample code H13, a new cloud is defined using a new set of randomized characteristics using the `createCloud()` function:

```
createCloud(c, clouds[c].image);
```

The `createCloud()` function, discussed earlier, is located in code section F of the example.

6. Position the new object for re-entry onto the Canvas.

Set the coordinate(s) of the new object so that it will begin moving onto the Canvas during the position changes in Step 3. In the example, only the *x* coordinate is used to move the clouds. In code section H14, the *x* coordinate is set to a distance to the left of the background image:

```
clouds[c].xPos = -cloudsWidth * cloudsSpace;
```

7. Set transparency for the Canvas based on the attribute stored in the object array.

See code section H15 for the cloud:

```
contextCL.globalAlpha = clouds[c].alpha;
```

8. Use the appropriate function to draw the object on your Canvas.

In code sample H16, the `drawImage()` function is used to draw each cloud:

```
contextC1.drawImage(clouds[c].image, clouds[c].xPos,  clouds[c].yPos,
                    clouds[c].width, clouds[c].height);
```

Testing Browser Animation Performance

Browser developers are continually improving the performance of Canvas animations. Better browser performance allows you to do more in your animation functions, which can translate into better graphics and more movement. It's important to keep abreast of browser enhancements and current performance levels.

Figure 9-7 and Listing 9-2 demonstrate an application that stresses browser performance and shows the resulting frame rate of the animation. You can use this application as is, or adapt the code for inclusion in your applications.

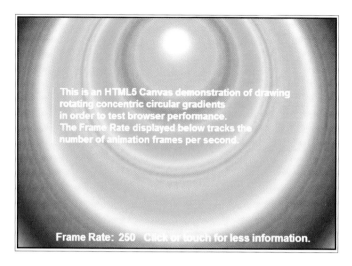

Figure 9-7: Testing browser animation performance.

Listing 9-2:   Testing Browser Animation Performance

```
<!DOCTYPE HTML> <html> <head> <script>

// A. ANIMATION variables.
    var interval   = 1;        var lastTime   = 0;

// B. GRADIENT variables.
    var gradC1X    = -140;     var gradC1Y    = 0;  var gradC1R   = 15;
    var gradC2X    = 0;        var gradC2Y    = 0;  var gradC2R   = 350;
    var gradSAngle = (Math.PI/180)*0;
    var gradEAngle = (Math.PI/180)*360;
    var gradRadius = 350;

// C. FRAME RATE variables.
    var fpsCounter  = 0;        var fpsDisplay  = 50;
    var fpsDisplayX = 60;       var fpsDisplayY = 340;
    var fpsPromptX  = 200;      var fpsPromptY  = 340;
    var fpsExplX    = 65;       var fpsExplY    = 100;
    var fpsExplYD1  = 6;        var fpsExplYD2  = 2;
    var fpsOffset   = 100;      var fps         = 0;
    var fpsMultMax  = 20;       var fpsColor    = "white";
    var fpsColorE   = "white"; var fpsColorL    = "white";
    var fpsWidthL   = 1;        var fpsScreen   = -1;
    var fpsAlphaL   = .5;       var fpsAlphaE   = 1;
    var fpsFont     = "bold 12pt arial";
    var fpsFontE    = "bold 11pt arial";
    var fpsTitle    = "Frame Rate:";
    var fpsPrompt1  = "Click or touch for more information."
```

```
    var fpsPrompt2  = "Click or touch for less information."
    var fpsLine1    = "This is an HTML5 Canvas demonstration of drawing"
    var fpsLine2    = "rotating concentric circular gradients "
    var fpsLine3    = "in order to test browser performance."
    var fpsLine4    = "The Frame Rate displayed below tracks the"
    var fpsLine5    = "number of animation frames per second."
    var fpsLineCt   = 5;
    var fpsLineSp   = 18;

// D. WINDOW LOAD function.
window.onload = function()
{
    // D1. CANVAS contexts.
    canvasFR  = document.getElementById("canvasFrameRate");
    contextFR = canvasFR.getContext("2d");
    canvasGR  = document.getElementById("canvasGradient");
    contextGR = canvasGR.getContext("2d");

    // D2. EVENT listeners.
    canvasFR.addEventListener("mousedown",  screenChange, false);
    canvasFR.addEventListener("touchstart", screenChange, false);
    canvasFR.addEventListener("touchmove",  screenChange, false);
    canvasFR.addEventListener("touchend",   screenChange, false);

    // D3. SCREEN CHANGE event.
    function screenChange(event) {fpsScreen = -fpsScreen;}

    // D4. START moving cloud scene.
    frameRateTest();
}
// E. CLOUD SCENE function.
function frameRateTest()
{
    // E1. TRANSLATE to middle of canvas.
    contextGR.translate(canvasGR.width/2, canvasGR.height/2);

    // E2. START animation.
    var intervalID = setInterval(drawFrameRate,interval);

    // F. DRAW FRAME RATE function.
    function drawFrameRate()
    {
        // F1. FRAME RATE calculation.
        var date     = new Date();
        var time     = date.getTime();
        var timeDiff = time - lastTime;
        fps          = 1000/Math.max(timeDiff, 1);
        lastTime     = time;

        // F2. FRAME COUNTER increment.
        fpsCounter++;
```

(continued)

Listing 9-2 *(continued)*

```
// F3. FRAME RATE display.
if((fpsCounter > fpsDisplay) && (timeDiff > 1))
{
    // F4. COUNTER reset.
    fpsCounter = 0;

    // F5. DISPLAY frame rate and click prompt.
    frameRateDisplay();
}
// F6. CLEAR canvas.
contextGR.clearRect(-canvasGR.width /2, -canvasGR.height/2,
                     canvasGR.width /2, canvasGR.height/2);
// F7. ROTATE canvas.
contextGR.rotate(((Math.PI)/180));

// F8. GRADIENT definition.
var gradRO = contextGR.createRadialGradient(gradC1X, gradC1Y, gradC1R,
                                            gradC2X, gradC2Y, gradC2R);
// F9. COLOR stops for gradient.
gradRO.addColorStop( 1, "silver"       );
gradRO.addColorStop(.9, "lightseagreen");
gradRO.addColorStop(.8, "purple"       );
gradRO.addColorStop(.7, "magenta"      );
gradRO.addColorStop(.6, "gold"         );
gradRO.addColorStop(.5, "darkturquoise");
gradRO.addColorStop(.4, "orange"       );
gradRO.addColorStop(.3, "lime"         );
gradRO.addColorStop(.2, "hotpink"      );
gradRO.addColorStop(.1, "springgreen"  );
gradRO.addColorStop( 0, "yellow"       );

// F10. FILL set to gradient.
contextGR.fillStyle = gradRO;

// F11. DRAW circle with gradient fill.
contextGR.beginPath();
contextGR.arc(0, 0, gradRadius, gradSAngle, gradEAngle, false);
contextGR.fill();

// G. FRAME RATE DISPLAY function.
function frameRateDisplay()
{
    // G1. CLEAR frame speed canvas.
    contextFR.clearRect(0, 0, canvasFR.width, canvasFR.height);

    // G2. ATTRIBUTES of counter.
    contextFR.font      = fpsFont;
    contextFR.fillStyle = fpsColor;
```

```
// G3. FIX precision of fps.
fps = fps.toFixed(0);

// G4. COUNTER text.
contextFR.fillText(fpsTitle, fpsDisplayX,                fpsDisplayY);
contextFR.fillText(fps,       fpsDisplayX + fpsOffset, fpsDisplayY);
// G5. MORE INFO prompt.
if(fpsScreen == -1)
{
    // G6. ATTRIBUTES of text.
    contextFR.font      = fpsFont;
    contextFR.fillStyle = fpsColor;

    // G7. DISPLAY text.
    contextFR.fillText(fpsPrompt1,fpsPromptX, fpsPromptY );
}
// G8. EXPLANATION text.
if(fpsScreen == 1)
{
    // G9. LESS info prompt.
    contextFR.fillText(fpsPrompt2,fpsPromptX, fpsPromptY );
    // G10. LINE drawing.
    contextFR.strokeStyle = fpsColorL;
    contextFR.globalAlpha = fpsAlphaL;
    contextFR.lineWidth   = fpsWidthL;
    contextFR.beginPath();
    contextFR.moveTo(fpsExplX-10, fpsExplY + fpsExplYD1);
    contextFR.lineTo(fpsExplX-10, fpsExplY + fpsExplYD2 +
                              (fpsLineCt * fpsLineSp));
    contextFR.stroke();

    // G11. TEXT display.
    explanationText(fpsLine1, 1);     explanationText(fpsLine2, 2);
    explanationText(fpsLine3, 3);     explanationText(fpsLine4, 4);
    explanationText(fpsLine5, 5);
}
}
// H. EXPLANATION TEXT function.
function explanationText(text, lineNumber)
{
    // H1. SPACING of line.
    var lineSpace = lineNumber * fpsLineSp;

    // H2. ATTRIBUTES of text.
    contextFR.globalAlpha = fpsAlphaE;   contextFR.font = fpsFontE;
    contextFR.fillStyle   = fpsColorE;
```

(continued)

Listing 9-2 *(continued)*

```
        // H3. DISPLAY text.

        contextFR.fillText(text, fpsExplX, fpsExplY + lineSpace);
      }
    }
}
</script> </head> <body> <div>

<!-- I. CANVAS DEFINITIONS  -->
<canvas id   = "canvasGradient"  width = "500"  height ="350"
        style = "border:2px solid black; position:absolute;
                 left:auto; top:auto; z-index: 2">
</canvas>
<canvas id   = "canvasFrameRate"  width = "500"  height ="350"
        style = "border:2px solid black; position:absolute;
                 left:auto; top:auto; z-index: 3">
Your browser doesn't currently support HTML5 Canvas.
</canvas> </div> </body> </html>
```

Creating the base code

The application in Listing 9-2 is based on the code from Listing 9-1. Before explaining how the two applications differ, I briefly touch on the code adapted from Listing 9-1.

To create the base code for testing browser performance, follow these steps:

1. **Define canvases and contexts as in Listing 9-2, code sections D1 and I.**

2. **Define an animation function as in code section F of Listing 9-2.**

3. **Calculate the frame rate as in Listing 9-2, code section F1.**

4. **Define a function for frame rate display as in Listing 9-2, code section G.**

5. **Prompt user interaction as in Listing 9-2, code sections D2, D3, G6, and G7.**

6. **Display a supplemental information screen as in Listing 9-2, code sections G8 and H.**

Defining an animation control function to stress the browser

The animation control function in Listing 9-2 differs from the one in Listing 9-1. The browser animation testing application only includes animation control via the setInterval() function. There is no option for using the request AnimationFrame() function. This is because the purpose of the application is to place a stress on browser performance, not to let the browser control the animation rate via the requestAnimationFrame() function.

To define an animation control function that places a stress on the browser, follow these steps:

1. **Define a variable specifying an animation interval that is *less* than a browser can satisfy.**

   This will cause the browser to return control to your callback function as rapidly as possible, thus demonstrating its maximum performance. In the example Listing 9-2, this is done in code section A, where the interval is set to 1 ms:

   ```
   var interval = 1;
   ```

2. **Define the `setInterval()` function call.**

   Define the function call to `setInterval()`, as in code section E2:

   ```
   var intervalID = setInterval(drawFrameRate,interval);
   ```

3. **Define the function that will perform animations when called at the interval specified in the `setInterval()` function.**

   See code section F of the example:

   ```
   function drawFrameRate()
   { . . . }
   ```

Drawing browser performance stressing images

The purpose of the application in Listing 9-2 is to stress the browser so that differences between browsers will show up in the displayed frame rate. If not enough work is being done for each animation frame, all browsers will perform at roughly the same level. They will all be able to keep up with the demands placed on them by the application code. In this application, you *want* to stress the browser. In the typical application, you want the code to be able to execute *without* stressing the browser. I've included this application in the book so that you can test browser performance under stressful situations. To see the application in action, open it in different browsers and watch the displayed frame rate.

In Listing 9-2, I've chosen a drawing function that places unusual stress on browsers. That is, drawing a radial, rotating, offset, multiple gradient with ten color levels. The browser (coupled with the graphics processing unit) has to generate shading between the gradients. In Listing 9-2, the gradients fill the Canvas. This means that every pixel on the Canvas has to be recalculated for each animation frame. The result is a psychedelic swirling circle. Be careful — don't let it hypnotize you.

To draw a radial, rotating, offset, multi-level gradient that stresses browser performance, follow these steps:

1. **Translate the (0,0) position to the center of the Canvas to facilitate drawing the rotating circle that will contain the gradient.**

See code section E1 of Listing 9-2:

```
contextGR.translate(canvasGR.width/2, canvasGR.height/2);
```

2. **Clear the Canvas.**

Clear the gradient display Canvas as in code section F6:

```
contextGR.clearRect(-canvasGR.width /2, -canvasGR.height/2,
                     canvasGR.width /2, canvasGR.height/2);
```

3. **To give the animation the appearance of movement, rotate the Canvas.**

See code section F7:

```
contextGR.rotate(((Math.PI)/180));
```

4. **Define the gradient that will fill the rotating circle.**

In Listing 9-2, this is a radial, offset gradient defined in code sections B and F8:

```
var gradC1X = -140;  var gradC1Y = 0;  var gradC1R = 15;
var gradC2X = 0;     var gradC2Y = 0;  var gradC2R = 350;

var gradRO = contextGR.createRadialGradient(gradC1X, gradC1Y, gradC1R,
                                            gradC2X, gradC2Y, gradC2R);
```

5. **Add the gradient colors.**

Add colors to the gradient as in code section F9:

```
gradRO.addColorStop( 1, "silver"       );
gradRO.addColorStop(.9, "lightseagreen");
gradRO.addColorStop(.8, "purple"       );
gradRO.addColorStop(.7, "magenta"      );
. . .
```

Including a large number of colors helps stress browser performance.

6. **Set the `fillStyle` to the gradient just created.**

See code section F10:

```
contextGR.fillStyle = gradRO;
```

7. **Use the `arc()` function to draw a circle and fill it with the gradient, as in code sections B and F11:**

```
var gradSAngle = (Math.PI/180)*0;
var gradEAngle = (Math.PI/180)*360;
var gradRadius = 350;

contextGR.beginPath();
contextGR.arc(0, 0, gradRadius, gradSAngle, gradEAngle, false);
contextGR.fill();
```

It's the `fill()` function that puts a heavy load on the browser and graphics processing unit, which must recalculate and draw every gradient image pixel.

10

Sounding Off with Audio

In This Chapter

- Configuring Canvas spaces to include audio
- Defining audio elements
- Using built-in playback controls or creating your own custom controls
- Responding to user interaction with audio

*H*TML5 takes a big step forward in handling browser-based audio. HTML5 audio doesn't require the use of a plug-in utility for audio playback; player capabilities are built into the browser. In addition, you can integrate audio elements with Canvas applications to create powerful combinations of effects.

In this chapter, you find out how to blend audio with Canvas capabilities described in previous chapters, such as objects, text, images, and user interaction.

Including Audio in Your Canvas Application

First the good news: You have *lots* of options for adding audio to your Canvas applications. Now the challenge: You have *lots* of options for adding audio to your Canvas applications. This chapter helps you understand these options and make good design and implementation choices.

You can implement audio in your Canvas applications in two ways:

- ✓ **With HTML tags:** Using HTML is the more traditional method. You define the audio file and player with HTML tags. Changes to audio playback are controlled using an audio player displayed with your Canvas.

- ✓ **With JavaScript code:** Audio is triggered by events and dynamically loaded within your application. You can generate audio as a result of application events such as colliding objects or the user clicking an object. Playback is controlled by your JavaScript code.

When designing your Canvas application, you can offer users two ways to control audio playback:

✓ **Using an audio player:** An audio player with standard controls for playback position, volume, pause, and mute.

✓ **Using custom controls:** Custom controls integrated with your Canvas graphics.

The application in Listing 10-1 and shown in Figure 10-1 demonstrates how to use these audio playback options. This application plays the following audio:

✓ **Water in the background:** In the application, the audio for the background sound of water is defined with HTML. The user can control playback with either the player control bar below the Canvas area or by clicking text within the Canvas area (via JavaScript).

✓ **Sounds of animals:** My dog Daisy barks, and the pelican (don't know his name) squawks when clicked. These recordings are defined and controlled via JavaScript without any associated HTML tags. Notice that the application user can trigger the animal sounds by clicking the mouse on the animal images so that they both play simultaneously over the water sound.

Figure 10-1: Using audio in an application.

As of this writing, multiple simultaneous sounds may not work on all your mobile devices' browsers. In my test of the Listing 10-1 application on mobile browsers, I found that the latest versions of desktop browsers could produce multiple simultaneous sounds while working with only certain mobile browsers such as Chrome and Opera. As mobile browser developers continue to improve HTML5 implementation, this situation is likely to change.

Listing 10-1:   Using Audio in an Application

```
<!DOCTYPE HTML> <html> <head>

<!-- A. STYLE for audio player. -->
<style   type="text/css" media="screen">
#audio1 {display:    inline;
         float:      left;
         margin-top: 510px;
         width:      304px;}
#audio2 {width:      304px;}
</style>
<script>

// B. VARIABLES.
   // B1. COORDINATES.
   var xPos       = 0;      var yPos       = 0;
   var dogX1      = 1;      var dogX2      = 150;
   var dogY1      = 250;    var dogY2      = 450;
   var birdX1     = 150;    var birdX2     = 230;
   var birdY1     = 150;    var birdY2     = 250;
   var menuX      = 15;     var menuY      = 85;
   var volumeX    = 60;

   // B2. MENU.
   var menuWidth  = 100;    var menuHeight   = 24;

   // B3. VOLUME.
   var volumeLevel = 0;     var volumeIncr   = .1;
   var volumeInit  = .7;
   var volumeDog   = .9;    var volumePelican = .9;

   // B4. AUDIO ELEMENTS.
   var audio2EL;            var audio3EL;
   var audio4EL;            var audioType;

   // B5. FONT.
   var textFont    = "12pt arial";
   var textColor   = "white";

   // B6. PROMPT COORDINATES.
   var promptY     = menuY + (0 * menuHeight);
   var soundY      = menuY + (1 * menuHeight);
   var playerY     = menuY + (2 * menuHeight);
   var volumeY     = menuY + (3 * menuHeight);
   var pauseY      = menuY + (4 * menuHeight);
   var loopY       = menuY + (5 * menuHeight);
```

(continued)

Listing 10-1 *(continued)*

```
// B7. TEXT.
var promptText  = "CLICK or TOUCH";
var volumeText  = "Volume";

var soundText1  = "Sound ON/off";
var playerText1 = "Player VISIBLE/hidden";
var pauseText1  = "Pause/PLAY";
var loopText1   = "Loop ON/off";

var soundText2  = "Sound on/OFF";
var playerText2 = "Player visible/HIDDEN";
var pauseText2  = "PAUSED/Play";
var loopText2   = "Loop on/OFF";

var soundText   = soundText1;
var playerText  = playerText1;
var pauseText   = pauseText1;
var loopText    = loopText1;


// B8. FILES.
var server          = "http://marketimpacts.com/storage/";
var backgroundFile  = "Pelican2";
var backgroundType  = ".jpg";
var dogAudFile      = "Dog";
var pelicanAudFile  = "Pelican";


// B9. IMAGES.
var backgroundImage = new Image();

// C. WINDOW LOAD function.
window.onload = function()
{
    // C1. CANVAS definition standard variables.
    canvasIM  = document.getElementById("canvasImage");
    contextIM = canvasIM.getContext("2d");
    canvasTX  = document.getElementById("canvasText");
    contextTX = canvasTX.getContext("2d");

    // C2. RETRIEVE AUDIO element for player.
    audio2EL  = document.getElementById("audio2");

    // C3. CREATE AUDIO element for animal sounds.
    audio3EL  = document.createElement("audio");
    audio4EL  = document.createElement("audio");

    // C4. AUDIO FILE type settings.
    audioType = audioExtensionType(audio3EL);

    // C5. AUDIO FILE source settings.
    audio3EL.setAttribute("src",server + pelicanAudFile + "." + audioType);
    audio4EL.setAttribute("src",server + dogAudFile     + "." + audioType);
```

```
// C6. INITIALIZE settings.
volumeLevel     = volumeInit;
audio2EL.volume = volumeLevel;
audio3EL.volume = volumeDog;
audio4EL.volume = volumePelican;
audio2EL.muted  = false;
audio2EL.paused = false;
audio2EL.loop   = true;
audio2EL.play();

// C7. LISTENERS.
canvasTX.addEventListener("mousedown",  clickTouch, false);
canvasTX.addEventListener("touchstart", clickTouch, false);
canvasTX.addEventListener("touchmove",  clickTouch, false);
canvasTX.addEventListener("touchend",   clickTouch, false);

// C8. GRAPHICS.
backgroundImage.src = server + backgroundFile + backgroundType;
backgroundImage.onload = function()
{
   // C9. IMAGE drawing.
   contextIM.drawImage(backgroundImage,0,0,canvasIM.width,canvasIM.height);

   // C10. TEXT display.
   textDisplay();
}
// C11. PLAYER state change functions.
audio2EL.onpause = function()
{
   pauseText = pauseText2;
   textDisplay();
}
audio2EL.onplay = function()
{
   pauseText = pauseText1;
   textDisplay();
}
audio2EL.onvolumechange = function()
{
   volumeLevel = audio2EL.volume;
   if(audio2EL.muted) {soundText = soundText2}
   else               {soundText = soundText1}
   textDisplay();
}
}
// D. CLICK/TOUCH function.
function clickTouch(event)
{
   // D1. COORDINATES retrieval.
   clickTouchEvent(event);
```

(continued)

Listing 10-1 *(continued)*

```
// D2. SOUND on/off.
if(positionTest(1))
{
    // D3. STATUS change.
    audio2EL.muted =       !audio2EL.muted;

    // D4. TEXT change.
    if(audio2EL.muted)     {soundText = soundText2}
    else                   {soundText = soundText1}
    textDisplay();
}
// D5. PLAYER visible/hidden.
if(positionTest(2))
{
    // D6. STATUS change.
    audio2EL.controls =    !audio2EL.controls;

    // D7. TEXT change.
    if(audio2EL.controls) {playerText = playerText1}
    else                  {playerText = playerText2}
    textDisplay();
}
// D8. LOOP on/off.
if(positionTest(5))
{
    // D9. STATUS change.
    audio2EL.loop =        !audio2EL.loop;

    // D10. TEXT change.
    if(audio2EL.loop)      {loopText = loopText1}
    else                   {loopText = loopText2}
    textDisplay();
}
// D11. PAUSE on/off.
if(positionTest(4))
{
    // D12. STATUS change & TEXT change.
    if(audio2EL.paused)    {audio2EL.play();  pauseText = pauseText1;}
    else                   {audio2EL.pause(); pauseText = pauseText2;}
    textDisplay();
}
// D13. VOLUME change.
if(positionTest(3))
{
    // D14. INCREMENT volume level.
    volumeLevel += volumeIncr;

    // D15. LIMIT.
    if(volumeLevel >1) {volumeLevel = 0}
```

```
      // D16. TEXT display.
      textDisplay();

      // D17. PLAYER setting.
      audio2EL.volume = volumeLevel;
   }
   // D18. BIRD event.
   if(objectTest(birdX1, birdX2, birdY1, birdY2))  {audio3EL.play()}

   // D19. DOG event.
   if(objectTest(dogX1, dogX2, dogY1, dogY2))      {audio4EL.play()}
}
// E. CLICK/TOUCH EVENT function.
function clickTouchEvent(event)
{
   // E1. BROWSERS except Firefox.
   if (event.x != undefined && event.y != undefined)
      {xPos = event.x;  yPos = event.y;}

   // E2. FIREFOX.
   else
   {  xPos = event.clientX + document.body.scrollLeft +
                  document.documentElement.scrollLeft;
      yPos = event.clientY + document.body.scrollTop +
                  document.documentElement.scrollTop;
   }
   // E3. CURSOR position.
   xPos -= canvasTX.offsetLeft;  yPos -= canvasTX.offsetTop;
}
// F. TEXT DISPLAY function.
function textDisplay()
{
   // F1. CLEAR canvas.
   contextTX.clearRect(0, 0, canvasTX.width, canvasTX.height);

   // F2. ATTRIBUTES.
   contextTX.font      = textFont;
   contextTX.fillStyle = textColor;

   // F3. FIX precision of volume.
   var volumeLev = volumeLevel.toFixed(1);

   // F4. DISPLAY text.
   contextTX.fillText(promptText, menuX, promptY);
   contextTX.fillText(soundText,  menuX, soundY );
   contextTX.fillText(playerText, menuX, playerY);
   contextTX.fillText(volumeText, menuX, volumeY);
   contextTX.fillText(pauseText,  menuX, pauseY );
   contextTX.fillText(loopText,   menuX, loopY  );
   contextTX.fillText(volumeLev,  menuX + volumeX, volumeY);
}
```

(continued)

Listing 10-1 *(continued)*

```
// G. POSITION TEST function.
function positionTest(position)
{
   // G1. INITIALIZE return value to false.
   var returnValue = false;

   // G2. TEST position.
   if (
       (xPos > (menuX)) &&
       (xPos < (menuX + menuWidth)) &&
       (yPos > (menuY + (position * menuHeight) - (menuHeight/2))) &&
       (yPos < (menuY + (position * menuHeight) + (menuHeight/4)))
       )
       {returnValue = true;}

   // G3. RETURN returnValue.
   return returnValue;
}
// H. OBJECT TEST function.
function objectTest(x1, x2, y1, y2)
{
   // H1. INITIALIZE return value to false.
   var returnValue = false;

   // H2. TEST position.
   if ((xPos > x1) && (xPos < x2) && (yPos > y1) && (yPos < y2))
       {returnValue = true;}

   // H3. RETURN returnValue.
   return returnValue;
}
// I. AUDIO EXTENSION TYPE function.
function audioExtensionType(audioElement)
{
   // I1. INITIALIZE return type.
   var returnType = "";

   // I2. TYPE test and setting.
   if (audioElement.canPlayType("audio/wav") == "probably"){returnType = "wav";}
   if (audioElement.canPlayType("audio/ogg") == "probably"){returnType = "ogg";}
   if (audioElement.canPlayType("audio/mp3") == "probably"){returnType = "mp3";}
   if (audioElement.canPlayType("audio/wav") == "maybe")    {returnType = "wav";}
   if (audioElement.canPlayType("audio/ogg") == "maybe")    {returnType = "ogg";}
   if (audioElement.canPlayType("audio/mp3") == "maybe")    {returnType = "mp3";}

   // I3. RETURN type.
   return returnType;
}
</script> </head> <body> <div>
```

```
<!-- J. CANVAS elements  -->
<canvas id    = "canvasImage"
        width = "300"  height = "500"
        style = "border:2px solid black;  position:absolute;
                 left:auto; top:auto; z-index: 1">
</canvas>
<canvas id    = "canvasText"
        width = "300"  height = "500"
        style = "border:2px solid black;  position:absolute;
                 left:auto; top:auto; z-index: 2">
Your browser doesn't currently support HTML5 Canvas.
</canvas>
</div>
<!-- K. AUDIO element  -->
<div    id=audio1>
<audio  id="audio2" controls autoplay loop>
<source src="http://marketimpacts.com/storage/WaterLapping_02.mp3">
<source src="http://marketimpacts.com/storage/WaterLapping_02.ogg">
<source src="http://marketimpacts.com/storage/WaterLapping_02.wav">
Your browser doesn't currently support the audio element.
</audio> </div> </body> </html>
```

Creating Audio Recordings

Creating great audio is by itself a big topic. Audio can vary from basic recordings made with handheld devices to sophisticated recordings made in studios with rooms full of high-priced equipment. I've done both, and either end of the spectrum can produce good results. Covering all the ins and outs of audio recording is beyond the scope of this book, but you can check out *Home Recording For Musicians For Dummies* and *PC Recording Studios For Dummies,* both written by Jeff Strong (Wiley). In the following sections, I give you a starter guide to creating audio recordings.

Recording or downloading audio

You can acquire or create recordings in several different ways:

- **Digital recorder:** It doesn't have to be a digital device, but creating a digital file while recording makes a better quality recording. It's also easier to access than an analog file.

- **Desktop sound recorder app:** Use a built-in sound-recording application, or download one for your desktop computer. One open source recording application is at

    http://audacity.sourceforge.net

🖋 **Smartphone sound recorder app:** Download a sound recorder app for your smartphone and use it to create digitally recorded sounds. To transfer the recorded files to your computer, you can then use a USB connection or e-mail the files from your smartphone:

> *iPhone:* `www.bluemic.com/mikey_digital/`
>
> *Android:* `https://play.google.com/store/apps/ details?id=com.needom.recorder`

🖋 **Soundtrack from a video recorder:** Extract the soundtrack from a recorded video, and import it into your computer, as described at `www. aoamedia.com/audioextractor.htm`.

🖋 **Downloaded recordings:** Use a website such as `www.audiosparx. com` to purchase/download audio recordings. Make sure you check the permissions for the recordings to verify you can legally include them in your application.

Creating supported audio file types

As of this writing, different browsers support different audio file types. Three major types supported include `mp3`, `ogg`, and `wav`. To make sure that your application will function in any of the major browsers, include an audio file for each audio recording for each of these supported file types.

To create supported file types, follow these steps:

1. **Create copies of your recordings in each supported file type (`mp3`, `ogg`, and `wav`).**

   Use software such as `www.audacity.sourceforge.net` to create the alternative file types from your original recording.

2. **Upload your audio files to a folder on a server.**

   Usually the server used is the one hosting the website containing your application.

To track the latest browser audio file support status, see

`http://en.wikipedia.org/wiki/HTML5_Audio`

Controlling Audio Recordings

When included in your Canvas application, each audio recording has a number of properties that can be accessed and modified. By manipulating these properties with HTML, JavaScript, and onscreen player controls, you can control audio:

✏ **Files:** File source locations on a server

✏ **Player:** Whether the player controls are visible and their status

✏ **Playback:** Playback volume, muting, pause, play, and loop control

As shown in Figure 10-2, a number of entities (applications, users, browsers) affect audio, and there's a lot of communication (events, attributes, functions, interactions) back and forth between these entities. Reference Figure 10-2 as you read through this chapter for help in understanding this flow of activity and information.

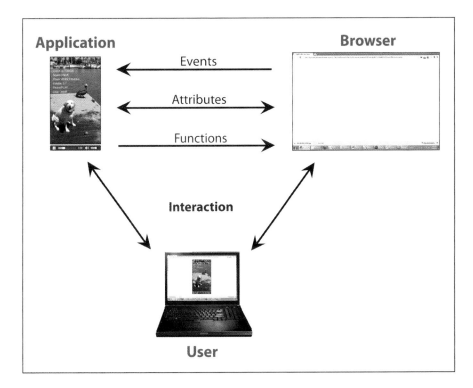

Figure 10-2: Controlling audio recordings.

Audio attributes

The attributes of an audio recording describe aspects of the audio files, player, and playback.

Table 10-1 lists the most commonly used audio attributes and indicates whether they can be accessed via HTML and/or JavaScript.

For a more complete list, visit www.w3.org/TR/webaudio/#AudioParam.

Table 10-1	Accessing Commonly Used Audio Attributes		
Attribute	*HTML*	*JavaScript*	*What It Specifies*
autoplay	autoplay	true, false	That the audio will start playing as soon as it is ready
controls	controls	true, false	That audio controls should be displayed
duration		Floating-point number	The length of the audio recording in seconds
ended		true, false	Whether the playback has completed
id	"name"		The name used to reference the audio element
loop	loop	true, false	That the audio will continually restart when it finishes
muted	muted	true, false	Whether the sound of the audio should be off (muted)
paused		true, false	Whether the sound should be temporarily stopped
preload	auto, metadata, none	auto, metadata, none	How the audio should be loaded when the web page containing it loads
src	"URL"	"URL"	The location of the audio file using a character string
volume		Floating-point number	The level of sound between 0 and 1 (for example, .5)

To access or manipulate audio attributes, or both, follow these steps:

1. **Set the initial audio attributes by using the parameters of the `<audio>` tag.**

For more on the `<audio>` tag, see the section "Defining audio elements using HTML tags," later in this chapter.

Here's an example of setting the initial audio attributes in code section K of Listing 10-1:

```
<audio id="audio2" controls autoplay loop>
```

2. **Test the value of an attribute in JavaScript by referencing the associated audio element.**

   Audio elements are used by the browser to store your audio attributes. (For more on using JavaScript to manipulate audio elements, see "Defining audio elements with JavaScript code," later in this chapter.) To access the value of an attribute, append the attribute name to the appropriate audio element with dot syntax (separating the attribute and value with a period), as in this example of accessing the muted attribute using JavaScript from code section D4:

   ```
   if(audio2EL.muted)
   ```

3. **Change the value of a property in JavaScript using an assignment statement.**

   To change the value of an attribute using JavaScript, append the attribute name to the appropriate audio element with dot syntax and use an assignment operator with the new value, as in this example of setting the muted property from code section C6 of Listing 10-1:

   ```
   audio2EL.muted = false;
   ```

4. **Set the `src` attribute using the `setAttribute()` function.**

   As of this writing, the `setAttribute()` function is only working properly on all browsers for setting the `src` attribute. Conversely, setting the `src` attribute using the technique in Step 3 is also not working properly. Therefore, use the `setAttribute()` function to set the `src` attribute and the method in Step 3 to set the other attributes. Here's an example from code section C5 using the `setAttribute()` function:

   ```
   audio3EL.setAttribute("src",server+pelicanAudFile+"."+audioType);
   ```

Audio functions

Browsers have several built-in standard audio functions that return information or cause an action with your audio file or player.

Table 10-2 lists commonly used audio functions.

Table 10-2		Commonly Used Audio Functions	
Function	*Parameter*	*Return*	*What It Does*
`canPlayType()`	File MIME type	`maybe`, `probably`, `" "`	Determines whether a given type of audio file is supported by the browser
`load()`	none	none	Specifies that the audio start playing as soon as it's ready
`pause()`	none	none	Pauses the playback
`play()`	none	none	Starts playing the audio file

To use an audio function, use dot syntax to append the function to the name of the appropriate audio element. Here's an example to start playing audio from D18 of Listing 10-1:

```
audio3EL.play();
```

Audio events

Audio events are triggered by circumstances related to the audio file and audio player. When the device operating system and browser detect these circumstances, event handlers look for application functions that have been registered via JavaScript as callback functions for the given event. Control is then passed to any registered callback functions.

Table 10-3 lists commonly referenced audio events.

Table 10-3	Commonly Used Audio Events
This Event Type . . .	*. . . Is Dispatched When This Happens*
`canplay`	The audio can start playing but might be interrupted by buffering.
`canplaythrough`	The audio can be played to the end without having to pause for buffering.
`ended`	Playback has stopped because the end of the file has been reached.
`error`	An error has occurred while accessing the audio file.
`pause`	Playback has been paused.

This Event Type . . .	. . . Is Dispatched When This Happens
play	The play() function has been initiated, or the auto-play attribute has caused playback to begin.
playing	Playback has started. The timing of this event may differ from the play event because of file load delays.
volumechange	Either the volume attribute or the muted attribute has changed.

Each event type has a browser event handler. The name of the event handler is created by appending *on* to the front of the type. For example, the event handler for pause is onpause.

To detect and respond to events such as those listed in Table 10-3, follow these steps:

1. **Define a function in your application that will be called when a given event takes place.**

   Append the event handler to the audio element using dot syntax, and then assign this combination to your callback function. Here's an example for handling a pause event from code section C11 of Listing 10-1:

   ```
   audio2EL.onpause = function () { . . . }
   ```

2. **Respond when the callback is triggered.**

   Within the function called, take the appropriate action, as in this example for handling a pause event, also from code section C11:

   ```
   {pauseText=pauseText2;  textDisplay()}
   ```

Defining Audio Elements

Audio elements act as an intermediary between your HTML/JavaScript code and audio recordings. An audio element is a component of an HTML document, which describes the structure of the web page containing your Canvas application using the Document Object Model (DOM) conventions.

Defining audio elements using HTML tags

Defining audio elements using HTML will cause the audio player to display on the web page if the controls parameter is included in the <audio> tag settings. You can include all the information necessary in your HTML to play and control audio. You can use JavaScript code to gain greater control over HTML tag–defined audio. For example, in the Listing 10-1 application, the user can control the background sound of water with the audio player defined in HTML or with the Canvas area text controls.

To define audio elements using HTML tags, follow these steps:

1. **Define an HTML5 `<audio>` tag enclosed in a `<div>` for the audio recording you're associating with an audio player (such as the water background in Listing 10-1).**

   The `<div>` enables you to control where the player will be placed on the web page relative to the Canvas. The `<audio>` tag defines the initial player settings, source files for the audio recording, and a message that will be displayed if the audio element isn't supported by the user's browser. Include an audio recording for each of the supported file types: mp3, ogg, and wav.

   If you're going to dynamically load an audio recording via JavaScript code (such as the animal sounds in Listing 10-1), you don't need to define an `<audio>` or `<div>` tag, as shown in this step.

   The code to define `<audio>` and `<div>` elements is shown in code section K of Listing 10-1:

```
<div    id= audio1>
<audio id="audio2" controls autoplay loop>
        <source src="http://marketimpacts.com/storage/WaterLapping_02.mp3">
        <source src="http://marketimpacts.com/storage/WaterLapping_02.ogg">
        <source src="http://marketimpacts.com/storage/WaterLapping_02.wav">
    Your browser doesn't support the audio element.
    </audio>
    </div>
```

2. **Use a `<style>` tag to control where the audio player is placed on the web page.**

   The ID #audio1 refers to the `<audio>` element, and the ID #audio2 refers to the `<div>` element defined in Step 1. The following sample code, located in code section A of Listing 10-1, places the audio player below the Canvas area using the margin-top parameter:

```
<style    type="text/css"    media="screen">
#audio1 {display: inline;
float: left; margin-top: 510px;
width: 304px;}
#audio2 {width:    304px;}
</style>
```

3. **Using the `getElementById()` function, retrieve the audio element that you defined in Step 1.**

   Here's an example in code section C2 of Listing 10-1:

```
audio2EL = document.getElementById("audio2");
```

4. **Initialize settings for the audio element and player.**

   Here's an example in code section C6 of Listing 10-1:

   ```
   volumeLevel      = volumeInit;
   audio2EL.volume = volumeLevel;
   audio2EL.muted  = false;
   audio2EL.paused = false;
   audio2EL.loop   = true;
   audio2EL.play();
   ```

Defining audio elements with JavaScript code

Defining audio elements using JavaScript code is particularly useful for play-ing audio as a result of dynamic events such as:

- ✒ **Object interactions:** For example, colliding and exploding objects

- ✒ **User interactions:** For example, in response to user clicks and touches

To define audio elements using JavaScript code, follow these steps:

1. **Define audio recording variables for server names and filenames.**

   See code section B8 of Listing 10-1:

   ```
   var server       = "http://marketimpacts.com/storage/";
   var dogAudFile   = "Dog";
   var pelicanAudFile = "Pelican";
   ```

2. **Create audio elements using the `createElement("audio")` function.**

   Create elements as shown in code section C3:

   ```
   audio3EL = document.createElement("audio");
   audio4EL = document.createElement("audio");
   ```

3. **Determine the file type supported by the user's browser:**

   Using the `canPlayType()` function, test the `audioElement` parameter for each type of audio and return the appropriate result.

   Here is a sample from code sections C4 and I of Listing 10-1:

   ```
   audioType = audioExtensionType(audio3EL);

   function audioExtensionType(audioElement)
   {
      var returnType = "";
      if(audioElement.canPlayType("audio/wav")=="probably")
        {returnType = "wav";}
      if(audioElement.canPlayType("audio/wav")=="maybe")
        {returnType = "wav";}
      return returnType;

      . . .

   }
   ```

4. **Using the `setAttribute()` function, set the source of each file location on the server.**

   Here's an example from code section C5 in Listing 10-1:

   ```
   audio3EL.setAttribute("src",
   server + pelicanAudFile + "." + audioType);
   audio4EL.setAttribute("src",
   server + dogAudFile    + "." + audioType);
   ```

5. **Initialize settings for audio elements.**

   See code section C6:

   ```
   audio3EL.volume = volumeDog;
   audio4EL.volume = volumePelican;
   ```

Responding to User Interaction

Users can interact with your application to affect audio playback in two ways: through the Canvas area or audio player. To keep your Canvas display in sync with the audio player (if you're using one), when one is altered, change the other. In the application in Listing 10-1, this means keeping the audio player for the background sound in sync with Canvas text.

Understanding this section of code requires some non-linear thinking. Responding to user interaction is very event driven — the user is clicking and touching, and your code is responding.

Normally, you probably wouldn't have a complete set of controls in both the Canvas area and a visible audio player. I did this in the Listing 10-1 application to demonstrate the range of audio capabilities.

Responding to Canvas area interaction

To respond to Canvas area interaction, define listeners for mouse and touch events and take the appropriate actions when your callback function is given control. Follow these steps:

1. **Define listeners for user interaction events. Use the `addEvent Listener()` function to specify the function to be called when a user event take place.**

   Listeners are your "lookouts" for Canvas user interaction. This is how you know when the user clicks or touches your Canvas.

   In Listing 10-1, the `clickTouch()` function (explained in Step 2) is specified for mouse and touch events in code section C7:

```
canvasTX.addEventListener("mousedown",  clickTouch, false);
canvasTX.addEventListener("touchstart", clickTouch, false);
cánvasTX.addEventListener("touchmove",  clickTouch, false);
canvasTX.addEventListener("touchend",   clickTouch, false);
```

2. **Define the callback function to be invoked when an event listener is triggered.**

   Within that callback function, first determine the position on the Canvas of the click/touch by using the clickTouchEvent() function (explained in Step 3). Then handle each type of event per Steps 4 and 5. In Listing 10-1, the callback function is defined in code section D:

```
function clickTouch(event)
{
    // Determine position on Canvas of click/touch.
    clickTouchEvent(event);

    // Code to handle each control selection.
}
```

3. **Create a function that will determine the *x* and *y* coordinate positions of a click or touch event.**

   See code section E of Listing 10-1:

```
function clickTouchEvent(event)
{
    // E1. BROWSERS except Firefox.
    if (event.x != undefined && event.y != undefined)
    {
        xPos = event.x;
        yPos = event.y;
    }

    // E2. FIREFOX.
    else
    {
        xPos = event.clientX + document.body.scrollLeft +
                    document.documentElement.scrollLeft;
        yPos = event.clientY + document.body.scrollTop +
                    document.documentElement.scrollTop;
    }
    // E3. CURSOR position.
    xPos -= canvasTX.offsetLeft;
    yPos -= canvasTX.offsetTop;
}
```

4. **Using the positionTest() function (explained in Step 6), determine which audio controls should be altered; then make changes using the appropriate audio function.**

Refer to code sections D2–D17 in Listing 10-1. Here is one example from D2–D4:

```
if(positionTest(1))
{
    audio2EL.muted =    !audio2EL.muted;
    if(audio2EL.muted) {soundText = soundText2}
    else               {soundText = soundText1}
    textDisplay();
}
```

This code example tests for selection of the Sound On/Off control and, if selected, changes the muted attribute of the audio element and alters the display text to the appropriate setting.

5. **Play the sound associated with an object.**

   This is where you trigger sounds that are typically not associated with an audio player. You might want to play sounds of colliding objects or, as in the Listing 10-1 application, trigger the sound associated with an image.

   Using the `objectTest()` function (explained in Step 7), determine which object has been selected by the user; then make changes using the appropriate audio function, as shown in code sections D18–19. Here is an example from D18 of my very wet dog Daisy barking for more attention:

   ```
   if(objectTest(dogX1, dogX2, dogY1, dogY2))
   {audio4EL.play();}
   ```

6. **Test to see whether the *x* and *y* coordinate positions selected on the Canvas by the user are within a given `position` in the audio controls area of the Canvas. Return a value of `true` or `false` depending on the results.**

   See code section G in Listing 10-1:

   ```
   function positionTest(position)
   {
       var returnValue = false;
       if (
           (xPos > (menuX)) &&
           (xPos < (menuX + menuWidth)) &&
           (yPos > (menuY + (position * menuHeight) - (menuHeight/2))) &&
           (yPos < (menuY + (position * menuHeight) + (menuHeight/4)))
           )
           {returnValue = true;}
       return returnValue;
   }
   ```

7. **Test to see whether the *x* and *y* coordinate positions selected on the Canvas by the user are within a rectangular area of the Canvas defined by coordinate parameters `x1`, `x2`, `y1`, and `y2`. Return `true` or `false` depending on the results.**

You can see an example in code section H of Listing 10-1:

```
function objectTest(x1, x2, y1, y2)
{
   var returnValue = false;
   if ((xPos > x1) && (xPos < x2) &&
(yPos > y1) && (yPos < y2))
      {returnValue = true;}
   return returnValue;
}
```

8. **Using a call to the `textDisplay()` function (defined in Step 9), change the text display after values have changed.**

   In the example, this is done in code sections C10, C11, D4, D7, D10, D12, and D16:

   ```
   textDisplay();
   ```

9. **Display the text that defines the status of the audio player settings.**

   This text is also used to define the areas for user interaction to change player settings.

   You can also control player settings with button images. See Listing 11-1, in Chapter 11, for an example of using button control images.

   In Listing 10-1, the text display function is defined in code section F:

   ```
   function textDisplay()
   {
      // F1. CLEAR canvas.
      contextTX.clearRect(0, 0, canvasTX.width, canvasTX.height);

      // F2. ATTRIBUTES.
      contextTX.font      = textFont;
      contextTX.fillStyle = textColor;

      // F3. FIX precision of volume.
      var volumeLev = volumeLevel.toFixed(1);

      // F4. DISPLAY text.
      contextTX.fillText(promptText, menuX, promptY);
      contextTX.fillText(soundText,  menuX, soundY );
      contextTX.fillText(playerText, menuX, playerY);
      contextTX.fillText(volumeText, menuX, volumeY);
      contextTX.fillText(pauseText,  menuX, pauseY );
      contextTX.fillText(loopText,   menuX, loopY  );
      contextTX.fillText(volumeLev,  menuX + volumeX, volumeY);
   }
   ```

Responding to audio player interaction

To be able to respond to changes a user makes in an audio player, you must define a callback function that will gain control when specific player changes are made. When a user changes settings in the audio player, reflect these changes in the appropriate settings within your application.

To respond to audio player interaction, follow these steps:

1. **For each audio player function you're tracking in your application, define a listener that will be called when the user changes the control.**

   Here's an example from code section C11 of Listing 10-1:

   ```
   audio2EL.onpause = function () { . . . }
   ```

2. **Change variables tracking the audio player value.**

   Within the function defined in Step 1, change the appropriate variable, as in this example from code section C11 in Listing 10-1:

   ```
   pauseText = pauseText1;
   ```

3. **Change the display text.**

   Using a call to the textDisplay() function defined in code section F, change the custom controls display.

   In Listing 10-1, this is done in code sections C10, C11, D4, D7, D10, D12, and D16:

   ```
   textDisplay();
   ```

Defining Other Application Components

You can combine audio with other Canvas capabilities. In the Listing 10-1 example, two Canvas areas are defined:

- **Background image:** Creates a backdrop for demonstrating audio capabilities
- **Text display:** Provides custom controls for audio playback

Use the following steps to define these Canvases:

1. **Upload your image file to a folder on a server.**

   In the sample application in Listing 10-1, this is a background image. Usually the server used is the one hosting the website containing your application.

2. Define variables and load functions for images.

In the sample application, the background image variable is defined in code section B9 and is drawn after it is loaded in code section C9:

```
var backgroundImage    = new Image();
backgroundImage.src    = server + backgroundFile +
backgroundType;
backgroundImage.onload = function()
   {contextIM.drawImage(backgroundImage, 0, 0,
                       canvasIM.width, canvasIM.height);}
```

3. Define the function that contains the main sequence of code that's called when the web page is loaded.

See code section C of Listing 10-1:

```
window.onload = function() { . . . }
```

4. Define Canvas elements.

In the code section J of Listing 10-1, there is a Canvas for the background image and a Canvas for the text:

```
<canvas id    = "canvasImage"
width = "300"  height = "500"
       style = "border:2px solid black; position:absolute;
                 left:auto;
top:auto; z-index: 1">
</canvas>
<canvas id    = "canvasText"
width = "300"  height = "500"
       style = "border:2px solid black; position:absolute;
                 left:auto; top:auto; z-index: 2">
Your browser doesn't currently support HTML5 Canvas.
</canvas>
```

5. Define Canvas variables and contexts.

In Listing 10-1, these variables and contexts are defined in code section C1:

```
canvasIM   = document.getElementById("canvasImage");
contextIM  = canvasIM.getContext("2d");
canvasTX   = document.getElementById("canvasText");
contextTX  = canvasTX.getContext("2d");
```

Part IV
Developing More Complex Applications

The 5th Wave   By Rich Tennant

"You know, I've asked you a dozen times NOT to animate the torches on our Web site."

In this part . . .

In Part IV, you discover how to combine the fundamentals from the first three parts with advanced techniques to create more complex, enhanced applications, such as a Canvas fireworks display. You also find out how to put your personal stamp of creativity on your Canvas application.

11

Grabbing Attention with Video

In This Chapter

- Configuring Canvas spaces to include video
- Defining video elements
- Creating custom playback controls
- Responding to user interaction

*I*t's no secret — video is a powerful medium. According to Google, 72 hours of video are presently being uploaded to YouTube every *minute.* Three billion hours of YouTube video are watched each month. And when a video goes viral, it can spread around the world at an astonishing rate, reaching tens of millions of viewers in just days.

HTML5 video builds on this success. Like HTML5 audio (described in Chapter 10), HTML5 video is a big advance over HTML4. Playing video doesn't require the use of a plug-in utility; player capabilities are built into the browser. The inclusion of video in Canvas enables you to manipulate video images or display them without modification.

In this chapter, you find out how to blend video with the Canvas capabilities described in previous chapters, such as objects, images, and user interaction.

Including Video in Your Application

You can implement video in your Canvas applications in two ways:

- **Using HTML tags:** You define the video file and player using HTML tags. Users can control video playback by using a video player displayed with your Canvas.

- **Using JavaScript code:** Video is triggered by events and dynamically loaded within your application. You can generate video as a result of application events such as colliding objects or the user clicking an object. Your JavaScript code controls playback.

You can allow users to control video playback in two ways:

- **Using a video player:** A video player with standard controls for playback position and pause
- **Using custom controls:** Custom controls integrated with your Canvas graphics

The application shown in Figure 11-1 and defined in Listing 11-1 demonstrates using custom controls via JavaScript code.

As of this writing, there are some inconsistencies across browsers in video implementation. I'm finding that automatic video replay isn't working in the Opera browser and video playback can be a bit choppy in Internet Explorer. These issues should abate as HTML5 standards and implementations move forward.

Figure 11-1: Using video in an application.

Listing 11-1:   Using Video in an Application

```
<!DOCTYPE HTML> <html> <head> <script>

// A. VARIABLES.

   // A1. ANIMATION.
   var xPos          = 0;                var yPos          = 0;
   var interval      = 15;
   var startAngle    = (Math.PI/180)*0;
   var endAngle      = (Math.PI/180)*360;

   // A2. AUDIO.
   var volumeX       = 60;               var volumeOffsetX = 21;
   var volumeInit    = .7;               var volumeOffsetY = 30;
   var volumeLevel   = 0;                var volumeIncr    = .1;

   // A3. VIDEO.
   var videoWidth    = 250;              var videoHeight   = 200;
   var videoX        = 335;              var videoY        = 20;
   var video1EL;                         var video1Type;

   // A4. FILES.
   var server        = "http://marketimpacts.com/storage/";
   var video         = "DaisyDiving";
   var backgroundFile = "DaisyWaiting";
   var soundOffFile  = "PlayerSoundOff";
   var soundOnFile   = "PlayerSoundOn";
   var pauseFile     = "PlayerPause";
   var playFile      = "PlayerPlay";
   var repeatOnFile  = "PlayerRepeatOn";
   var repeatOffFile = "PlayerRepeatOff";
   var soundLevelFile = "PlayerSoundLevel";
   var buttonFileType = ".png";
   var backgroundType = ".jpg";

   // A5. IMAGES.
   var backgroundImage = new Image();    var soundOffImage   = new Image();
   var soundOnImage  = new Image();      var pauseImage      = new Image();
   var playImage     = new Image();      var repeatOnImage   = new Image();
   var repeatOffImage = new Image();     var soundLevelImage = new Image();

   // A6. BUTTONS.
   var playButton    = new Image();      var repeatButton    = new Image();
   var soundButton   = new Image();      var levelButton     = new Image();
   var buttonsX      = 360;              var buttonsY        = 375;
   var buttonInit    = false;            var buttonLoad      = false;
   var buttonCount   = 0;                var buttonQuant     = 7;
   var buttonWidth   = 50;               var buttonHeight    = 50;
   var textFont      = "12pt arial";     var textColor       = "black";
```

(continued)

Listing 11-1 *(continued)*

```
// B. WINDOW LOAD function.
window.onload = function()
{
    // B1. CANVAS definition standard variables.
    canvasIM = document.getElementById("canvasImage");
    contextIM = canvasIM.getContext("2d");
    canvasVI = document.getElementById("canvasVideo");
    contextVI = canvasVI.getContext("2d");
    canvasBT = document.getElementById("canvasButtons");
    contextBT = canvasBT.getContext("2d");

    // B2. CREATE video elements.
    video1EL = document.createElement("video");

    // B3. VIDEO FILE setup.
    videoType = videoExtensionType(video1EL);
    video1EL.setAttribute("src", server + video + "." + videoType);
    video1EL.addEventListener("canplaythrough", videoDisplay, false);

    // B4. SETTINGS initialization.
    volumeLevel    = volumeInit;   video1EL.volume = volumeLevel;
    video1EL.muted = false;        video1EL.paused = false;
    video1EL.loop  = true;

    // B5. GRADIENT for halo around video.
    video1Gradient = contextVI.createRadialGradient(
                    videoWidth/2, videoHeight/2, .7*videoHeight,
                    videoWidth/2, videoHeight/2, 0);
    video1Gradient.addColorStop( 0, "white"      );
    video1Gradient.addColorStop(.05, "white"      );
    video1Gradient.addColorStop(.20, "white"      );
    video1Gradient.addColorStop(.50, "transparent");
    video1Gradient.addColorStop( 1, "transparent");

    // B6. TRANSLATE video canvas to video location.
    contextVI.translate(videoX, videoY);

    // B7. PLAY video.
    video1EL.play();

    // B8. MOUSE/TOUCH listeners.
    canvasBT.addEventListener("mousedown",  clickTouch, false);
    canvasBT.addEventListener("touchstart", clickTouch, false);
    canvasBT.addEventListener("touchmove",  clickTouch, false);
    canvasBT.addEventListener("touchend",   clickTouch, false);

    // B9. BACKGROUND IMAGE.
    backgroundImage.src    = server + backgroundFile + backgroundType;
    backgroundImage.onload = function()
    {contextIM.drawImage(backgroundImage, 0, 0, canvasIM.width, canvasIM.height)}
```

```
      // B10. BUTTON/TEXT display.
      buttonTextDisplay();

      // B11. BUTTON SOURCES.
      soundOffImage.src     = server + soundOffFile   + buttonFileType;
      soundOnImage.src      = server + soundOnFile    + buttonFileType;
      pauseImage.src        = server + pauseFile      + buttonFileType;
      playImage.src         = server + playFile       + buttonFileType;
      repeatOnImage.src     = server + repeatOnFile   + buttonFileType;
      repeatOffImage.src    = server + repeatOffFile  + buttonFileType;
      soundLevelImage.src   = server + soundLevelFile + buttonFileType;

      // B12. BUTTON LOAD functions.
      soundOffImage.onload   = function() {buttonIncrement()}
      soundOnImage.onload    = function() {buttonIncrement()}
      pauseImage.onload      = function() {buttonIncrement()}
      playImage.onload       = function() {buttonIncrement()}
      repeatOnImage.onload   = function() {buttonIncrement()}
      repeatOffImage.onload  = function() {buttonIncrement()}
      soundLevelImage.onload = function() {buttonIncrement()}
}
// C. BUTTON INCREMENT function.
function buttonIncrement()
{
      // C1. INCREMENT.
      buttonCount++;

      // C2. TEST for all buttons loaded.
      if(buttonCount = buttonQuant)
      {
          // C3. SET buttons loaded variable.
          buttonLoad = true;

          // C4. DISPLAY buttons and text.
          buttonTextDisplay();
      }
}
// D. VIDEO DISPLAY function.
function videoDisplay()
{
      // D1. CLIPPING circle around video.
      contextVI.beginPath();
      contextVI.arc(videoWidth/2, videoHeight/2, videoHeight/2,
                    startAngle, endAngle, false);
      contextVI.fill();
      contextVI.clip();

      // D2. ANIMATION loop function.
      (function animLoop()
      {
          // D3. REQUEST ANIMATION FRAME
          requestAnimFrame(animLoop);
```

(continued)

Listing 11-1 *(continued)*

```
        // D4. DRAW video.
        drawVideo();
    }
    ) ();
}
// E. DRAW VIDEO function.
function drawVideo()
{
    // E1. IMAGE drawing of video frame.
    contextVI.drawImage(video1EL, 0, 0, videoWidth, videoHeight);

    // E2. GRADIENT CIRCLE for halo around video.
    contextVI.fillStyle = video1Gradient;
    contextVI.beginPath();
    contextVI.arc(videoWidth/2, videoHeight/2, videoHeight,
                  startAngle, endAngle, false);
    contextVI.fill();

    // E3. BUTTON load check.
    if(buttonLoad && !buttonInit)
    {
        // E4. INITIALIZE buttons when all have loaded.
        playButton   = pauseImage;
        repeatButton = repeatOnImage;
        soundButton  = soundOnImage;
        levelButton  = soundLevelImage;

        // E5. BUTTON LOAD status.
        buttonInit   = true;

        // E6. DRAW buttons.
        buttonTextDisplay();
    }
}
// F. CLICK/TOUCH function.
function clickTouch(event)
{
    // F1. COORDINATES retrieval.
    clickTouchEvent(event);

    // F2. SOUND on/off.
    if(positionTest(2))
    {
        // F3. STATUS change.
        video1EL.muted =      !video1EL.muted;

        // F4. BUTTON change.
        if(video1EL.muted)    {soundButton = soundOffImage}
        else                  {soundButton = soundOnImage }
        buttonTextDisplay();
    }
```

```
      // F5. REPEAT on/off.
   if(positionTest(1))
   {
      // F6. STATUS change.
      video1EL.loop =        !video1EL.loop;

      // F7. BUTTON change.
      if(video1EL.loop)      {repeatButton = repeatOnImage;  video1EL.play()}
      else                   {repeatButton = repeatOffImage};
      buttonTextDisplay();
   }
   // F8. PAUSE on/off.
   if(positionTest(0))
   {
      // F9. STATUS change & BUTTON change.
      if(video1EL.paused)    {video1EL.play();  playButton = pauseImage}
      else                   {video1EL.pause(); playButton = playImage }
      buttonTextDisplay();
   }
   // F10. VOLUME change.
   if(positionTest(3))
   {
      // F11. INCREMENT volume level.
      volumeLevel += volumeIncr;

      // F12. LIMIT.
      if(volumeLevel > 1.01){volumeLevel = 0}

      // F13. TEXT display.
      buttonTextDisplay();

      // F14. PLAYER volume setting.
      video1EL.volume = volumeLevel;
   }
}
// G. CLICK/TOUCH EVENT function.
function clickTouchEvent(event)
{
   // G1. BROWSERS except Firefox.
   if (event.x != undefined && event.y != undefined)
      {xPos = event.x;   yPos = event.y;}

   // G2. FIREFOX.
   else
   {  xPos = event.clientX + document.body.scrollLeft +
                  document.documentElement.scrollLeft;
      yPos = event.clientY + document.body.scrollTop +
                  document.documentElement.scrollTop;
   }
   // G3. CURSOR position.
   xPos -= canvasBT.offsetLeft;  yPos -= canvasBT.offsetTop;
}
```

(continued)

Listing 11-1 *(continued)*

```
// H. BUTTON/TEXT DISPLAY function.
function buttonTextDisplay()
{
    // H1. CLEAR canvas.
    contextBT.clearRect(0, 0, canvasBT.width, canvasBT.height);

    // H2. BUTTON LOAD check.
    if(buttonLoad)
    {
        // H3. BUTTON DISPLAY.
        contextBT.drawImage(playButton,   buttonsX + (buttonWidth * 0),
                            buttonsY, buttonWidth, buttonHeight);
        contextBT.drawImage(repeatButton, buttonsX + (buttonWidth * 1),
                            buttonsY, buttonWidth, buttonHeight);
        contextBT.drawImage(soundButton,  buttonsX + (buttonWidth * 2),
                            buttonsY, buttonWidth, buttonHeight);
        contextBT.drawImage(levelButton,  buttonsX + (buttonWidth * 3),
                            buttonsY, buttonWidth, buttonHeight);
    }
    // H4. VOLUME.
    contextBT.font      = textFont;
    contextBT.fillStyle = textColor;
    var volumeLev       = volumeLevel.toFixed(1);
    contextBT.fillText( volumeLev, buttonsX + volumeOffsetX + (buttonWidth * 3),
                                   buttonsY + volumeOffsetY);
}
// I. POSITION TEST function.
function positionTest(position)
{
    // I1. INITIALIZE return value to false.
    var returnValue = false;

    // I2. TEST position.
    if (
        (yPos > (buttonsY)) &&
        (yPos < (buttonsY + buttonHeight)) &&
        (xPos > (buttonsX + (position * buttonWidth))) &&
        (xPos < (buttonsX + (position * buttonWidth) + buttonWidth))
        )
        {returnValue = true;}

    // I3. RETURN returnValue.
    return returnValue;
}
// J. VIDEO EXTENSION TYPE function.
function videoExtensionType(videoElement)
{
    // J1. INITIALIZE return type.
    var returnType = "";
```

```
        // J2. TYPE test and setting.
        if (videoElement.canPlayType("video/webm" )=="probably"){returnType = "webm"}
        if (videoElement.canPlayType("video/ogg"  )=="probably"){returnType = "ogg" }
        if (videoElement.canPlayType("video/mp4"  )=="probably"){returnType = "mp4" }
        if (videoElement.canPlayType("video/webm" )=="maybe"    ){returnType = "webm"}
        if (videoElement.canPlayType("video/ogg")  =="maybe"    ){returnType = "ogg" }
        if (videoElement.canPlayType("video/mp4"  )=="maybe"    ){returnType = "mp4" }


        // J3. RETURN type.
        return returnType;
}
// K. REQUEST ANIMATION FRAME function.
    window.requestAnimFrame = (function()
    {
        // K1. RETURN function available.
        return window.requestAnimationFrame        ||
                window.webkitRequestAnimationFrame  ||
                window.mozRequestAnimationFrame     ||
                window.oRequestAnimationFrame       ||
                window.msRequestAnimationFrame      ||

        // K2. FALLBACK setTimeout function.
        function(callback) {window.setTimeout(callback, interval)};
    })();
</script> </head> <body> <div>

<!-- L. CANVAS elements -->
<canvas id     = "canvasImage"  width  = "600"  height = "450"
        style  = "border:2px solid black;  position:absolute;
                    left:auto; top:auto; z-index: 1">
</canvas>
<canvas id     = "canvasVideo"  width  = "600"  height = "450"
        style  = "border:2px solid black;  position:absolute;
                    left:auto; top:auto;  z-index: 2">
</canvas>
<canvas id     = "canvasButtons"  width  = "600"  height = "450"
        style  = "border:2px solid black;  position:absolute;
                    left:auto; top:auto; z-index: 3">
You're browser doesn't currently support HTML5 Canvas.
</canvas> </div> </body> </html>
```

Creating Video Recordings

Making your own video is a lot easier now that video recorders are included with many smartphone models. This is one big reason behind the explosion in uploads to YouTube and other video sites.

Use the information in the following section as a starter guide to creating your video recordings.

Recording or downloading your video

You can create or acquire videos in a number of ways:

- **Smartphone:** Many smartphones have built-in apps that you can use to create your videos. You can transfer the recorded files via a USB connection to your computer or e-mail smaller files from your phone to your PC.

- **Camcorder:** Camcorders generally produce better video quality than smartphones. Many camcorder models have motion stabilization and other advanced features and offer a USB connection to transfer videos to your computer.

- **Desktop video recording application:** Use a built-in video recording application or download one for your desktop computer. One video recording option is available at www.innoheim.com/camverce.php.

- **Downloaded videos:** Use a website such as www.gettyimages.com/footage to purchase and download videos. Make sure you check the permissions for the recordings to verify you can legally include them in your application.

Creating supported video file types

As of this writing, different browsers support different video file types. Three major types supported include mp4, ogg, and webm. To make sure that your application will function in any of the major browsers, include a video file for each of the supported file types.

To track the latest browser video file support status, see http://en.wikipedia.org/wiki/HTML5_video#Browser_support.

To create supported file types, follow these steps:

1. **Create copies of your video recordings in each supported file type (mp4, ogg, and webm).**

   Use software such as www.mirovideoconverter.com to create the alternative file types from your original recording.

2. **Upload your video files to a folder on a server.**

   Usually, you use the server hosting the website containing your application.

Controlling Video Recordings

When included in your application, each video recording will have a number of properties that can be accessed and modified. By manipulating these properties using HTML, JavaScript, and onscreen player controls, you can control video:

✔ **Files:** File source locations on a server

✔ **Player:** Visibility, whether the player controls are visible, and their status

✔ **Playback:** Playback volume, muting, pause, play, loop control

As shown in Figure 11-2, several entities (applications, users, browsers) affect video, and there is a lot of communication (events, attributes, functions, interactions) back and forth between these entities. Reference Figure 11-2 as you read through this chapter for help in understanding this flow of activity and information.

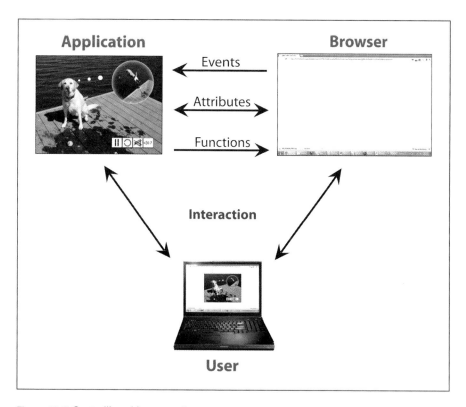

Figure 11-2: Controlling video recordings.

Video attributes

The attributes of a video recording describe aspects of the video files, player, and playback. Table 11-1 lists the most commonly used attributes and shows whether they can be accessed via HTML and/or JavaScript.

For a more complete list, see `www.w3.org/wiki/HTML/Elements/video`.

Table 11-1	Commonly Used Video Attributes and How They Can Be Accessed		
Attribute	*HTML*	*JavaScript*	*Description*
autoplay	autoplay	true, false	Specifies that the video will start playing as soon as it is ready.
controls	controls	true, false	Specifies that video controls should be displayed.
duration		Floating point number	Specifies the length of the video recording in seconds.
ended		true, false	Specifies whether the playback has completed.
id	"name"		Specifies a name used to reference the video element.
loop	loop	true, false	Specifies that the video will continually restart when it finishes.
muted	muted	true, false	Specifies whether the sound of the video should be off (muted.)
paused		true, false	Specifies whether the video should be temporarily stopped.
preload	auto, metadata, none	auto, metadata, none	Specifies how the video should be loaded when the web page containing it loads.
src	"URL"	"URL"	Specifies the location of the video file using a character string.
volume		Floating point number	Specifies the level of sound between 0 and 1 (for example, .5).

To access and/or manipulate video attributes, follow these steps:

1. **Set the initial video attributes using the parameters of the `<video>` tag.**

   ```
   <video id="video1" controls autoplay loop>
   ```

   For more on the <video> tag, see the section "Defining Video Elements," later in this chapter.

2. **Test the value of an attribute in JavaScript by referencing the associated video element.**

   Video elements are used by the browser to store your video attributes. (See the section "Defining video elements using HTML," for more on using HTML video definitions.) To access the value of an attribute, append the attribute name to the appropriate video element with dot syntax, as in this example of accessing the muted attribute using JavaScript from code section F4 of Listing 11-1:

   ```
   if(video1EL.muted)
   ```

3. **Change the value of a property in JavaScript using an assignment statement.**

   To change the value of an attribute using JavaScript, append the attribute name to the appropriate video element with dot syntax and use an assignment operator with the new value, as in this example of setting the muted property from code section F3:

   ```
   video1EL.muted = !video1EL.muted;
   ```

4. **Set the `src` attribute using the `setAttribute()` function.**

   As of this writing, the `setAttribute()` function is only working properly on all browsers for setting the `src` attribute. Setting the `src` attribute using the technique in Step 3 is also not working properly. Therefore, use the `setAttribute()` function to set the `src` attribute and the method in Step 3 to set the other attributes. Here is an example from sample code section B3 using the `setAttribute()` function:

   ```
   video1EL.setAttribute("src", server + video + "." + video1Type);
   ```

Video functions

There are a number of standard video functions built into the browser that return information or cause an action with your video file or player. Table 11-2 lists the commonly used video functions.

Table 11-2		Commonly Used Video Functions	
Function	*Parameter*	*Return*	*Description*
canPlay Type()	File MIME type	maybe, probably, " "	Determines whether a given type of video file is supported by the browser.
load()	none	none	Specifies that the video will start playing as soon as it is ready.
pause()	none	none	Pauses the playback.
play()	none	none	Starts playing the video file.

To use a video function, append the function to the name of the video element associated with the video file you want to affect using dot syntax. Here's an example to start playing video from B7 of Listing 11-1:

```
video1EL.play();
```

Video events

Video events are triggered by circumstances related to the video file and video player. When the device operating system and the browser detect these circumstances, event handlers look for application functions that have been registered via JavaScript as callback functions for the given event. Control is then passed to any registered callback functions.

Table 11-3 lists commonly used video events.

Table 11-3	Commonly Used Video Events
This Event Type . . .	*. . . Is Dispatched When This Happens*
canplay	The video can start playing but might be interrupted by buffering.
canplaythrough	The video can be played through to the end without having to pause for buffering.
ended	Playback has stopped because the end of the file has been reached.
error	An error has occurred accessing the video file.
pause	Playback has been paused.
play	The play() function has been initiated, or the autoplay attribute has initiated playback.

This Event Type . . .	. . . Is Dispatched When This Happens
playing	Playback has started. The timing of this event may differ from the play event due to file load delays.
volumechange	Either the volume attribute or the muted attribute has changed.

Each event type has a browser event handler. The name of the event handler is created by appending *on* to the front of the event type. Therefore, the event handler for pause is onpause.

To detect and respond to events such as those listed in Table 11-3, follow these steps:

1. **Register a callback function for a video element event handler.**

   Define a function in your application that is to be called when a given event takes place.

   Register a callback using the addEventListener() function, as in code section B3:

   ```
   video1EL.addEventListener("canplaythrough", videoDisplay, false);
   ```

2. **Respond when the callback is triggered.**

   Within the function called in Step 1, take the appropriate action, as in this example for handling a canplaythrough event from code section D:

   ```
   function videoDisplay() { . . . code to respond to callback }
   ```

Defining Video Elements

Video elements act as an intermediary between your HTML/JavaScript code and video recordings. A video element is a component of an HTML document, which describes the structure of the web page containing your Canvas application using the Document Object Model (DOM) conventions.

Defining elements using HTML tags

Defining video elements using HTML will cause the video player to display on the web page. You can include all the information necessary in your HTML to play and control video. And you can have further control over HTML tag–defined video with JavaScript code.

The video in Listing 11-1 is defined using JavaScript only, so you won't see HTML tags for it. If you're displaying a video within your Canvas area, as in the example application, it will be more typical to use only JavaScript.

If you do want to define video elements using HTML tags, here's the way to do it:

1. **Define an HTML5 `<video>` tag enclosed in a `<div>` for the video recording you're associating with a video player, such as the water background in Listing 11-1.**

   Here's the lowdown on the tags:

   - The `<div>` enables you to control where the player will be placed on your web page relative to your Canvas.

   - The `<video>` tag defines the initial player settings, source files for the video recording, and a message that will be displayed if the video element isn't supported by the user's browser. Include a video recording for each of the supported file types: `mp4`, `ogg`, and `webm`.

   An example of the code to define `<video>` and `<div>` elements is

   ```
   <div     id = video0>
   <video   id = "video1" controls autoplay loop>
   <source src = "http://marketimpacts.com/storage/Daisy2.mp4">
   <source src = "http://marketimpacts.com/storage/Daisy2.ogg">
   <source src = "http://marketimpacts.com/storage/Daisy2.webm">
   Your browser doesn't support the video element.
   </video>
   </div>
   ```

2. **Define the video player location on the web page. Use a `<style>` tag placed after the `<head>` tag to control where the video player is placed on the web page.**

   The ID `#video0` refers to the `<div>` element defined in Step 1. The following sample code places the video player below the Canvas area using the `margin-top` parameter:

   ```
   <style   type="text/css"  media="screen">
   #video0 {display:inline;  float:left;  margin-top:510px;  width:304px;}
   </style>
   ```

3. **Using the `getElementById()` function, retrieve the video element defined in Step 1.**

   Here's an example from Listing 11-1:

   ```
   video1EL = document.getElementById("video1");
   ```

4. **Initialize settings for the video element and player.**

   Here's an example:

   ```
   volumeLevel    = volumeInit;      video2EL.volume = volumeLevel;
   video2EL.muted = false;           video2EL.paused = false;
   video2EL.loop  = true;            video2EL.play();
   ```

Defining elements using JavaScript code

Defining video elements using JavaScript code gives you complete control over placing and manipulating your video frames on your Canvas area. In the Listing 11-1 application, I've used these capabilities to play a video inside a "thought bubble" that my dog Daisy has as she waits for me to throw her a ball. (She loves to swim, as you can see if you watch the video.) JavaScript code is used to clip the video frames to a round shape and place a circle with a gradient over the frames to render the bubble appearance.

You have access to every bit in the video frame. You can do shaping and enhancement as I've done. You can also change the bit to alter the appearance of the images, such as changing image colors.

To define video elements using JavaScript code, follow these steps:

1. **Define video recording variables for server names and filenames.**

   Here's an example from code section A4 of Listing 11-1:

   ```
   var server = "http://marketimpacts.com/storage/";
   var video  = "DaisyDiving";
   ```

2. **Create video elements using the `createElement("video")` function.**

   Create elements as shown in code section B2:

   ```
   video1EL = document.createElement("video");
   ```

3. **Determine the file type supported by the user's browser. Using the `canPlayType()` function, test the `videoElement` parameter for each type of video and return the appropriate result.**

   Here is a sample from code sections B3 and J of Listing 11-1:

   ```
   videoType = videoExtensionType(video1EL);
   . . .
   function videoExtensionType(videoElement)
   {
     var returnType = "";
     if(videoElement.canPlayType("video/mp4") == "probably")
       {returnType="webm";}
      . . .
     if(videoElement.canPlayType("video/mp4") == "maybe")
       {returnType="webm";}
      . . .
     return returnType;
   }
   ```

4. **Using the `setAttribute()` function, set the source of each video file located on the server.**

   In Listing 11-1, there's only one video file, as in code section B3:

   ```
   video1EL.setAttribute("src", server + video + "." + videoType);
   ```

5. **Initialize video element settings.**

   Initialize settings for video elements, as in code section B4:

   ```
   video1EL.volume = volumeLevel;
   ```

Using Animation to Draw Video Frames

The video doesn't play directly on the Canvas. When a video is started, the individual frame images are stored in the video element. The `drawImage()` function is then used to draw these frames on a Canvas. This multistep process gives you access to the video frames in your application. You can draw them on your Canvas without modification (as is done in Listing 11-1), or alter the pixels before drawing.

To animate your video images on a Canvas, follow the steps described in the following sections.

Starting the video

Follow these steps to tell the browser to begin playing the video and to notify your JavaScript code when play can continue without interruption:

1. **Add an event listener for the `canplaythrough` condition.**

   This event listener transfers control to the function you specify when enough of the video has loaded that it should be able to play without interruption. The `canplaythrough` event listener is added in code section B3 of Listing 11-1 specifying the `videoDisplay` callback function:

   ```
   video1EL.addEventListener("canplaythrough", videoDisplay, false);
   ```

2. **Play the video. Use the `play()` function to cause the browser to begin playing the video file and transfer control to your event listener callback function in Step 1 when enough is loaded to play the video without interruption.**

   In Listing 11-1, this code is in section B7:

   ```
   video1EL.play();
   ```

Setting up the animation loop

You found out all about animation loops in previous chapters. Here, you use an animation loop to draw frames from a video on your Canvas:

1. **Define the callback function to be executed when the video is loaded.**

   In Listing 11-1, the callback function is `videoDisplay()` in code section D:

   ```
   function videoDisplay() { . . . }
   ```

2. **Within the callback function, do any Canvas context path creation related to the video that doesn't have to be repeated during every animation frame.**

   During execution of the animation loop, you will want to do as little drawing as possible so that the video frames can be drawn fast enough to keep up with the callbacks, producing a smooth-looking video. So, before starting the animation loop, perform path creation that can be done once and not repeated for each frame. In Listing 11-1 code section D1, a clipping circle is set up around the video frames to help simulate the doggie thought bubble:

   ```
   contextVI.beginPath();
   contextVI.arc(videoWidth/2, videoHeight/2, videoHeight/2,
                 startAngle, endAngle, false);
   contextVI.fill();
   contextVI.clip();
   ```

3. **Within the callback function, start your animation loop.**

   Start the animation loop using the `requestAnimationFrame()` function as in code section D2–D4. This section of code is shown here:

   ```
   (function animLoop()
   {
     requestAnimFrame(animLoop);
     drawVideo();
   }
   ) ();
   ```

Drawing the video images

During each animation frame callback from the browser, your designated function (`drawVideo()` in Listing 11-1) is given control. This is when you draw the individual video frames and anything else you want to include during your animation cycle. In Listing 11-1, I've drawn the video, an imaginary bubble surrounding it, and the video control buttons. Follow these steps to draw your individual video frame images:

1. **Define the drawing function that will be executed during each animation frame.**

In Listing 11-1, this is the `drawVideo()` function in code section E:

```
function drawVideo();
```

2. **If you want to, modify pixels in the video frame.**

   It's at this point that you can modify the pixels of the individual Canvas video image if you want to. In Listing 11-1, the image is on the `contextVI` Canvas starting at the coordinates (`videoX`, `videoY`) with width `video Width` and height `videoHeight`. The Listing 11-1 application doesn't directly modify any image pixels. Instead, it uses a gradient per Step 4 to shade the edges of the thought bubble around the video frame.

3. **Within the `drawVideo()` function, draw a single video frame using the `drawImage()` function.**

   Here's an example from code section E1 of Listing 11-1:

```
contextVI.drawImage(video1EL, videoX, videoY, videoWidth, videoHeight);
```

4. **Draw other objects you want in the frame.**

   This is where I drew the gradient on top of the video image to enhance the bubble appearance in code sections E2:

```
contextVI.fillStyle   = video1Gradient;
contextVI.beginPath();
contextVI.arc(videoWidth/2, videoHeight/2, videoHeight,
              startAngle, endAngle, false);
contextVI.fill();
```

   To keep as much processing out of the animation loop as possible, the gradient `video1Gradient` used in the preceding code block is defined in code section B5:

```
video1Gradient   = contextVI.createRadialGradient(
                   videoWidth/2, videoHeight/2,.7*videoHeight,
                   videoWidth/2, videoHeight/2, 0);
video1Gradient.addColorStop( 0, "white"       );
video1Gradient.addColorStop(.05, "white"       );
video1Gradient.addColorStop(.20, "white"       );
video1Gradient.addColorStop(.50, "transparent");
video1Gradient.addColorStop( 1, "transparent");
```

   To facilitate drawing in the animation loop, `contextVI` is translated to the position of the video in the overall image in code section B6:

```
contextVI.translate(videoX, videoY);
```

5. **Draw control buttons when loaded. Check to see whether the buttons have been loaded but not yet initialized. Set initial values and display them.**

Here's an example from code section E3:

```
if(buttonLoad && !buttonInit)
{
// E6. INITIALIZE buttons when all have loaded.
    playButton   = pauseImage;
    repeatButton = repeatOnImage;
    soundButton  = soundOnImage;
    levelButton  = soundLevelImage;

    // E7. BUTTON LOAD status.
    buttonInit   = true;

    // E8. DRAW buttons.
    buttonTextDisplay();
}
```

Responding to User Interaction

There are two ways the user can interact with your application to affect video playback: through the Canvas area or video player. To keep your Canvas display in sync with the video player (if you're using one), when one is altered, change the other. In the Listing 11-1 example, this means keeping the video player for the background sound in sync with Canvas text.

Keep in mind that this section of code requires some non-linear thinking. Responding to user interaction is very event driven: The user clicking and touching, and your code is responding.

Normally, you probably wouldn't have a complete set of controls in both the Canvas area and a visible video player. In the Listing 11-1 example I used only Canvas area controls. In Listing 10-1 example demonstrating audio, I used both Canvas area and a visible video player.

Responding to Canvas area interaction

To respond to Canvas area interaction, define listeners for mouse and touch events and take the appropriate actions when your callback function is given control. Follow these steps:

1. **Define video control graphics.**

   In the Listing 11-1 example, I used buttons as graphics for controlling video playback. To include graphic elements for control, define their sources and load functions as in code sections A4, A5, A6, B11, B12 and C. Here is the sample code for the play button from those sections:

```
var playFile    = "PlayerPlay";
var playImage   = new Image();
var playButton  = new Image();
playImage.src   = server + playFile + buttonFileType;
playImage.onload = function() {buttonIncrement()}
function buttonIncrement()
{
   buttonCount++;
   if(buttonCount = buttonQuant) {buttonLoad = true;  buttonTextDisplay()}
}
```

2. Define listeners for user interaction events.

Listeners are your "lookouts" for Canvas user interaction. This is how you know when the user clicks or touches your Canvas. Use the addEventListener() function to specify the function to be called when a user event takes place. In Listing 11-1, the clickTouch() function defined in Step 3 is specified for mouse and touch events in code section B8:

```
canvasBT.addEventListener("mousedown",  clickTouch, false);
canvasBT.addEventListener("touchstart", clickTouch, false);
canvasBT.addEventListener("touchmove",  clickTouch, false);
canvasBT.addEventListener("touchend",   clickTouch, false);
```

3. Define the callback function that will respond to interaction events.

Define the callback function to be invoked when an event listener is triggered. Within that function, first determine the position on the Canvas of the click/touch using the clickTouchEvent() function defined in Step 4. Then handle each type of event per Steps 5 and 6. In Listing 11-1, the callback function is defined in code section F:

```
function clickTouch(event)
{
   // Determine position on Canvas of click/touch.
   clickTouchEvent(event);

   // Code to handle each control selection.
}
```

4. Determine the Canvas location of a click/touch event. Create a function that will determine the *x* and *y* coordinate positions of a click or touch event.

Here's an example from code section G of Listing 11-1:

```
function clickTouchEvent(event)
{
   // G1. BROWSERS except Firefox.
   if (event.x != undefined && event.y != undefined)
      {xPos = event.x;  yPos = event.y;}

   // G2. FIREFOX.
   else
```

```
    {xPos = event.clientX + document.body.scrollLeft +
                        document.documentElement.scrollLeft;
     yPos = event.clientY + document.body.scrollTop +
                        document.documentElement.scrollTop}

  // G3. CURSOR position.
  xPos -= canvasTX.offsetLeft;   yPos -= canvasTX.offsetTop;
}
```

5. Change the selected video controls.

Using the `positionTest()` function defined in Step 6, determine which video controls should be altered; then make changes using the appropriate video function, as shown in code sections F2–F14. Here is one example from F2–F4:

```
if(positionTest(2))
{
   video1EL.muted =    !video1EL.muted;
   if(video1EL.muted) {soundButton = soundOffImage}
   else               {soundButton = soundOnImage }
   buttonTextDisplay();
}
```

This code tests for selection of the Sound On/Off control and, if selected, changes the muted attribute of the video element and alters the button to the appropriate setting.

6. Test for player control position. Test to see whether the *x* and *y* coordinate positions selected on the Canvas by the user are within a given `position` in the video controls area of the Canvas. Return a value of `true` or `false` depending on the results.

See code section I:

```
function positionTest(position)
{
   // I1. INITIALIZE return value to false.
   var returnValue = false;

   // I2. TEST position.
   if (
      (yPos > (buttonsY)) &&
      (yPos < (buttonsY + buttonHeight)) &&
      (xPos > (buttonsX + (position * buttonWidth))) &&
      (xPos < (buttonsX + (position * buttonWidth) + buttonWidth))
      )
      {returnValue = true;}

   // I3. RETURN returnValue.
   return returnValue;
}
```

7. **Change the display buttons and text. Using a call to the `buttonText-Display()` function (defined in Step 8), change the display after values have changed.**

   In Listing 11-1, this is done in code sections B10, C4, E6, F4, F7, F8, F9 and F13:

   ```
   buttonTextDisplay();
   ```

8. **Display the text that defines the status of the video player settings.**

   This text is also used to define the areas for user interaction to change player settings.

   In Listing 11-1, the text display function is defined in code section H:

   ```
   function buttonTextDisplay()
   {
       // H1. CLEAR canvas.
       contextBT.clearRect(0, 0, canvasBT.width, canvasBT.height);

       // H2. BUTTON LOAD check.
       if(buttonLoad)
       {
           // H3. BUTTON DISPLAY.
           contextBT.drawImage(playButton, buttonsX + (buttonWidth * 0),
                         buttonsY, buttonWidth, buttonHeight);
           . . .
       }
       // H4. VOLUME.
       contextBT.font      = textFont;
       contextBT.fillStyle = textColor;
       var volumeLev       = volumeLevel.toFixed(1);
       contextBT.fillText(   volumeLev,  buttonsX + volumeOffsetX +
                         (buttonWidth * 3), buttonsY + volumeOffsetY);
   }
   ```

Responding to video player interaction

In order to respond to changes a user makes in a video player, define a call-back function that will gain control when specific player changes are made. When a user changes settings in the video player, reflect these changes in the appropriate settings within your application.

To respond to video player interaction, follow these steps:

1. **For each video player function you're tracking in your application, define a listener that will be called when the user changes the control.**

   Here's an example:

   ```
   Video1EL.onpause = function () { . . . }
   ```

2. **Change variables tracking the video player value.**

   Within the function defined in Step 1, change the appropriate variable:

   ```
   pauseText = pauseText1;
   ```

3. **Using a call to the `buttonTextDisplay()` function (defined in Step 8 in the preceding section), change the custom controls display.**

   Here's an example:

   ```
   buttonTextDisplay();
   ```

Defining Other Application Components

You can combine video with other Canvas capabilities. In the Listing 11-1 example, a Canvas is defined for a background image, as demonstrated in the following steps:

1. **Upload your image file to a folder on a server.**

   In the sample application, this is a background and button images. Usually the server used is the one hosting the website containing your application.

2. **Define variables and load functions for images.**

   In the sample application in Listing 11-1, the background and button image variable is defined in code section A4 and drawn after it is loaded in code section B9:

   ```
   var backgroundImage     = new Image();
   backgroundImage.src     = server + backgroundFile + backgroundType;
   backgroundImage.onload = function()
   {contextIM.drawImage(backgroundImage,0,0,canvasIM.width,canvasIM.height)}
   ```

3. **Define the function to be called when your web page is loaded.**

   Define the function that contains the main sequence of code that's called when the web page is loaded, as in code section B of the example:

   ```
   window.onload = function() { . . . }
   ```

4. **Define Canvas elements.**

   In the example code section L, a Canvas is defined for the background image:

   ```
   <canvas id = "canvasImage" width = "300"  height = "500"
        style = "border:2px solid black; position:absolute;
                 left:auto; top:auto;  z-index: 1">
   </canvas>
   ```

5. Define Canvas variable and context.

In the example, these are defined in code section B1:

```
canvasIM  = document.getElementById("canvasImage");
contextIM = canvasIM.getContext("2d");
```

12

Enhancing Canvas Applications

To me, this is a very exciting chapter. It's an opportunity to build an application that demonstrates what Canvas can really do. Options for enhancing Canvas applications are virtually limitless — and every application can benefit from different enhancement techniques. My objective for this chapter is to spark your thinking about innovative ways you can enhance your own applications. Get creative. Don't limit your thinking. Go for it.

In this chapter, I use two elements to approach the topic of enhancement:

- **The use of an enhanced application example:** Listing 12-1 and Figure 12-1 demonstrate an application that simulates a fireworks display. It builds on techniques covered in previous chapters.

- **A discussion of key aspects of enhancement:** A look at some general principles of enhancement and how they've been applied to Listing 12-1.

Figure 12-1: Fireworks — an enhanced Canvas application.

Listing 12-1: Fireworks — an Enhanced Canvas Application

```
<!DOCTYPE HTML> <html> <head> <script>

// A. VARIABLES.

    // A1. ANIMATION.
    var interval      = 15;         var intervalT     = 70;
    var intervalI     = 5;          var intervalB     = 5;
    var showBG        = false;      var intervalID    = 0;
    var xStart        = 350;        var yStart        = 400;
    var xVecStart     = -1;         var yVecStart     = -.5;
    var lastTime      = 1;          var fps           = 0;
    var animType      = 1;          var moveAdj       = 1;
    var fpsCounter    = 0;          var fpsDisplay    = 1000;
    var fpsMaxAdj     = 5;          var fpsMaxPct     = 300;
    var partLimit     = 100;        var mute          = false;
    var fire          = true;       var key;
    var reqAnimOn     = false;
```

```
// A2. ENVIRONMENT.
var frictionS     = .02;        var frictionB     = 0;
var frictionL     = 0;          var frictionT     = .09;
var frictionI     = .01;
var gravityS      = .003;       var gravityB      = .0;
var gravityL      = 0;          var gravityT      = .01;
var gravityI      = .001;
var sunset        = 1;          var sunsetT       = 10;
var sunsetI       = 1;          var sunsetB       = 1;
var sunsetHorizon = 60;         var sunsetFactor  = 600;
var skyNight      = 0;          var skyCount      = 0;
var skyAlpha      = .2;         var skyInterval   = 0;
var smokeOn       = 1;          var smokeFactor   = 1200;
var smokeLimit    = 250;        var smokeStart    = 375;
var smokeGrad     = 0;          var smokeColor    = "hotpink";
var cityScapeY    = 350;

// A3. FIREWORKS.
var massMin       = 1;          var massMax       = 2;
var lifeMin       = 75;         var lifeMax       = 150;
var glowMin       = 150;        var glowMax       = 250;
var sizeMin       = 1;          var sizeMax       = 3;
var quantMin      = 5;          var quantMax      = 30;
var decayMin      = .1;         var decayMax      = 1;
var spreadMin     = 0;          var spreadMax     = 30;
var radMin        = .5;         var radMax        = 2;
var newMin        = 30;         var newMax        = 100;
var newCount      = 0;          var newCreate     = 0;
var wait          = 300;        var waitT         = 1000;
var waitI         = 100;        var waitB         = 100;
var accelerS      = .01;        var accelerB      = .0;
var accelerL      = 0;          var accelerT      = .1;
var accelerI      = .01;
var altitMin      = 300;        var serialExpl    = 10;
var tailJitter    = 2;          var fadeJitter    = 5;
var angleJitter   = 1;          var vectJitter    = 2;
var tailMin       = 500;        var glowMin       = 100;
var explThrot     = .8;         var launchThrot   = .7;
var xLaunchLeft   = 8;          var xLaunchRight  = 4;
var yLaunchLower  = 2;          var yLaunchUpper  = 3;

var colors =
["aqua", "red", "blue", "fuchsia","crimson", "cyan", "lime", "lightpink",
 "chartreuse", "greenyellow", "olive", "purple","red", "deeppink",
 "silver","teal", "yellow", "azure", "hotpink", "gold", "pink", "orange",
 "lawngreen", "white", "salmon", "magenta", "springgreen", "orchid",
 "green", "green", "green", "green", "green", "green", "green", "green"];
```

(continued)

Listing 12-1 *(continued)*

```
var numColors = colors.length;

var launchColors =
["aliceblue", "azure", "blanchedalmond", "gainsboro", "lavender",
 "lightcyan", "mistyrose", "silver", "white", "lightblue", "lightskyblue",
 "paleturquoise", "red", "orangered", "gold", "yellow"];

var numLaunchColors = launchColors.length;

var part   = new Array();

var pathX = new Array();
var pathY = new Array();

// A4. TRAFFIC.
var trafficXMin   = 0;     var trafficXMax   = 700;
var trafficY      = 400;   var trafficChange = 6;
var trafficColors =
["bisque", "bisque", "bisque", "bisque",
 "black", "black", "black", "black", "black"];

var numTrafficColors = trafficColors.length;

// A5. TEXT.
var welcomeText   = "Welcome to a night of fireworks!
                     Press the Ctrl key to enable & display menu.";
var welcomeFont   = "10pt arial";
var welcomeColor  = "purple";
var menuFont      = "9pt courier";
var menuColor     = "slateblue";
var fpsDisplayX   = 625;   var fpsDisplayY = 20;
var fpsXOffset    = 40;    var numYOffset    = 20;

// A6. FILES.
var server        = "http://marketimpacts.com/storage/";
var cityScapeType = ".png";
var cityScapeFile = "NightCityScape1000px";
var darkSkyType   = ".png";
var darkSkyFile   = "DarkSky1000px";
var expl1AudFile  = "Fireworks";
var expl2AudFile  = "FireworksMultiple";
var expl3AudFile  = "FireworksBassBoost";
var expl4AudFile  = "FireworksLowPitch";
var expl5AudFile  = "FireworksSlow";
var crowdAudFile  = "FireworksCrowd";
var crowd2AudFile = "FireworksCrowd2";

// A7. AUDIO.
var crowdVolume   = .2;
var explVolumeMin = .2;    var explVolumeMax = .5;
var explNumMin    = 1;     var explNumMax    = 4;
```

```
    var audio1EL;          var audio5EL;
    var audio2EL;          var audio6EL;
    var audio3EL;          var audio7EL;
    var audio4EL;

// B. WINDOW LOAD function.
window.onload = function()
{
    // B1. CANVAS contexts.
    canvasFW  = document.getElementById("canvasFireworks");

    contextFW = canvasFW.getContext("2d");
    canvasTR  = document.getElementById("canvasTraffic");
    contextTR = canvasTR.getContext("2d");
    canvasSK  = document.getElementById("canvasSky");
    contextSK = canvasSK.getContext("2d");
    canvasDS  = document.getElementById("canvasDarkSky");
    contextDS = canvasDS.getContext("2d");
    canvasIM  = document.getElementById("canvasImage");
    contextIM = canvasIM.getContext("2d");
    canvasBG  = document.getElementById("canvasBackground");
    contextBG = canvasBG.getContext("2d");
    canvasFS  = document.getElementById("canvasFrameSpeed");
    contextFS = canvasFS.getContext("2d");
    canvasSM  = document.getElementById("canvasSmoke");
    contextSM = canvasSM.getContext("2d");

    // B2. AUDIO files.
    audio1EL = document.createElement("audio");
    audio2EL = document.createElement("audio");
    audio3EL = document.createElement("audio");
    audio4EL = document.createElement("audio");
    audio5EL = document.createElement("audio");
    audio6EL = document.createElement("audio");
    audio7EL = document.createElement("audio");
    audioType = audioExtensionType(audio1EL);
    audio1EL.setAttribute("src",server + crowdAudFile  + "." + audioType);
    audio2EL.setAttribute("src",server + expl1AudFile  + "." + audioType);
    audio3EL.setAttribute("src",server + expl2AudFile  + "." + audioType);
    audio4EL.setAttribute("src",server + expl3AudFile  + "." + audioType);
    audio5EL.setAttribute("src",server + expl4AudFile  + "." + audioType);
    audio6EL.setAttribute("src",server + expl5AudFile  + "." + audioType);
    audio7EL.setAttribute("src",server + crowd2AudFile + "." + audioType);

    // B3. CROWD audio settings.
    audio1EL.volume = crowdVolume;  audio1EL.loop = true; audio1EL.play();
    audio7EL.volume = crowdVolume;  audio7EL.loop = true; audio7EL.play();

    // B4. CITY image source.
    var cityNight = new Image();
    cityNight.src = server + cityScapeFile + cityScapeType;
```

(continued)

Listing 12-1 *(continued)*

```
   // B5. CITY image load function.
   cityNight.onload = function()
   {
      // B6. DRAW image.
      contextIM.drawImage(cityNight, 0, cityScapeY, canvasIM.width,
                                     canvasIM.height-cityScapeY);

      // B7. WELCOME text.
      contextIM.fillStyle    = welcomeColor;
      contextIM.font         = welcomeFont;
      contextIM.textAlign    = "center";

      contextIM.textBaseline = "middle";
      contextIM.fillText(welcomeText ,canvasIM.width/2, canvasIM.height-15);
   }
   // B8. SKY image source.
   var darkSky = new Image();
   darkSky.src = server + darkSkyFile + darkSkyType;


   // B9. SKY image load function.
   darkSky.onload = function()
   {
      var test1 = darkSky;
      contextDS.drawImage(darkSky, 0, 0, canvasDS.width, canvasDS.height);
      var test2 = darkSky;
   }
   // C. FIREWORKS start.
   fireworks();
}
// D. KEY functions.
document.onkeydown = function(event)
{
   // D1. EVENT.
   event = event || window.event;

   // D2. KEY code.
   key = event.keyCode;

   // D3. MENU toggle using the Ctrl key.
   if (key == 17) {
      showBG = !showBG;
      clearInterval(intervalID);
      fire = false;  fireworks();
      }
   // D4. GRAVITY change using the g key.
   if ((key == 71) && (showBG)) {gravityS += gravityI;
      if (gravityS > gravityT)  {gravityS = gravityB};
      clearInterval(intervalID);
      fire = false;  fireworks();
      }
```

```
// D5. FRICTION change using the f key.
if ((key == 70) && (showBG)) {frictionS += frictionI;
    if (frictionS > frictionT){frictionS = frictionB};
    clearInterval(intervalID);
    fire = false;  fireworks();
    }
// D6. INTERVAL change using the i key.
if ((key == 73) && (showBG)) {interval += intervalI;
    if (interval > intervalT) {interval = intervalB};
    clearInterval(intervalID);
    fire = false;  fireworks();
    }
// D7. WAIT change using the w key.
if ((key == 87) && (showBG)) {wait += waitI;
    if (wait > waitT)          {wait = waitB};
    clearInterval(intervalID);
    fire = false;  fireworks();
    }
// D8. SUNSET change using the s key.
if ((key == 83) && (showBG)) {sunset += sunsetI;
    if (sunset > sunsetT)      {sunset = sunsetB};
    skyAlpha = 0;
    clearInterval(intervalID);
    fire = false;  fireworks();
    }
// D9. MUTE change using the m key.
if ((key == 77) && (showBG)) {mute = !mute; background();
    if(mute) {muting(true)} else {muting(false)}
    }
// D10. LAUNCH fireworks using the l key.
if ((key == 76) && (showBG)) {
    clearInterval(intervalID);
    fireworks();
    }
}
// E. FIREWORKS function.
function fireworks()
{
    // E1. RESET variables.
    frictionL = frictionS;
    gravityL  = gravityS;
    accelerL  = accelerS;
    newMax    = wait;
    newCount  = 0;
    newCreate = 0;

    // E2. BACKGROUND text shown if turned on.
    contextBG.clearRect(0, 0, canvasBG.width, canvasBG.height);
    if(showBG) {background()}
```

(continued)

Listing 12-1 *(continued)*

```
    // E3. SMOKE generation.
    smoke();

    // E4. MUTING.
    if(mute) {muting(true)}   else {muting(false)}

    // E5. TRAFFIC clear.
    contextTR.clearRect(0, 0, canvasTR.width, canvasTR.height);

    // E6. START DRAWING fireworks using setInterval.
    if(animType == 0) {intervalID = setInterval(drawFireworks,interval)}

    // E7. START DRAWING fireworks using request animation frame.
    if((animType == 1) && !reqAnimOn)
    {
        // E8. ANIMATION ON indicator.
        reqAnimOn = true;

        // E9. ANIMATION LOOP.
        (function animloop(){requestAnimFrame(animloop); drawFireworks()})();
    }
}
// F. DRAW FIREWORKS function.
function drawFireworks()
{
    // F1. SUNSET increment & check for change.
    skyInterval = sunset*sunsetFactor;
    skyCount    = skyCount + interval;
    if(skyCount > skyInterval)
    {
        // F2. SKY ALPHA increase if reached skyInterval.
        skyAlpha = skyAlpha + .01;
        if(skyAlpha > 1) {skyApha = 1}
        skyCount = 0;

        // F3. SKY alpha setting.
        contextSK.globalAlpha = skyAlpha;
        if(skyNight == 1) {contextSK.globalAlpha = 1}

        // F4. SKY gradient.
        var skyGrad = contextSK.createLinearGradient(0, 0, 0, canvasSK.height-
                                                           sunsetHorizon);
        skyGrad.addColorStop( 0, "black");
        skyGrad.addColorStop(.8, "black");
        skyGrad.addColorStop( 1, "transparent");

        // F5. SKY fill.
        contextSK.fillStyle = skyGrad;
        contextSK.clearRect(0, 0, canvasSK.width, canvasSK.height);
        contextSK.fillRect( 0, 0, canvasSK.width, canvasSK.height);
    }
```

```
// F6. INCREMENT count for new fireworks.
newCount++;

// F7. CHECK for creating a new fireworks.
if(newCount > newCreate)
{
   // F8. RESET counter for launch of new fireworks.
   newCount = 0;

   // F9. INTERVAL for launching next new fireworks.
   newCreate = newMin+(Math.random()*(newMax-newMin));

   // F10. NEW FIREWORKS if particle limit not exceeded.
   if(part.length < partLimit) {newFireworks()}
}
// F11. PROCESS individual particles.
var partLength = part.length;
for(var p=0; p<partLength; p++)
{
   // F12. AGE increase.
   part[p].age++;

   // F13. END OF LIFE check.
   if (part[p].age > (part[p].life + part[p].glow))
   {
      // F14. REMOVE particle.
      part.splice(p,1); pathX.splice(p,1);  pathY.splice(p,1);

      // F15. SMOKE generation.
      smoke();
   }
   // F16. ALIVE check.
   if (part[p].age < part[p].life)

      // F17. MOVE particle.
      {moveParticle(p)}

   // F18. EXPLOSION CRITERIA check.
   if ((part[p].age >  part[p].life) && ( part[p].explode == 1)  &&
       (part[p].yPos <  altitMin)     && ((part[p].quant+ part.length) <
                                                           partLimit))
   {
      // F19. EXPLODE particle.
      part[p].explode = 0;      explodeParticle(p);
   }
}
// F20. CLEAR fireworks canvas.
contextFW.clearRect(0,0,canvasFW.width, canvasFW.height);

// F21. LOOP through particles.
partLength = part.length-1;
for(var p=0; p<partLength; p++)
```

(continued)

Listing 12-1 *(continued)*

```
        // F22. DRAW particle.
        {drawParticle(p)}

    // F23. TRAFFIC loop.
    for(var t=0; t<trafficChange; t++)
    {
        // F24. COLOR.
        var colorIndex      = Math.random()*(numTrafficColors-1);
        colorIndex          = Math.round(colorIndex);
        contextTR.fillStyle = trafficColors[colorIndex];

        // F25. POSITION.
        var trafficXPos = trafficXMin + (Math.random()*(trafficXMax-trafficXMin));

        // F26. DRAW.
        contextTR.fillRect(trafficXPos, trafficY, 1, 1);
    }
}
// G. DRAW PARTICLE function.
function drawParticle(p)
{
    // G1. ALIVE check.
    if (part[p].age < part[p].life)
    {
        // G2. LOOP through path.
        var pathLength = Math.min(1*pathX[p].length, tailMin);
        for(var t=0; t<pathLength; t++)
        {
            // G3. COLOR setting.
            contextFW.fillStyle = part[p].color;

            // G4. TRANSPARENCY setting.
            var ga = 1/(part[p].decay*t);
            contextFW.globalAlpha = ga;

            // G5. X POSITION/JITTER setting.
            var x = pathX[p][t] + (tailJitter*Math.random());

            // G6. Y POSITION setting.
            var y = pathY[p][t];

            // G7. DRAW particle.
            contextFW.fillRect(x, y, part[p].size, part[p].size);
        }
    }
    // G8. GLOW check.
    if ((part[p].age > part[p].life) &&
        (part[p].age < (part[p].life+part[p].glow)))
    {
        // G9. STILL GLOWING variable.
        var stillGlowing = 0;
```

```
   // G10. LOOP through tail.
   for(var t=0; t<Math.min(pathX[p].length, glowMin); t++)
   {
       // G11. COLOR setting.
       contextFW.fillStyle = part[p].color;

       // G12. TRANSPARENCY setting.
       var ga = 1/(.5*(t + (part[p].age)-(part[p].life)));
       contextFW.globalAlpha = ga;

       // G13. X POSITION/JITTER setting.
       var x = pathX[p][t] + (fadeJitter*Math.random());

       // G14. Y POSITION setting.
       var y = pathY[p][t];

       // G15. DRAW particle.
       contextFW.fillRect(x, y, part[p].size, part[p].size);

       // G16. STILL GLOWING setting.
       stillGlowing = ga;
   }
   // G17. GLOWING check.
   if(stillGlowing < .003)
   {
       // G18. REMOVE particle.
       part.splice(p,1);  pathX.splice(p,1);  pathY.splice(p,1);

       // G19. SMOKE generation.
       smoke();
   }
  }
}
// H. MOVE PARTICLE function.
function moveParticle(p)
{
   // H1. ANIMATION RATE check.
   var date     = new Date();
   var time     = date.getTime();
   var timeDiff = time - lastTime;
   fps          = 1000/timeDiff;
   lastTime     = time;

   // H2. FRAME COUNTER increment.
   fpsCounter++;

   // H3. FRAME RATE display.
   if((fpsCounter > fpsDisplay) && (timeDiff > 20))
   {
       // H4. CLEAR frame speed canvas.
       contextFS.clearRect(0, 0, canvasFS.width, canvasFS.height);
```

(continued)

Listing 12-1 *(continued)*

```
// H5. ATTRIBUTES of display.
contextFS.font      = menuFont;
contextFS.fillStyle = menuColor;
fps                 = fps.toFixed(0);

// H6. COUNTER reset.
fpsCounter = 0;

// H7. PARTICLE COUNT.
var particleCount = part.length;

// H8. SHOW BACKGROUND check.
if(showBG)
{
    // H9. DISPLAY frame rate and particle count.
    contextFS.fillText("fps:", fpsDisplayX, fpsDisplayY);
    contextFS.fillText( fps,   fpsDisplayX + fpsXOffset, fpsDisplayY);
    contextFS.fillText("num:", fpsDisplayX, fpsDisplayY + numYOffset);
    contextFS.fillText( particleCount, fpsDisplayX + fpsXOffset,
                                       fpsDisplayY + numYOffset);

}
}
// H10. FPS factor.
var fpsTarget   = 1000/interval;
var fpsDiff     = fpsTarget - fps;
var fpsPercent  = fpsDiff/fps;
var fpsAdjustX  = 0;
var fpsAdjustY  = 0;
if(fpsDiff > Math.abs(fpsMaxAdj))
{
    var adjust  = Math.min(fpsPercent, fpsMaxPct/100);
    fpsAdjustX  = adjust * part[p].xVec * moveAdj;
    fpsAdjustY  = adjust * part[p].yVec * moveAdj;
}
// H11. FRICTION & ACCELERATION factor.
faFactor = (1-((frictionL/(part[p].mass+accelerL))));

// H12. VECTOR & POSITION change.
part[p].xVec  *= faFactor;
part[p].xPos  += (part[p].xVec + fpsAdjustX);
part[p].yVec  *= faFactor;
part[p].yVec  += gravityL/2;
part[p].yPos  += (part[p].yVec + fpsAdjustY);

// H13. PATH recording.
pathX[p].unshift(part[p].xPos);
pathY[p].unshift(part[p].yPos);
}
// I. NEW FIREWORKS function.
function newFireworks()
{
```

```
   // I1. FIRE check.
   if(fire)
   {
      // I2. ADD new particle to array.
      var newPart        = part.length;
      part[newPart]      = {};

      // I3. PATH arrays.
      pathX[newPart]     = new Array();
      pathY[newPart]     = new Array();

      // I4. AGE.
      part[newPart].age  = 0;

      // I5. POSITION.
      part[newPart].xPos = xStart;
      part[newPart].yPos = yStart;

      // I6. X VECTOR.
      part[newPart].xVec = xLaunchRight-(Math.random()*(xLaunchLeft));

      // I7. X VECTOR THROTTLE.
      part[newPart].xVec = part[newPart].xVec * launchThrot;

      // I8. Y VECTOR.
      part[newPart].yVec = -(yLaunchLower+Math.random()*(yLaunchUpper));

      // I9. Y VECTOR THROTTLE.
      part[newPart].yVec = part[newPart].yVec * launchThrot;

      // I10. COLOR.
      var colorIndex       = Math.random()*(numLaunchColors-1);
      colorIndex           = Math.round(colorIndex);
      var newColor         = launchColors[colorIndex];
      part[newPart].color = newColor;

      // I11. CHARACTERISTICS.
      part[newPart].mass  = massMin +(Math.random()*(massMax-massMin));
      part[newPart].life  = lifeMin +(Math.random()*(lifeMax-lifeMin));
      part[newPart].size  = sizeMin +(Math.random()*(sizeMax-sizeMin));
      part[newPart].quant = quantMin+(Math.random()*(quantMax-quantMin));
      part[newPart].radius= radMin  +(Math.random()*(radMax-radMin));
      part[newPart].glow  = part[newPart].life+glowMin +
                                     (Math.random()*(glowMax-glowMin));
      part[newPart].decay = 1;

      // I12. EXPLODE at end of life.
      part[newPart].explode = 1;
   }
   // I13. FIRE set to true.
   else {fire = true}
}
```

(continued)

Listing 12-1 *(continued)*

```
// J. EXPLODE PARTICLE function.
function explodeParticle(particle)
{
    // J1. CHARACTERISTICS using random factor.
    var mass   = massMin  + (Math.random()*(massMax-massMin));
    var life   = lifeMin  + (Math.random()*(lifeMax-lifeMin));
    var glow   = glowMin  + (Math.random()*(glowMax-glowMin));
    var size   = sizeMin  + (Math.random()*(sizeMax-sizeMin));
    var decay  = decayMin + (Math.random()*(decayMax-decayMin));
    var quant  = quantMin + (Math.random()*(quantMax-quantMin));
    var radius = radMin   + (Math.random()*(radMax-radMin));
    var colorIndex = Math.random()*(numColors-1);
    colorIndex     = Math.round(colorIndex);
    var newColor   = colors[colorIndex];
    var vectJitterN = Math.random()*vectJitter;

    // J2. SPREAD of new particles in degrees.
    var spread = 360/(part[particle].quant);

    // J3. NEW PARTICLES generation.
    for (var i=1; i<(part[particle].quant); i++)
    {
        // J4. ADD to particle array.
        var newPart  = part.length;
        part[newPart] = {};

        // J5. PATH arrays.
        pathX[newPart] = new Array();
        pathY[newPart] = new Array();

        // J6. POSITION using current position.
        part[newPart].xPos = part[particle].xPos;
        part[newPart].yPos = part[particle].yPos;

        // J7. ANGLE.
        var angle = (Math.PI/180)*i*spread;
        angle     = (angleJitter*Math.random())+angle;

        // J8. SPEED LIMIT.
        var speedLimit = 1;

        // J9. JITTER SHAPING for selected colors.
        if(newColor == "red"   ) {vectJitterN = 0 }
        if(newColor == "gold"  ) {vectJitterN = 1 }
        if(newColor == "orange") {vectJitterN = .5}

        // J10. X VECTOR ANGLE.
        part[newPart].xVec = part[particle].xPos + (part[particle].radius *
                                                    Math.cos(angle));
        // J11. X VECTOR JITTER.
        part[newPart].xVec = part[newPart].xVec - part[newPart].xPos +
            (vectJitterN*Math.random()) - (vectJitterN*Math.random());
```

```
// J12. X VECTOR THROTTLE.
part[newPart].xVec = part[newPart].xVec * explThrot;


// J13. Y VECTOR ANGLE.
part[newPart].yVec = part[particle].yPos + (part[particle].radius *
                                                Math.sin(angle));
// J14. Y VECTOR JITTER.
part[newPart].yVec = part[newPart].yVec - part[newPart].yPos +
        (vectJitterN*Math.random()) - (vectJitterN*Math.random());


// J15. Y VECTOR THROTTLE.
part[newPart].yVec = part[newPart].yVec * explThrot;


// J16. CHARACTERISTICS of new particle.
part[newPart].age    = 0;
part[newPart].mass   = mass;
part[newPart].life   = life;
part[newPart].glow   = glow + (Math.random()*(glow/1));
part[newPart].size   = size;
part[newPart].decay  = decay;
part[newPart].quant  = quant;
part[newPart].radius = radius;
part[newPart].color  = newColor;


// J17. COLOR VARIETY check.
if(newColor == "green")
{
    // J18. RANDOM color setting.
    var colorIndex     = Math.random()*(numColors-1);
    colorIndex         = Math.round(colorIndex);
    var newColorV      = colors[colorIndex];
    part[newPart].color = newColorV;
}
// J19. EXPLODE turned off.
part[newPart].explode = 0;


// J20. SERIAL EXPLOSION check.
if(part[particle].quant < serialExpl)
{
    // J21. EXPLOSION turned on.
    part[newPart].explode = 1;


    // J22. PREVENT further explosions.
    part[newPart].quant = serialExpl;
    }
}
// J23. SMOKE generation.
smoke();


// J24. SOUND of explosion.
if(part[particle].quant < serialExpl)
{
```

(continued)

Listing 12-1 *(continued)*

```
      // J25. MULTIPLE explosions.
      soundExplosion(audio3EL);
   }
   else
   {
      // J26. SINGLE randomly chosen explosion.
      var r = explNumMin + (Math.random()*(explNumMax-explNumMin));
      var n = Math.round(r);

      // J27. SWITCH to explosion.
      switch(n)
      {
         case 1: soundExplosion(audio2EL); break;
         case 2: soundExplosion(audio4EL); break;
         case 3: soundExplosion(audio5EL); break;
         case 4: soundExplosion(audio6EL); break;
      }
   }
}
// K. SOUND EXPLOSION function.
function soundExplosion(element)
{
   element.volume = explVolumeMin+(Math.random()*(explVolumeMax-explVolumeMin));
   element.play();
}
// L. SMOKE function.
function smoke()
{if (smokeOn == 1)
   {
      // L1. TRANSPARENCY setting.
      contextSM.globalAlpha = Math.min(part.length, smokeLimit)/smokeFactor;

      // L2. GRADIENT settings.
      smokeGrad = contextSK.createLinearGradient(0, 0, 0, smokeStart);
      smokeGrad.addColorStop( 0, "transparent");
      smokeGrad.addColorStop(.4,  smokeColor  );
      smokeGrad.addColorStop(.8,  smokeColor  );
      smokeGrad.addColorStop( 1,  "transparent" );
      contextSM.fillStyle = smokeGrad;

      // L3. CLEAR and FILL canvas.
      contextSM.clearRect(0,0, canvasSM.width, canvasSM.height);
      contextSM.fillRect( 0,0, canvasSM.width, canvasSM.height);
   }
}
// M. BACKGROUND text function.
function background()
{
   // M1. ATTRIBUTES.
   contextBG.font       = menuFont;
   contextBG.textAlign  = "left";
```

```
    contextBG.textBaseline = "middle";
    contextBG.fillStyle    = menuColor;

    // M2. POSITIONS.
    var xPos1 = 15;   var xPos2 = 120;  var xPos3 = 250;   var yPos  = 13;

    // M3. CLEAR canvas.
    contextBG.clearRect(0, 0, canvasBG.width, canvasBG.height);

    // M4. FIX decimal points.
    var gravityFix  = gravityL.toFixed(3);
    var frictionFix = frictionL.toFixed(3);

    // M5. TEXT display.
    contextBG.fillText("Key Factor",     xPos1, yPos*1);
    contextBG.fillText("Value",          xPos2, yPos*1);
    contextBG.fillText("--- ---------",  xPos1, yPos*2);
    contextBG.fillText("-----",          xPos2, yPos*2);
    contextBG.fillText("g - gravity:",   xPos1, yPos*3);
    contextBG.fillText(gravityFix,       xPos2, yPos*3);
    contextBG.fillText("f - friction:",  xPos1, yPos*4);
    contextBG.fillText(frictionFix,      xPos2, yPos*4);
    contextBG.fillText("i - interval:",  xPos1, yPos*5);
    contextBG.fillText(interval,         xPos2, yPos*5);
    contextBG.fillText("w - wait:",      xPos1, yPos*6);
    contextBG.fillText(wait,             xPos2, yPos*6);
    contextBG.fillText("s - sunset:",    xPos1, yPos*7);
    contextBG.fillText(sunset,           xPos2, yPos*7);
    contextBG.fillText("m - mute:",      xPos1, yPos*8);
    contextBG.fillText(mute,             xPos2, yPos*8);
    contextBG.fillText("l - launch",     xPos1, yPos*9);
}
// N. REQUEST ANIMATION FRAME function.
    window.requestAnimFrame = (function(callback){
        return window.requestAnimationFrame ||
        window.webkitRequestAnimationFrame ||
        window.mozRequestAnimationFrame     ||
        window.oRequestAnimationFrame      ||
        window.msRequestAnimationFrame     ||
        function(callback){
            window.setTimeout(callback, interval);};};})();

// O. AUDIO EXTENSION TYPE function.
function audioExtensionType(audioElement)
{
    // O1. INITIALIZE return type.
    var returnType = "";

    // O2. TYPE test and setting.
    if (audioElement.canPlayType("audio/wav")=="probably"){returnType = "wav";}
    if (audioElement.canPlayType("audio/ogg")=="probably"){returnType = "ogg";}
    if (audioElement.canPlayType("audio/mp3")=="probably"){returnType = "mp3";}
```

(continued)

Listing 12-1 *(continued)*

```
    if (audioElement.canPlayType("audio/wav")=="maybe"   ){returnType = "wav";}
    if (audioElement.canPlayType("audio/ogg")=="maybe"   ){returnType = "ogg";}
    if (audioElement.canPlayType("audio/mp3")=="maybe"   ){returnType = "mp3";}

    // O3. RETURN type.
    return returnType;
}
// P. MUTING function.
function muting(setting)
{
    audio1EL.muted = setting;   audio5EL.muted = setting;
    audio2EL.muted = setting;   audio6EL.muted = setting;
    audio3EL.muted = setting;   audio7EL.muted = setting;
    audio4EL.muted = setting;
}
</script> </head> <body> <div>

<!-- Q. CANVAS DEFINITIONS -->
<canvas id    = "canvasTraffic"

        width = "700"  height ="500"  style = "border:2px solid black;
                position:absolute; left:auto; top:auto;  z-index: 5">
</canvas>
<canvas id    = "canvasFrameSpeed"
        width = "700"  height ="500"  style = "border:2px solid black;
                position:absolute; left:auto; top:auto;  z-index: 7">
</canvas>
<canvas id    = "canvasFireworks"
        width = "700"  height ="500"  style = "border:2px solid black;
                position:absolute; left:auto; top:auto;  z-index: 6">
</canvas>
<canvas id    = "canvasSmoke"
        width = "700"  height ="500"  style = "border:2px solid black;
                position:absolute; left:auto; top:auto;  z-index: 5">
</canvas>
<canvas id    = "canvasSky"
        width = "700"  height ="500"  style = "border:2px solid black;
                position:absolute; left:auto; top:auto;  z-index: 2">
</canvas>
<canvas id    = "canvasDarkSky"
        width = "700"  height ="500"  style = "border:2px solid black;
                position:absolute; left:auto; top:auto;  z-index: 1">
</canvas>
<canvas id    = "canvasImage"
        width = "700"  height ="500"  style = "border:2px solid black;
                position:absolute; left:auto; top:auto;  z-index: 3">
</canvas>
<canvas id    = "canvasBackground"
        width = "700"  height ="500"  style = "border:2px solid black;
                position:absolute; left:auto; top:auto;  z-index: 4">
Your browser doesn't currently support HTML5 Canvas.
</canvas> </div> </body> </html>
```

Aspects of Enhancement

To make your application truly shine , you can add and enhance objects, colors, images, sound, and user interaction. In this section, I show you how to attract and retain user attention.

Before I dive into the details of the fireworks application in Listing 12-1, the following sections give you an overview of why and how enhancements were used in its development.

Reasons for enhancement

Stated briefly, add enhancements and complexity to your application when it's appropriate, not just for their own sake.

When I developed the Listing 12-1 application, early versions had an artificial feel to them. The fireworks were too uniform and not realistic. The background was a bit flat. Exploding fireworks didn't make any noise. I added enhancements until the Canvas fireworks display had the look and feel of a real and interesting fireworks display.

I added enhancements to the fireworks application to:

- **Generate interest:** Enhancements and complexity can help draw attention to a Canvas. People like fireworks. Variations in color, motion, and sound enhance the experience and keep the viewer's attention.

- **Create emotion:** Combinations of sights and sounds evoke the emotion of a good fireworks display.

- **Simulate reality:** The world is a complex place. Fireworks displays have lots of varied colors, sounds, and movement.

- **Serve a purpose:** The fundamental purpose of the application is to help you understand Canvas development technology. I added enough complexity for the application to serve as a foundation for this chapter.

Techniques of enhancement

The Listing 12-1 application uses a number of techniques to add complexity:

- **Multiplicity:** Fireworks are made of multiple particles, each moving on its own trajectory. Explosions spawn new particles.

- **Variation:** Variations in fireworks size, color, motion, and sound help simulate the real thing.

✔ **Layering:** Multiple Canvases are used to layer fireworks on top of background images.

✔ **Randomization:** Random variations in size, color, motion, and sound add to the realism of the overall effect.

Application of enhancement

The preceding techniques are applied to a number of Canvas elements in the fireworks application:

✔ **Images:** Images of fireworks, car traffic, and a background scene are blended for an overall impression.

✔ **Objects:** Fireworks particles are generated using a variety of sizes and colors.

✔ **Motion:** Particle paths have varied trajectories, speeds, and life spans. Real world forces of friction, acceleration, and gravity are simulated.

✔ **Color:** Particle colors are chosen randomly from a colors array.

✔ **Sound:** Multiple background sound tracks are played and multiple exploding fireworks sounds are layered over each other and the background.

Constructing an Application Base

The Listing 12-1 application is built on a number of fundamental Canvas capabilities that have been explained in detail in previous chapters. Following is a list of these components and references to their code sections in Listing 12-1.

On load function

The `onload` function is called when the application is opened in a browser window. The main code is in section B of Listing 12-1. The `onload` function is called only once, so it's here that you perform actions that are only required a single time:

✔ Defining canvas elements: B1, Q

✔ Defining images and audio variables: A6, A7, B2–B9, O

✔ Calling the setup function: C

Animation setup function

The animation setup function is called to initialize variables and start animation. The animation setup function in the example is `fireworks()` in code section E. It's called multiple times from code sections D and once from code section B5. It includes

- Initializing variables: E1
- Displaying text: E2
- Initializing muting: E4
- Starting an animation loop: E6–E9

Animation loop

The animation loop instructs the browser to call the specified drawing function once for each animation frame:

- Defining the `setInterval` option: E6
- Defining the `requestAnimationFrame` option: E7–E9, N

Drawing function

The drawing function creates images on Canvases that the viewer sees as animated movement. In Listing 12-1, the drawing function is `drawFireworks()` in code section F:

- Making time-dependent scene changes: F1–F10
- Processing individual objects: F11–F26

Object movement

During each animation frame, each object is moved to its new position. In Listing 12-1, this is done in the `moveParticle()` function in code section H:

- Adjusting for animation time interval variations: H1, H10, H12
- Adjusting for real world forces: H11, H12
- Changing position and vector: H12

Object drawing

In the example, fireworks particles are drawn as small rectangles in code section G:

- Setting object attributes: G3, G4, G11, G12
- Drawing on a Canvas: G7, G15

Playing audio

In the example, the sound of a crowd is played as a background and the sounds of explosions are played to coincide with fireworks.

✔ Defining audio elements and their sources: A6, A7, B2, B3

✔ Determining audio extension types: O

✔ Setting audio attributes: B2, D9, E4, P

✔ Playing audio files: B3, K

User interaction

Users are given the option of displaying a menu of keystrokes in code section D, and information is displayed in code section M:

✔ Handling key presses: D1–D10

✔ Displaying information: M1–M5

Enhancing Background Canvas Layers

Although not the focus of attention, background Canvas layers can have a powerful influence on the overall impact of an application. Following are techniques for enhancing your background scenes.

Shading a background

In the sample application in Listing 12-1, the sky of the background image is progressively shaded to simulate nightfall. Follow these steps to shade a background:

1. **Check for shading conditions.**

   In the example in code section F1, a sky change counting interval is checked during each animation frame:

   ```
   skyInterval = sunset * sunsetFactor;
   skyCount    = skyCount + interval;
   if(skyCount > skyInterval) { . . . }
   ```

2. **Define transparency.**

   If the counting interval conditions in Step 1 are met, `globalAlpha` is increased by 1%, as in code sections F2 and F3:

```
skyAlpha = skyAlpha + .01;
if(skyAlpha > 1) {skyAlpha = 1}
skyCount = 0;
contextSK.globalAlpha = skyAlpha;
if(skyNight == 1) {contextSK.globalAlpha = 1}
```

3. **Define a gradient that contains the color to be used for shading.**

   In the example, a transparent portion of the gradient is used to feather in simulated evening dusk. The gradient is defined in code section F4:

```
var skyGrad = contextSK.createLinearGradient(0, 0, 0, canvasSK.height-
                                                       sunsetHorizon);
skyGrad.addColorStop( 0, "black");
skyGrad.addColorStop(.8, "black");
skyGrad.addColorStop( 1, "transparent");
```

4. **Clear and fill the Canvas.**

   Finally, clear and fill the Canvas with the gradient and `globalAlpha`, as in code section F5:

```
contextSK.fillStyle = skyGrad;
contextSK.clearRect(0,0, canvasSK.width, canvasSK.height);
contextSK.fillRect( 0,0, canvasSK.width, canvasSK.height);
```

Creating reflected light on a background

In Listing 12-1, a simulation of reflected light is used to emulate the light cast on smoke created by exploding fireworks. This adds to the sense of depth and realism. To simulate reflected light, use these steps:

1. **Call a light reflection function at the appropriate times.**

   In the example, the `smoke()` function is called in a number of code sections to produce a smoke effect that looks as real as possible. This is an example of coding for aesthetics, not for only technical accuracy. See code E3, F15, G19, and J23:

```
smoke();
```

2. **Set transparency.**

   The amount of reflected light should be based on a combination of factors related to activity in the animation. In the example code section L1, `globalAlpha` transparency is calculated by dividing the particle length by the variable `smokeFactor`. The variable `smokeLimit` limits the amount of light.

```
contextSM.globalAlpha = Math.min(part.length, smokeLimit)/smokeFactor;
```

3. **Define a gradient to shape the reflected light.**

   Here an example from code section L2:

   ```
   smokeGrad = contextSK.createLinearGradient(0, 0, 0, smokeStart);
   smokeGrad.addColorStop( 0, "transparent");
   smokeGrad.addColorStop(.4, smokeColor  );
   smokeGrad.addColorStop(.8, smokeColor  );
   smokeGrad.addColorStop( 1, "transparent");
   contextSM.fillStyle = smokeGrad;
   ```

4. **Clear and fill a Canvas with the light.**

   Here's an example in code section L3:

   ```
   contextSM.clearRect(0,0, canvasSM.width, canvasSM.height);
   contextSM.fillRect( 0,0, canvasSM.width, canvasSM.height);
   ```

Creating simulated background movement

Adding a bit of movement to a background improves the realism of what would otherwise be a scene. In Listing 12-1, the background image of the San Francisco skyline is interesting, but without some movement can look artificial and "dead." Because it's a background, it's not necessary to be totally accurate in simulated movement. In the example, I added a simple line of single pixel colors, some of which are changed during each animation frame to simulate the twinkling of auto headlights in the distance.

To simulate movement on a background, use these steps:

1. **Define an array of colors for your objects.**

   Choose a color for the headlights (bisque in the example) and a background color (black in the example). These colors will be alternately drawn on the Canvas to simulate the auto headlights. Multiple array entries for the same color are used to control the ratio of colors chosen in Step 4.

   ```
   var trafficColors   = ["bisque", "bisque", "bisque", "bisque",
                          "black", "black", "black", "black", "black"];
   var numTrafficColors = trafficColors.length;
   ```

2. **Clear the Canvas you'll use for your simulated background.**

   Here's an example in code section E5:

   ```
   contextTR.clearRect(0, 0, canvasTR.width, canvasTR.height);
   ```

   This makes the Canvas fully transparent, allowing the layers underneath to show through. In the example, simulated traffic will appear to be on top of these layers.

3. **Loop through the objects.**

Use a `for()` loop to process the number of light changes made (per the `trafficChange` variable) in each animation frame, as in F23:

```
for(var t=0; t<trafficChange; t++)  { . . . }
```

4. **Set the color of the object.**

Use the `Math.random()` function to select a color from the colors array, as in code section F24:

```
var colorIndex      = Math.random()*(numTrafficColors-1);
colorIndex          = Math.round(colorIndex);
contextTR.fillStyle = trafficColors[colorIndex];
```

5. **Set the Canvas position of the object.**

Use the `Math.random()` function to select a position on the *x* axis, as in code section F25:

```
var trafficXPos = trafficXMin + (Math.random()*(trafficXMax-trafficXMin));
```

6. **Draw the object.**

Use the `fillRect()` function to draw the pixel (or pixels), as in code section F26:

```
contextTR.fillRect(trafficXPos, trafficY, 1, 1);
```

Creating Multiple and Multifaceted Objects

Increasing the number of objects and number of object characteristics can enhance the impact of your application. In the fireworks example in Listing 12-1, each fireworks particle is treated as an object that has multiple characteristics.

Storing variables in an array

In an application with multiple objects, using an array for variable storage and organization quickly becomes essential. Use these steps to store your variables in an array:

1. **Define an array to hold your objects and their characteristics.**

In Listing 12-1, the `part` array for fireworks particles is defined in code section A3:

```
var part = new Array();
```

2. **Add objects to the array.**

   In the example, new fireworks particles are added to the end of the particles array, as in code sections I2 and J4:

   ```
   var  newPart  = part.length;
   part[newPart] = {};
   ```

3. **Define object characteristics.**

   For each object characteristic you're defining for a new object, add a variable to the object array using dot syntax, as in this example from code section I5:

   ```
   part[newPart].xPos = xStart;
   part[newPart].yPos = yStart;
   ```

   In Listing 12-1, particle characteristics are defined in code sections I3–I12 and J4–J22 for position, age, vectors, color, mass, life, size, quantity (for explosion), radius (for explosion), glow, decay indicator, and explosion indicator.

4. **Delete each object at the end of its life.**

   First, check for the conditions you use to limit the life of your object. In the example, particle life span is the sum of the `life` and `glow` after it dies out. If the conditions are met, use the `splice()` function to remove the entry from your array, as in code section F13–F14 of the example:

   ```
   if(part[p].age > (part[p].life + part[p].glow)) {part.splice(p,1) . . .}
   ```

Using randomized object characteristics

The world is a very non-uniform place. Nothing travels in an exactly straight path. No two objects are exactly the same. Events don't take place at exact intervals. So if one goal of your application is to simulate the real world, you need a way to mimic the non-uniformity of nature. You're in luck. There's a function you can use to introduce any level of non-uniformity (randomness) you choose. It's the `Math.random()` function.

In Listing 12-1, `Math.random()` is used extensively to introduce random variation in variables such as size, quantities, speed, direction, life span, sounds, and colors.

Randomizing variables

You can randomize any numeric variable by following these steps:

1. **For each variable to be randomized, define a minimum and maximum value.**

Here's an example from code section A3:

```
var lifeMin = 75;     var lifeMax = 150;
```

2. **Calculate a random value by adding the random difference between the maximum and minimum values to the minimum value.**

   Here's an example from code section I11:

   ```
   part[newPart].life = lifeMin + (Math.random()*(lifeMax-lifeMin));
   ```

Using random jitter

Jitter is a special form of random variation that doesn't require minimum and maximum values. The `Math.random()` function is simply applied directly to a variable. This is typically used to create small random variations, as in this example from code section J1 to generate small variations in the vector of particles:

```
var vectJitterN = Math.random()*vectJitter;
```

Randomizing non-numeric variables

Randomizing non-numeric variables requires a different technique than numeric variables. Instead of applying the `Math.random()` function directly to a variable, the variables, such as colors in Listing 12-1, are stored in an array, and the `Math.random()` function is used to choose a random entry in the array.

Use these steps to randomize non-numeric values:

1. **Define an array to hold the variable values.**

   Store your variable values in an array, as in this example of a colors array from code section A3:

   ```
   var colors = ["aqua", "red", "blue", "fuchsia", . . . ];
   ```

2. **Define the length of the array.**

   Define the length of the array, as in A3:

   ```
   var numColors = colors.length;
   ```

3. **Use the `Math.random()` function to select a value from the array.**

   Here's an example from code section J18:

   ```
   var colorIndex      = Math.random()*(numColors-1);
   colorIndex          = Math.round(colorIndex);
   var newColor        = colors[colorIndex];
   part[newPart].color = newColor;
   ```

Spawning new objects

Spawning refers to the creation of new objects as the result of animation events. For example, in the Listing 12-1 fireworks application, new objects are created based on time elapsing and the explosion of previously created fireworks.

Time dependent object spawning

In the example, new fireworks are launched after an animation frame count if the maximum number of particles has not been reached. To perform time dependent object spawning, follow these steps:

1. **Define time dependent spawning variables.**

   In the example, the following variables are defined in code section A3:

   ```
   var wait     = 300;   // Initial wait between fireworks launch.
   var newMin   = 30;    // Minimum wait between fireworks launch.
   var newMax   = 100;   // Maximum wait between fireworks launch.
   var partLimit = 100;  // Maximum number of particles.
   var newCount = 0;     // Count of animation frames between launches.
   var newCreate = 0;    // Frame count trigger for fireworks launch.
   ```

2. **Check for spawning conditions.**

   In code section E1 and F6–F10, the `newCount` frame counter is incre-mented and checked for reaching the `newCreate` trigger for fireworks launch. The `newCreate` variable is reset to a new random number, and if the `partLimit` hasn't been reached, `newFireworks()` is called to create a fireworks particle for launch:

   ```
   newMax = wait;
   newCount++;
   if(newCount > newCreate)
   {
      newCount  = 0;
      newCreate = newMin+(Math.random()*(newMax-newMin));
      if(part.length < partLimit)  {newFireworks()}
   }
   ```

Event dependent object spawning

In Listing 12-1, new objects are created when a fireworks explodes. The gen-erated objects create the familiar spread of new fireworks particles. To per-form event dependent object spawning, follow these steps:

1. **Define the event dependent spawning variables.**

   In the example, the explode variable associated with each particle in the part array is set to indicate an explosion should take place. This is done when the particle is created in code sections I12 and J21:

   ```
   part[newPart].explode = 1;
   ```

2. **Check for spawning conditions.**

In the example code section F18–F19, a number of conditions are checked, including the particle `age`, `explode` setting, `yPos`, and `partLimit`. If all conditions are met, the `explodeParticle()` function is called:

```
if ((part[p].age>part[p].life) && (part[p].explode == 1) &&
    (part[p].yPos<altitMin) && ((part[p].quant+part.length)<partLimit))
    {part[p].explode = 0;  explodeParticle(p)}
```

Creating Object Tails

Object tails follow behind an object as it moves across a Canvas. In the sample application in Listing 12-1, object tails are used to simulate fireworks as they die out over time. To create an object tail, use these steps:

1. **Define arrays to store tail positions.**

In Listing 12-1, arrays are defined for the *x* and *y* coordinates in code section A3:

```
var pathX = new Array();    var pathY = new Array();
```

2. **Store object coordinates as the object moves.**

Store the coordinates of the object to generate a tail, as in code section H13:

```
pathX[p].unshift(part[p].xPos);
pathY[p].unshift(part[p].yPos);
```

3. **Check conditions you're using to determine if the tail should be drawn.**

In the example, the `age` of the particle is checked against the `life` and `glow` variables in code section G8:

```
if ((part[p].age >  part[p].life) &&
    (part[p].age < (part[p].life + part[p].glow)))  { . . . }
```

4. **Loop through tail coordinates.**

In the example code section G10, the tail is drawn until the minimum of the length of the path or the `glowMin` is reached:

```
for(var t=0; t<tailLength; t++)  { . . . }
```

5. **Set the color of the tail particle.**

In the example, the color variable is used in code section G11:

```
contextFW.fillStyle = part[p].color;
```

6. **Set the transparency of the tail particle using the `globalAlpha` attribute.**

In example code section G12, `globalAlpha` is set based on a formula using the `age` and `life` of the particle:

```
var ga = 1/(.5*(t + (part[p].age)-(part[p].life)));
contextFW.globalAlpha = ga;
```

7. **Set the *x* and *y* coordinates of the tail particle based on the particle path.**

In example code sections G13 and G14, the *x* coordinate is varied from the path using a random jitter factor. The *y* coordinate is based on the path without modification:

```
var x = pathX[p][t] + (fadeJitter*Math.random());
var y = pathY[p][t];
```

8. **Using the `fillRect()` function and the size variable for the particle, draw the tail.**

Here's an example from Listing 12-1 code section G15:

```
contextFW.fillRect(x, y, part[p].size, part[p].size);
```

9. **Set an indicator based on the `globalAlpha` setting.**

Here's an example from code section G16:

```
stillGlowing = ga;
```

10. **Check to see if the glowing indicator has dropped below a minimum level.**

See this example in code section G17:

```
if(stillGlowing < .003) { . . . }
```

11. **If the glowing indicator has dropped below the minimum, remove the particle and path coordinates from their arrays.**

Here's an example in code section G18:

```
part.splice(p,1);  pathX.splice(p,1);  pathY.splice(p,1);
```

Creating Layered Audio

You know how to play audio. Playing multiple audio tracks one on top of the other is useful for enhancing application realism. Canvas audio enables you to play simultaneous audio files, but not with the same audio element. To layer multiple audio sounds, follow these steps:

1. **Define the elements, sources, and attributes of multiple audio files.**

   See these examples from sample code sections A7 and B2:

   ```
   var audio2EL;
   var audio3EL;
   audio2EL = document.createElement("audio");
   audio3EL = document.createElement("audio");
   audio2EL.setAttribute("src",server + expl1AudFile + "." + audioType);
   audio3EL.setAttribute("src",server + expl2AudFile + "." + audioType);
   ```

2. **Set a variable for a random explosion sound number.**

   In the fireworks application, the sounds of explosions are varied to add to animation realism. To do this, the Math.random() function was used to generate a random number for designating an audio file in code section J26:

   ```
   var r = explNumMin + (Math.random()*(explNumMax-explNumMin));
   var n = Math.round(r);
   ```

3. **Use the `switch()` function to select and play an audio file.**

   Here's an example from code section J27:

   ```
   switch(n)
   {
   case 1: soundExplosion(audio2EL); break;
   case 2: soundExplosion(audio4EL); break;
   case 3: soundExplosion(audio5EL); break;
   case 4: soundExplosion(audio6EL); break;
   }
   ```

4. **Using a reference to the `volume` attribute of the selected audio element, set the volume level. Then use the `play()` function to start the playback.**

   In the fireworks application, the Math.random() function was used to create variation in volume levels.

   The code to set volume and start playback is contained in the sound Explosion() function in code section K:

   ```
   function soundExplosion(element)
   {
       element.volume = explVolumeMin+(Math.random()*
                   (explVolumeMax-explVolumeMin));
       element.play();
   }
   ```

Managing Performance

As you add enhancements and complexity to your applications, performance may suffer. There are only a limited number of processor cycles available to your application code during each animation frame interval. The number of cycles available depends on the speed of the computer's CPU/GPU, the efficiency of the browser, and the length of your application animation interval.

Which code segments stress performance depends on the individual application. This list describes some common examples of object characteristics that can affect performance:

- **Quantity:** In Listing 12-1, the number of fireworks particles

- **Complexity:** In Listing 12-1, the characteristics of the fireworks particles, such as color, size, and lifespan

- **Movement:** In Listing 12-1, the trajectory and random fluctuation in movement of the fireworks particles

The fireworks example displays, in the upper right corner, the frames-per-second animation rate and number of active fireworks particles. This important information is used in monitoring and adjusting application performance.

To avoid application performance degradation, follow these steps:

1. **Define limits on object animation.**

   Here are some examples of limits in Listing 12-1, defined in code sections A1 and A3:

   ```
   var lifeMax   = 150;   // Limits the life of a particle.
   var glowMax   = 250;   // Limits the afterglow of a particle.
   var quantMax  = 30;    // Limits the number of explosion particles.
   var newMax    = 100;   // Limits the interval between new fireworks.
   var partLimit = 100;   // Limits the number of active particles.
   ```

2. **Use limits during animation.**

   In the example, these limits are used as follows in the indicated code sections:

   ```
   if(newCount > newCreate)                                         // F7
   newCreate = newMin+(Math.random()*(newMax-newMin));             // F9
   if(part.length < partLimit) {newFireworks()}                    // F10
   part[newPart].life  = lifeMin+ (Math.random()*(lifeMax-lifeMin));  // I11
   part[newPart].quant = quantMin+(Math.random()*(quantMax-quantMin)); // I11
   part[newPart].glow  = part[newPart].life+glowMin+
                         (Math.random()*(glowMax-glowMin));        // I11
   var life = lifeMin + (Math.random()*(lifeMax-lifeMin));         // J1
   var glow  = glowMin  + (Math.random()*(glowMax-glowMin));       // J1
   var quant = quantMin + (Math.random()*(quantMax-quantMin));     // J1
   ```

Part V
The Part of Tens

In this part . . .

*I*n Part V, I list ten Canvas applications and ten tools for Canvas development that can help you build on the knowledge and skills you acquired by reading this book. HTML5 Canvas is evolving into an important part of the World Wide Web and is supported by a growing global cadre of developers. Welcome aboard. Enjoy the ride. I look forward to seeing your apps join the ranks of those you find in these final chapters.

13

Ten Great Canvas Applications

*T*he number of interesting and entertaining Canvas applications grows steadily every day. Developers are connecting Canvas with activity on the web, experimenting with new techniques, and blending art with science.

In this chapter, I list a few of the best sites I've found, including some that are themselves Canvas application collections and great places to quickly scan for new apps.

To check out an application's source code, right-click (Ctrl+click on the Mac) and select View Page Source.

Bomomo

Bomomo (shown in Figure 13-1) is a painting application that combines controlled artistry with the semi-random movement of multi-faceted paint brushes. It's as though you have little Canvas processors on your fingertips. And it's very cool. Try it out at http://bomomo.com.

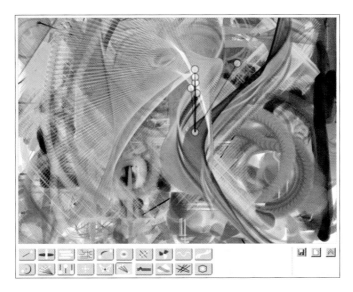

Figure 13-1: Bomomo drawing.

Canvas Cycle

The Canvas Cycle app demonstrates a series of scenes featuring moving images such as water and snow. It's a good way to get a quick perspective on the variety of backgrounds that can be created using Canvas. Get the picture at www.effectgames.com/demos/canvascycle/.

Chrome Experiments

Google is sponsoring a website that contains a collection of some of the best developer experiments using Canvas and related technologies. To find Canvas experiments, search the site for "Canvas." Maybe they'd include one of *your* masterpieces. Check them out at www.chromeexperiments.com.

Grow a Face

Why would anyone want to grow a face? There are plenty of reasons: to have a little fun, get some ideas for graphics, and get some help creating faces you might use in your own applications. Watch the evolution at `http://growaface.com`.

Burn Canvas

This is an open source demonstration project of pixel-based modification of a Canvas. Click and watch the burn at `http://guciek.github.com/burn_canvas.html`.

Canvas Sketch

This application demonstrates how traditional drawing programs can be implemented using HTML5 Canvas. Create your masterpiece at `http://gartic.uol.com.br/sketch/`.

Canvas 3D Engine

This site demonstrates how 2D Canvas can simulate 3D without the use of WebGL. Click on the floating squares to see images appear at `http://peterned.home.xs4all.nl/3d/`.

Canvas Raytracer

This site shows how you can draw sophisticated surfaces and reflections on a Canvas without WebGL or high computational loads. Raytracing is a technique for creating images reflected on virtual surfaces, as shown in Figure 13-2. Click the Random and Render buttons to see the scene perspective change at `http://jupiter909.com/mark/jsrt.html`.

Figure 13-2: Raytracer drawing.

Pocket Full of Canvas

This application demonstrates a number of Canvas effects alongside the code that generates them. It's a great demo and also useful for your toolkit. See it at www.nihilogic.dk/labs/pocket_full_of_canvas/#presets/hsl.js.

Plasma Tree

Have fun mimicking the branching growth of colorful trees. See them grow at: http://openrise.com/lab/PlasmaTree/.

14

Ten Great Tools

There aren't enough hours in the day to do everything by ourselves. We all need to leverage the work of others.

In this chapter, I list ten tools that can enhance your life as a Canvas application developer.

Audacity

Until all browsers support all audio file types, you need to include multiple versions of your audio files in your applications. Audacity (shown in Figure 14-1) is a free, open-source cross-platform software tool for converting an audio file to multiple formats, including MP3, OGG, and WAV. You can download the free software at `http://audacity.sourceforge.net`.

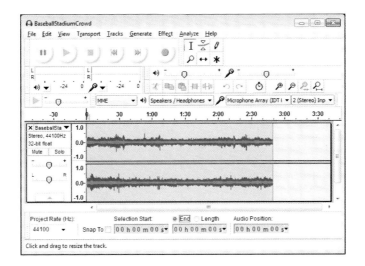

Figure 14-1: Audacity editing.

Can I Use

This website provides the latest status of browser support for a wide variety of features and capabilities, including HTML5 Canvas. See `http://caniuse.com`.

EaselJS

EaselJS is one of a number of JavaScript libraries that can be used to help simplify Canvas JavaScript development. See `www.createjs.com/#!/EaselJS`. Search your favorite search engine for *Canvas JavaScript libraries* to see other examples.

Electrotank

Electrotank provides a suite of software products that support the development of multiplayer social games for desktop and mobile devices. See `www.electrotank.com`.

Firebug

Firebug (`http://getfirebug.com/`) is a free software tool for debugging JavaScript and HTML code. It provides capabilities to set breakpoints, check variable values, and follow code execution. You can include as an add-on to most browsers, including Firefox, Chrome, Internet Explorer, and Opera. For additional information on installing it in various browsers, check out `www.makeuseof.com/tag/install-firebug-for-browsers-other-than-firefox/`.

Gamepad API

The Gamepad API is a specification for using game controllers via Canvas JavaScript code. See `https://wiki.mozilla.org/GamepadAPI`.

HTML5 Test

The html5test website tests desktop and mobile browsers for the status of their support for HTML5 features, including Canvas. It rates individual features and gives a score for the browser as a whole. See `http://html5test.com`.

Kuler

The Kuler website is an Adobe tool for developing color palettes and experimenting with color combinations. See `http://kuler.adobe.com`.

Micro Video Converter

As is the case with audio, until all browsers support all video file types, you need to include multiple versions of your video files in your applications. Micro Video Converter is a free, open-source cross-platform software tool for converting a video file to multiple formats, including MP4, OGG, and WebM. See `www.mirovideoconverter.com`.

WebGL

HTML5 Canvas doesn't currently support an integrated, 3D context. WebGL is a cross-platform, royalty-free web standard for a 3D graphics API. WebGL is growing as the de facto standard for Canvas 3D. For more information, see www.khronos.org/webgl.

The WebGL example in Figure 14-2 is from http://carvisualizer.plus 360degrees.com/threejs/. Check it out to experiment with different car models, colors, and viewpoints.

Figure 14-2: WebGL example.

Index

e & Mac

2 For Dummies,
Edition
1-118-17679-5

ne 4S For Dummies,
Edition
1-118-03671-6

touch For Dummies,
Edition
1-118-12960-9

OS X Lion
Dummies
1-118-02205-4

ging & Social Media

Ville For Dummies
1-118-08337-6

book For Dummies,
Edition
1-118-09562-1

n Blogging
Dummies
1-118-03843-7

ter For Dummies,
Edition
-0-470-76879-2

dPress For Dummies,
Edition
-1-118-07342-1

iness

h Flow For Dummies
-1-118-01850-7

sting For Dummies,
Edition
-0-470-90545-6

Job Searching with Social
Media For Dummies
978-0-470-93072-4

QuickBooks 2012
For Dummies
978-1-118-09120-3

Resumes For Dummies,
6th Edition
978-0-470-87361-8

Starting an Etsy Business
For Dummies
978-0-470-93067-0

Cooking & Entertaining

Cooking Basics
For Dummies, 4th Edition
978-0-470-91388-8

Wine For Dummies,
4th Edition
978-0-470-04579-4

Diet & Nutrition

Kettlebells For Dummies
978-0-470-59929-7

Nutrition For Dummies,
5th Edition
978-0-470-93231-5

Restaurant Calorie Counter
For Dummies,
2nd Edition
978-0-470-64405-8

Digital Photography

Digital SLR Cameras &
Photography For Dummies,
4th Edition
978-1-118-14489-3

Digital SLR Settings
& Shortcuts
For Dummies
978-0-470-91763-3

Photoshop Elements 10
For Dummies
978-1-118-10742-3

Gardening

Gardening Basics
For Dummies
978-0-470-03749-2

Vegetable Gardening
For Dummies,
2nd Edition
978-0-470-49870-5

Green/Sustainable

Raising Chickens
For Dummies
978-0-470-46544-8

Green Cleaning
For Dummies
978-0-470-39106-8

Health

Diabetes For Dummies,
3rd Edition
978-0-470-27086-8

Food Allergies
For Dummies
978-0-470-09584-3

Living Gluten-Free
For Dummies,
2nd Edition
978-0-470-58589-4

Hobbies

Beekeeping
For Dummies,
2nd Edition
978-0-470-43065-1

Chess For Dummies,
3rd Edition
978-1-118-01695-4

Drawing For Dummies,
2nd Edition
978-0-470-61842-4

eBay For Dummies,
7th Edition
978-1-118-09806-6

Knitting For Dummies,
2nd Edition
978-0-470-28747-7

Language & Foreign Language

English Grammar
For Dummies,
2nd Edition
978-0-470-54664-2

French For Dummies,
2nd Edition
978-1-118-00464-7

German For Dummies,
2nd Edition
978-0-470-90101-4

Spanish Essentials
For Dummies
978-0-470-63751-7

Spanish For Dummies,
2nd Edition
978-0-470-87855-2

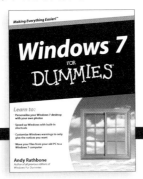

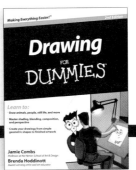

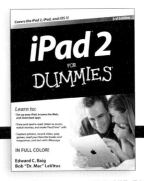

lable wherever books are sold. For more information or to order direct: U.S. customers visit www.dummies.com or call 1-877-762-2974.
U.K. customers visit www.wileyeurope.com or call (0) 1243 843291. Canadian customers visit www.wiley.ca or call 1-800-567-4797.

Connect with us online at www.facebook.com/fordummies or @fordummies

Math & Science

Algebra I For Dummies,
2nd Edition
978-0-470-55964-2

Biology For Dummies,
2nd Edition
978-0-470-59875-7

Chemistry For Dummies,
2nd Edition
978-1-1180-0730-3

Geometry For Dummies,
2nd Edition
978-0-470-08946-0

Pre-Algebra Essentials
For Dummies
978-0-470-61838-7

Microsoft Office

Excel 2010 For Dummies
978-0-470-48953-6

Office 2010 All-in-One
For Dummies
978-0-470-49748-7

Office 2011 for Mac
For Dummies
978-0-470-87869-9

Word 2010
For Dummies
978-0-470-48772-3

Music

Guitar For Dummies,
2nd Edition
978-0-7645-9904-0

Clarinet For Dummies
978-0-470-58477-4

iPod & iTunes
For Dummies,
9th Edition
978-1-118-13060-5

Pets

Cats For Dummies,
2nd Edition
978-0-7645-5275-5

Dogs All-in One
For Dummies
978-0470-52978-2

Saltwater Aquariums
For Dummies
978-0-470-06805-2

Religion & Inspiration

The Bible For Dummies
978-0-7645-5296-0

Catholicism For Dummies,
2nd Edition
978-1-118-07778-8

Spirituality For Dummies,
2nd Edition
978-0-470-19142-2

Self-Help & Relationships

Happiness For Dummies
978-0-470-28171-0

Overcoming Anxiety
For Dummies,
2nd Edition
978-0-470-57441-6

Seniors

Crosswords For Seniors
For Dummies
978-0-470-49157-7

iPad 2 For Seniors
For Dummies, 3rd Edition
978-1-118-17678-8

Laptops & Tablets
For Seniors For Dummies,
2nd Edition
978-1-118-09596-6

Smartphones & Tablets

BlackBerry For Dummies,
5th Edition
978-1-118-10035-6

Droid X2 For Dummies
978-1-118-14864-8

HTC ThunderBolt
For Dummies
978-1-118-07601-9

MOTOROLA XOOM
For Dummies
978-1-118-08835-7

Sports

Basketball For Dummies,
3rd Edition
978-1-118-07374-2

Football For Dummies,
2nd Edition
978-1-118-01261-1

Golf For Dummies,
4th Edition
978-0-470-88279-5

Test Prep

ACT For Dummies,
5th Edition
978-1-118-01259-8

ASVAB For Dummies,
3rd Edition
978-0-470-63760-9

The GRE Test For
Dummies, 7th Edition
978-0-470-00919-2

Police Officer Exam
For Dummies
978-0-470-88724-0

Series 7 Exam
For Dummies
978-0-470-09932-2

Web Development

HTML, CSS, & XHTML
For Dummies, 7th Editi•
978-0-470-91659-9

Drupal For Dummies,
2nd Edition
978-1-118-08348-2

Windows 7

Windows 7
For Dummies
978-0-470-49743-2

Windows 7
For Dummies,
Book + DVD Bundle
978-0-470-52398-8

Windows 7 All-in-One
For Dummies
978-0-470-48763-1

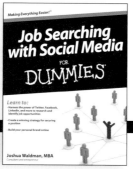

Available wherever books are sold. For more information or to order direct: U.S. customers visit www.dummies.com or call 1-877-762-2
U.K. customers visit www.wileyeurope.com or call (0) 1243 843291. Canadian customers visit www.wiley.ca or call 1-800-567-4797.
Connect with us online at www.facebook.com/fordummies or @fordummies

Wherever you are in life, Dummies makes it easier.

From fashion to Facebook®, wine to Windows®, and everything in between, Dummies makes it easier.

Visit us at Dummies.com and connect with us online at www.facebook.com/fordummies or @fordummies

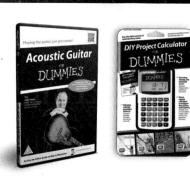